COLORADO
TRAVEL✦SMART™ TRIP PLANNER

How to Use This Book 1
Suggested Itineraries 2
Planning Map 10
Mileage Chart 12
Why Visit Colorado? 13
Practical Tips 23
❶ Denver 33
❷ Pawnee Grasslands 53
    ☆ Scenic Route: Pawnee Pioneer Trails Byway 65
❸ Rocky Mountain National Park 67
❹ Steamboat Springs 81
❺ Leadville 95
    ☆ Scenic Route: Leadville to Aspen over Independence Pass 107
❻ Roaring Fork Valley 109
❼ Grand Junction and the Colorado River Valley 123
    ☆ Scenic Route: Unaweep Tabeguache Scenic and Historic Byway .135
❽ Northern San Juan Mountains 137
❾ Durango and Cortez 151
❿ Upper Rio Grande Valley 165
    ☆ Scenic Route: The Alpine Loop 175
⓫ Upper Arkansas River Valley 177
⓬ San Luis Valley 189
⓭ Trinidad/La Junta 201
    ☆ Scenic Route: Highway of Legends 213
⓮ Colorado Springs 215
Appendix 229
Index 234
Maps Index 240

COLORADO

TRAVEL✦SMART™ TRIP PLANNER

Dianna Litvak

John Muir Publications
Santa Fe, New Mexico

Thank you to my family, friends, and co-workers who contributed so much to the completion of this book. I would especially like to thank Brian and David for an overflowing supply of support and encouragement. And, of course, a heartfelt scratch behind the ears goes out to Lumpy, my computer pal.

John Muir Publications, P.O. Box 613, Santa Fe, New Mexico 87504

Printed in the United States of America.
First printing October 1996

ISSN 1087-8327
ISBN 1-56261-296-4

Cover Photo: Unicorn/Ron Holt
Map Design: American Custom Maps—Albuquerque, NM USA
Editors: Dianna Delling, Peggy Schaefer, Elizabeth Wolf, Chris Hayhurst
Design: Janine Lehmann and Linda Braun
Graphics Coordination: Tom Gaukel
Typesetting: John Ericksen
Production: Marie Vigil, Nikki Rooker
Printing: Publishers Press

Distributed to the book trade by
Publishers Group West
Emeryville, California

While every effort has been made to provide accurate, up-to-date information, the author and publisher accept no responsibility for loss, injury, or inconvenience sustained by any person using this book.

HOW TO USE THIS BOOK

This *Colorado Travel♦Smart Trip Planner* is organized in 14 destination chapters, each covering the best sights and activities, restaurants, and lodging available in that specific destination. Thanks to thorough research and experience, the author is able to bring you only the best options, saving you time and money in your travels. The chapters are presented in geographic sequence so you can follow an easy route from one to the next. If you were to visit each destination in chapter order, you'd enjoy a complete tour of the best of Colorado.

Each chapter contains:
• User-friendly maps of the area, showing all recommended sights, restaurants, and accommodations.
• "A Perfect Day" description—how the author would spend her time if she had just one day in that destination.
• Sightseeing highlights, each rated by degree of importance: ✯✯✯ Don't miss; ✯✯ Try hard to see; ✯ See if you have time; and No stars—Worth knowing about.
• Selected restaurant, lodging, and camping recommendations to suit a variety of budgets.
• Helpful hints, fitness and recreation ideas, insights, and random tidbits of information to enhance your trip.

The Importance of Planning. Developing an itinerary is the best way to get the most satisfaction from your travels, and this guidebook makes it easy. First, read through the book and choose the places you'd most like to visit. Then, study the color map on the inside cover flap and the mileage chart (page 12) to determine which you can realistically see in the time you have available and at the travel pace you prefer. Using the Planning Map (pages 10–11), map out your route. Finally, use the lodging recommendations to determine your accommodations.

Some Suggested Itineraries. To get you started, six itineraries of varying lengths and based on specific interests follow. Mix and match according to your interests and time constraints, or follow a given itinerary from start to finish. The possibilities are endless. *Happy travels!*

SUGGESTED ITINERARIES

With the *Colorado Travel+Smart Trip Planner* you can plan a trip of any length—a one-day excursion, a getaway weekend, or a three-week vacation—around any special interest. To get you started, the following pages contain six suggested itineraries geared toward a variety of interests. For more information, refer to the chapters listed—chapter names are bolded and chapter numbers appear inside black bullets. You can follow a suggested itinerary in its entirety, or shorten, lengthen, or combine parts of each, depending on your starting and ending points.

Discuss alternative routes and schedules with your travel companions—it's a great way to have fun, even before you leave home. And remember: don't hesitate to change your itinerary once you're on the road. Careful study and planning ahead of time will help you make informed decisions as you go, but spontaneity is the extra ingredient that will make your trip memorable.

Tom Gaukel

The Best of Colorado Tour

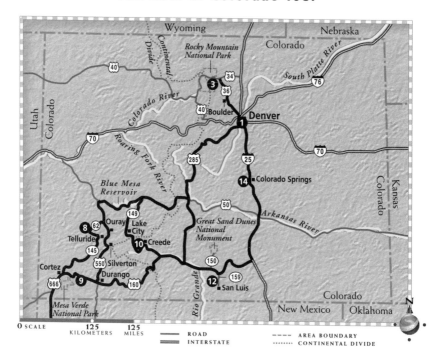

For those discerning travelers who want only the "crème de la crème" for their Colorado vacation, these are the places I recommend. You should know, however, that all of the destinations included in this book are "the best." Most everything about Colorado is superlative!

1 **Denver** (Civic Center Cultural Complex, Boulder, downtown Denver, Cherry Creek)

3 **Rocky Mountain National Park** (Trail Ridge Road)

8 **Northern San Juan Mountains** (Telluride, hiking, mountain biking rides, and scenic driving)

9 **Durango and Cortez** (Mesa Verde)

10 **Upper Rio Grande Valley** (Creede Repertory Theater, Wheeler Geologic Area, Silver Thread Scenic and Historic Byway)

12 **San Luis Valley** (San Luis, Stations of the Cross, Great Sand Dunes National Monument)

14 **Colorado Springs** (Pikes Peak, Garden of the Gods)

Time needed: 2 to 3 weeks

Nature Lover's Tour

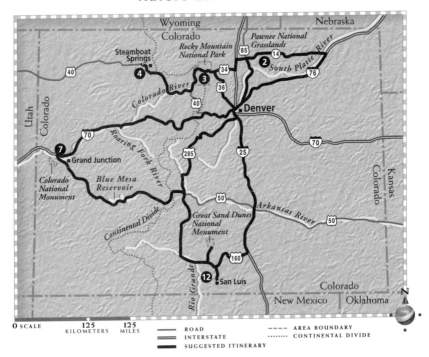

The variety of natural places found in Colorado is tremendous. This itinerary recommends a sampling of different regions, from prairie grasslands to 14,000-foot peaks, all bursting with a diversity of plant and animal life.

② **Pawnee Grasslands** (Pawnee Buttes, Crow Valley Recreation Area)

③ **Rocky Mountain National Park** (Trail Ridge Road, wildlife viewing, hiking)

④ **Steamboat Springs** (Flat Tops Wilderness Area, Mt. Zirkel Wilderness Area)

⑦ **Grand Junction and the Colorado River Valley** (Grand Mesa, Colorado National Monument)

⑫ **San Luis Valley** (Great Sand Dunes National Monument, Alamosa-Monte Vista National Wildlife Refuge)

Time needed: 1 to 2 weeks

Family Fun Tour

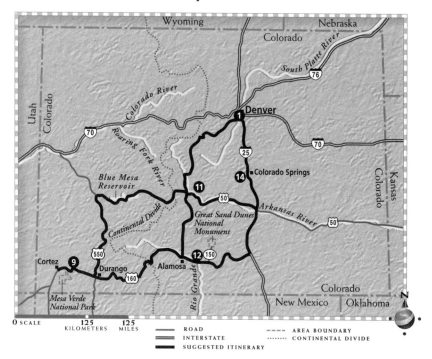

One thing everybody knows about kids is that they love dinosaurs. Families can visit the state's most famous paleontological specimens, embark on an exciting river-raft trip, wander through ancient dwellings, and stand on top of one of America's most famous mountains.

- **❶ Denver** (Denver Museum of Natural History, Denver Zoo, Elitch Gardens Amusement Park, United States Mint)
- **❾ Durango and Cortez** (Mesa Verde, Durango & Silverton Narrow Gauge Railroad)
- **⓫ Upper Arkansas River Valley** (river rafting)
- **⓬ San Luis Valley** (Great Sand Dunes National Monument, Splashland, alligator farm)
- **⓮ Colorado Springs** (Pikes Peak, Royal Gorge, United States Air Force Academy, Cheyenne Mountain Zoo, Cripple Creek)

Time needed: 10 days to 2 weeks

Arts and Cultures Tour

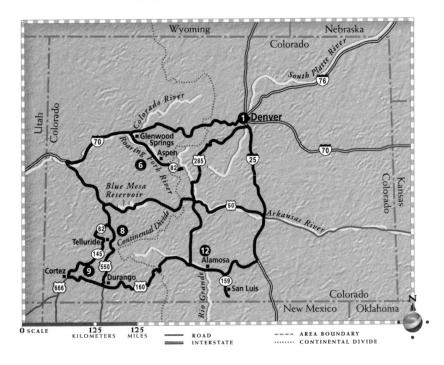

This itinerary gives you ideas for exploring the arts and cultures of Colorado—both past and present. The rich artistic traditions of several ethnic groups are especially highlighted.

❶ **Denver** (Civic Center Cultural Complex, Museo de las Americas, Black American West Museum, Denver Center for Performing Arts, festivals)

❻ **Roaring Fork Valley** (Aspen Music Festival, Anderson Ranch Arts Center, Glenwood Springs Center for the Arts, galleries, festivals)

❽ **Northern San Juan Mountains** (festivals, galleries in Telluride)

❾ **Durango and Cortez** (Anasazi sites, Ute reservations, Cortez Center)

⓬ **San Luis Valley** (galleries and museums in La Garita, San Luis, Alamosa; Stations of the Cross, Our Lady of Guadalupe Church)

Time needed: 2 weeks

Outdoor Sports Tour

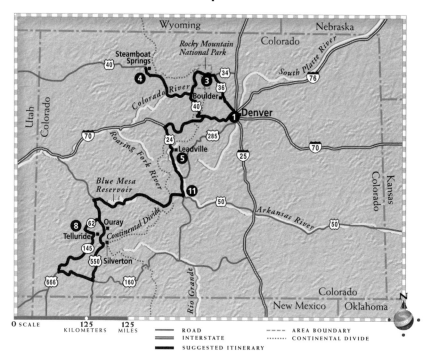

Colorado is famous for its staggering array of outdoor adventures. Wintertime is a skier's paradise; summer rewards outdoor enthusiasts with hikes up soaring peaks, white-water raft trips, and overnight outings in the beautiful Colorado wilderness.

❶ Denver (hiking near Boulder)

❸ Rocky Mountain National Park (hiking, backpacking, fishing, wildlife viewing, skiing)

❹ Steamboat Springs (Steamboat Ski Area, hiking, backpacking, mountain biking, dipping in hot springs)

❺ Leadville (Ski Cooper Ski Area, hiking, backpacking, fishing)

❽ Northern San Juan Mountains (Telluride Ski Area, hiking, mountain biking, jeep touring on four-wheel drive roads)

⓫ Upper Arkansas River Valley (Monarch Ski Area, river rafting, mountain biking, fishing)

Time needed: 2 to 3 weeks

History Tour

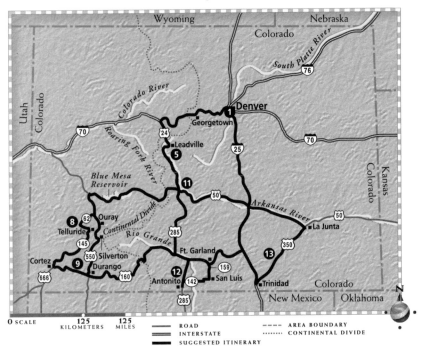

This itinerary guides you to significant historical sites in Colorado, steeped in the pasts of Anasazi Indians, fur trade forts, early Hispanic settlements, ghost towns, and mountain towns that survived the bust years after the mineral rush.

① **Denver** (Georgetown, Colorado History Museum)

⑤ **Leadville** (National Mining Museum, Tabor Opera House, Matchless Mine, Route of the Silver Kings)

⑧ **Northern San Juan Mountains** (scenic drives through former mining districts)

⑨ **Durango and Cortez** (Anasazi sites, Durango & Silverton Narrow Gauge Railroad)

⑪ **Upper Arkansas River Valley** (ghost towns)

⑫ **San Luis Valley** (San Luis, Fort Garland Museum, Pikes Stockade, Cumbres & Toltec Scenic Railroad)

⑬ **Trinidad/La Junta** (Bent's Fort, Corazon de Trinidad National Historic District, Boggsville, Ludlow, Highway of Legends)

Time needed: 2 weeks

USING THE PLANNING MAP

A major aspect of itinerary planning is determining your mode of transportation and the route you will follow as you travel from destination to destination. The Planning Map on the following pages will allow you to do just that.

First, read through the destination chapters carefully and note the sights that intrigue you. Then, photocopy the Planning Map so you can try out several different routes that will take you to these destinations. (The mileage chart that follows will allow you to calculate your travel distances.) Decide where you will be starting your tour of Colorado. Will you fly into Denver, Colorado Springs, or Grand Junction, or will you start from somewhere in between? Will you be driving from place to place or flying into major transportation hubs and renting a car for day trips? The answers to these questions will form the basis for your travel route design.

Once you have a firm idea of where your travels will take you, copy your route onto one of the additional Planning Maps in the Appendix. You won't have to worry about where your map is, and the information you need on each destination will always be close at hand.

Planning Map: Colorado

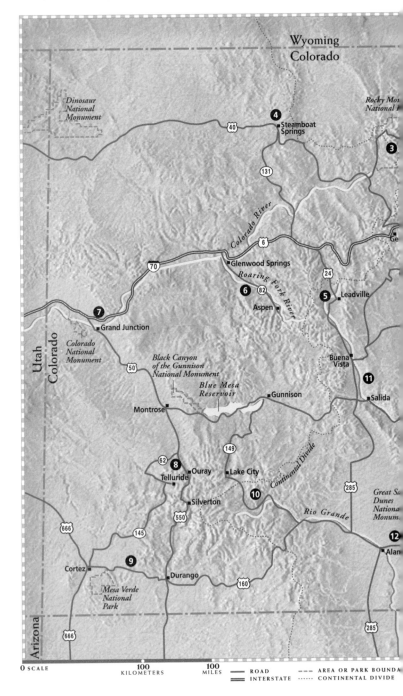

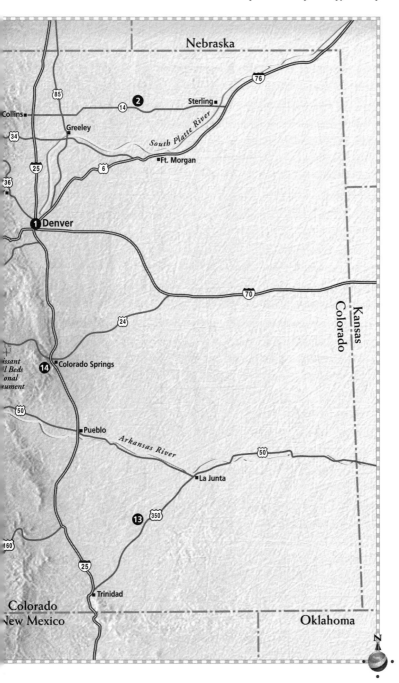

COLORADO MILEAGE CHART

	Grand Junction	Telluride	Durango	Leadville	Aspen	Salida	Alamosa	Creede	Trinidad	Colorado Spgs.	Denver	Estes Park	Greeley
Telluride	134												
Durango	168	124											
Leadville	179	245	264										
Aspen	134	281	321	60									
Salida	197	186	205	59	87								
Alamosa	268	268	150	141	169	68							
Creede	219	221	131	172	200	113	68						
Trinidad	380	367	261	252	268	181	111	179					
Colorado Spgs.	302	291	310	129	157	105	164	223	127				
Denver	258	340	359	113	173	154	213	262	195	68			
Estes Park	319	416	435	171	231	219	278	327	260	133	65		
Greeley	312	394	413	167	227	208	267	316	249	122	54	51	
Steamboat Spgs.	197	331	365	120	180	179	256	292	371	244	176	142	193

WHY VISIT COLORADO?

Pikes Peak, an imposing sentinel rising above Colorado's eastern plains, has intrigued Americans for generations. Zebulon Pike himself regarded it unclimbable, and believed it must reach at least 20,000 feet above the valley floor. In fact, at a little over 14,000 feet, it isn't even Colorado's highest mountain, ranking only thirty-first among 54 "Fourteeners." But its magnificence inspired a young poet to pen words that have become a part of the American soul: "O beautiful for spacious skies, for amber waves of grain, for purple mountain majesties above the fruited plain . . . " Although Katherine Lee Bates wrote these words many decades ago, Pikes Peak continues to inspire those seeing it for the first or the fiftieth time. And, like the sentiments expressed in "America the Beautiful," this great mountain is a stalwart symbol for all that is magnificent, unique, and inspirational about Colorado.

As a Colorado native, I am privileged to introduce you to my state—all of it—from the eastern plains country to the high mountain valleys and the plateau lands of the western slope. This guide will acquaint you with Colorado's wilderness, its past, and its everyday wonders. My suggestions, which are based on my own experiences, will help you plan your journey, show you many rare and unusual places, and allow you to discover all that Colorado has to offer. Take your time and really get to know a place before rushing off to the next. It will all be waiting for you the next time you come.

HISTORY AND CULTURES

Colorado's landscape holds many clues—for those patient enough to find them—that tell mysterious stories about early human habitation within the borders of the state. At least 12,000 years ago, Paleo-Indians roamed this land, hunting woolly mammoth and bison. Hunter-gatherers lived here at least 9,000 years ago, surviving by hunting game and gathering roots and berries. They also made pottery and used bows and arrows introduced by other nomadic bands to the east. The Fremont peoples lived in the red sandstone canyons of the Colorado Plateau near present-day Grand Junction from A.D. 500 to 1450. On the canyon walls they inscribed detailed scenes and figures, such as the mythical humpbacked flute player, Kokopelli, and drilled complex hole patterns on the mesa tops, revealing their sophisticated knowledge of the solar system.

The Anasazi are the most well known of Colorado's prehistoric peoples. Believed to be the ancestors of the modern Pueblo and Hopi tribes, their cliff dwellings and artifacts are concentrated in the canyon country of Colorado, Arizona, New Mexico, and Utah. By A.D. 1300, the Anasazi simply vanished from their homes in Colorado. Archaeologists continue to debate the possible reasons for their mysterious disappearance.

For thousands of years, the Utes lived within Colorado's extensive mountain ranges, typically traveling between the high and low country as the seasons changed. By 1600, the tribe had acquired horses brought to the New World by the Spanish. Horses dramatically increased their mobility and freedom. The Utes began to venture farther onto the foothills and plains, fighting with Plains Indians tribes over disputed territory and buffalo herds. The Comanche, Kiowa, Cheyenne, Arapaho, Plains Apache, Pawnee, and Shoshone competed against one another for control of the Great Plains region of Colorado, Kansas, and Nebraska. They followed the seasonal migration of gigantic herds of American buffalo, relying on the animals for clothing, shelter, and sustenance.

Hispanics from northern New Mexico first migrated into southern Colorado 450 years ago—more than three centuries before white settlers claimed the land for homesteads and cattle ranches. Extended families filtered into southern Colorado, establishing *plazas* and *placitas* along fertile river valleys such as *el Huerfano* ("the Orphan") and "*El Rio de las Animas Perdidas en Purgatorio*" ("the River of Souls Lost in Purgatory"). The rich legacy of these families lives on today in places like San Luis, Colorado's oldest incorporated town (1851).

In 1821, as a result of its independence from Spain, Mexico established an important trading relationship with the United States, a practice illegal under Spanish rule. The boundary between the United States and Mexico was the Arkansas River, which, from its headwaters in the central Rockies, traverses through the southeastern corner of present-day Colorado. Traders from Missouri traveled to and from Santa Fe on what became known as the Santa Fe Trail, sometimes using a branch of the trail along the Arkansas River. The most important stopping point on the Arkansas—in United States territory—was Bent's Fort, established in 1834 to trade buffalo robes and horses with Plains Indian tribes. The fort brought together three distinct groups of people that all played major roles in Colorado's rich and storied history: American Indians of the Great Plains, Mexicans, and Euro-Americans.

Zebulon Pike, an American explorer, entered the lands of present-day Colorado in 1806, followed by Stephen Long in 1820. Both believed the vast plains of Nebraska, Kansas, and eastern Colorado to be a wasteland, best left to the "wild" Indian tribes who inhabited it; the Rocky Mountains to the west were a wilderness where only seasoned mountain men and Indians could survive. This view of Colorado prevailed until 1858, when a prospector announced to an eager nation the discovery of "color" at the confluence of Cherry Creek and the South Platte River, today the very heart of Denver. As reports of "gold!" filtered back to the states, hundreds of thousands of people willing to risk everything for a chance to get rich quick flocked to Pikes Peak country.

As the United States became increasingly interested in the immense agricultural and mineral wealth of Colorado, the native tribes were forced, painfully and reluctantly, to relinquish their cherished ancestral lands. Of the vast territories once controlled by these tribes, only the Ute Mountain Ute and Southern Ute tribes today retain a minuscule portion of their original lands in the southwestern corner of the state.

Settlement, mining, and industry, all indications of the taming of the frontier, rapidly transformed Colorado's untouched landscape. Bonanza towns such as Aspen, Georgetown, and Cripple Creek left significant marks on history. They came into this life as infant mining camps and experienced the growing pains of adolescent towns, but once the minerals played out, these settlements became quaint relics of a bygone era. Several former boom towns languished until the joys of mountain living and tourism hastened in a new boom era.

In the twentieth century, Colorado still wrestles with its ever-expanding popularity. During the last decade alone, Colorado cities and towns have grown by leaps and bounds. More and more people, grown weary of the hustle and bustle of city life, have turned to Colorado as a place to escape, hoping life here will be simple, relaxed, and healthy. With the population boom, many Coloradans are scrambling to preserve the past and the remaining wilderness from the damaging effects of rapid growth.

THE ARTS

You'll find a refreshing variety of arts and culture in Colorado—from the time-honored and traditional to the cutting-edge and unconventional. Denver hosts a multitude of cultural events, including concerts, symphonies, gallery openings, museum exhibitions, and theater and dance performances. The Denver Center for the Performing Arts covers four city blocks, houses nine separate venues, and boasts an overall seating capacity second only to Lincoln Center in New York.

Festivals in Denver tend to be friendly neighborhood gatherings, such as the Cinco de Mayo fiesta along Santa Fe Drive, the Chile Festival in downtown Denver, or the Black Arts Festival in City Park in mid-July. Denver's Asian community sponsors the Cherry Blossom Festival in Sakura Square in downtown Denver in June. In addition, the Cherry Creek Arts Festival features the best in regional art and is held each Fourth of July. These festivals provide a tremendous opportunity to purchase art, such as weavings, paintings, jewelry, and clothing, and to learn about the diverse cultures that comprise metropolitan Denver.

But Denver doesn't hold a monopoly on Colorado arts; many communities feature a diverse selection of events, museums, and galleries. Aspen proudly hosts the world-acclaimed Aspen Music Festival each summer, a bonanza for classical music lovers, while Telluride is known for its Telluride Film Festival, one of the best small festivals in the country, and the innovative Telluride Bluegrass Festival, which draws thousands each summer. Other annual music festivals receive rave reviews and attract national and international entertainers. Glenwood Springs hosts an annual jazz festival, and the American Music Festival, held near Estes Park in late summer, features the latest alternative music bands.

The San Luis Valley is a haven for artists who continue to practice centuries-old arts passed down to them by their Hispanic ancestors. Their tinwork, religious objects, weavings, sculpture, and jewelry are widely available in many towns in the valley. Both the Ute Mountain Ute and Southern Ute Reservations display locally produced works at galleries, including silver jewelry, unique pottery, and visual arts.

Artists' collectives have sprouted in Boulder, Salida, Alamosa, and Glenwood Springs. Their presence has contributed to a statewide appreciation of the arts, and they present special art exhibits, workshops, classes, poetry readings, and theater and dance performances throughout Colorado.

CUISINE

During your Colorado visit, be prepared to sample many different foods, from barbecue to tequila-braised calamari. Traditional Colorado foods feature a variety of wild game—venison, buffalo, elk, rabbit, pheasant, quail, duck, goose, and even wild turkey. The Rocky Mountain trout is always a sumptuous dinner entree, often baked or sautéed in the lightest of oils and accented by lemon. And with hundreds of cattle ranches throughout the state, you can expect only the best cuts of aged beef.

During late summer and fall, farmers trumpet the availability of fresh vegetables and fruits at homemade stands lining the highways. Legendary Rocky Ford cantaloupes, grown in a small agricultural community in the Arkansas River Valley, are noted for their sweet aroma and taste. The fertile Colorado River Valley, east of Grand Junction, is prime orchard country. Here, Palisade peach orchards bask in the gentle "peach wind" that wafts through the valley, as do numerous vineyards that produce distinctive wines. Near the Grand Mesa, in Cedaredge, are seemingly endless rows of apple trees, sources of the most crisp and flavorful apples in the state.

Colorado chefs commonly use only the freshest ingredients in their creations, varying their menus according to the seasonal availability of produce grown by local farmers. Many restaurants employ an innovative cooking style that relies on old favorites prepared with a unique twist: such as grilled salmon rubbed with chipotle and red chile, pasta dishes enhanced by complex Asian flavors, T-bone steaks topped with a dollop of fresh salsa.

While traditional Mexican food has been in Colorado for decades, new Southwestern cuisine is a more recent arrival. Southwestern cooking features traditional pueblo foods from New Mexico (black beans, corn, and green chile) paired with unusual ingredients such as duck, lamb, or goat cheese. In addition, a plethora of ethnic restaurants in Colorado, ranging from Italian, Russian, Japanese, Thai, Vietnamese, and South American, to French, offers Coloradans and visitors the best in international cooking.

Resort towns such as Aspen, Telluride, and Steamboat Springs are known for their cafés and bistros, many started by European ski enthusiasts. Like most of the large cities in Colorado, these towns also have numerous health-food stores and restaurants specializing in flavorful and distinctive vegetarian cuisine. In the more rural areas, the food remains traditionally Western—just like the good old days—with the finest steaks and wild game accompanied with fresh vegetables and homemade potato dishes.

Although beer might not qualify as "cuisine," connoisseurs will appreciate the 60 or so microbreweries in the state. These masters of handcrafted beers have vaulted the once-ordinary beverage to new heights. Microbreweries feature a range of beers to please any taste, from light ales to heavy porters, and often vary them according to season. The hearty fare served at many pubs is in a class by itself, with tempting appetizers, pastas, soups, and main-course selections featuring beer as a central ingredient.

FLORA AND FAUNA

The High Plains that blanket eastern Colorado are generally too dry for trees, except along streams or rivers. Swaying grasses and prickly cacti cover the prairie, which erupts with an assortment of wildflowers each spring. Grassland birds have adapted to the scarcity of trees by nesting and rearing their young on the ground. Colorado's state bird, the lark bunting, is frequently seen, as are hawks and eagles, which feast on rattlesnakes and small rodents scampering through the brush. Rabbits, coyotes, foxes, pronghorn antelope, prairie dogs, gophers, and owls are other significant species living in the prairie landscape.

Much of Colorado is a semi-arid desert, found at elevations between 5,000 and 10,000 feet. The San Luis Valley, the Yampa River Valley near Steamboat Springs, and the Dolores River Canyon west of Grand Junction are all examples of Colorado's high deserts. Desert shrubs such as rabbit brush, sagebrush, and greasewood have uniquely adapted to the region, using long roots to capture moisture deep under the ground.

Piñon-juniper woodlands, such as those found at Mesa Verde, are often referred to as "pygmy forests" because their trees are stunted and gnarled, soaking up only 10 to 20 inches of moisture each year. Juniper berries and piñon nuts provide nourishment for several species, such as elk, mule deer, bighorn sheep, quail, chipmunks, and squirrels.

Ponds, lakes, marshes, creeks, and rivers cover only 3 percent of the state but support a wide diversity of wildlife. Lush vegetation marks the location of water in this arid land, with tangles of cattails, bulrushes, willows, and cottonwoods lining the waterways. Migrating birds rest near water during the spring and fall, when sightings of great blue herons, waterfowl, and sandhill cranes delight wildlife viewers. Beavers inventively build dams on the streams, while fish—both native and introduced species—thrive in Colorado's waters.

Denver and Colorado Springs are situated on the eastern fringe of foothills where thickets of scrub oak and mountain mahogany present beautiful fall colors. Beyond the foothills, ponderosa pines (with a bark that smells like vanilla), Douglas firs, and lodgepole pines begin to make their first appearance. Mice, chipmunks, foxes, black bears, scrub jays, and warblers harvest abundant seeds, fruits, and nuts from the vegetation during the fall, while mountain lions, bobcats, owls, and mule deer scavenge year-round.

At altitudes of approximately 10,000 feet, in places like the northern San Juan mountains and the Creede and Lake City regions, are Colorado's subalpine forests. The temperature here is much cooler, and abundant snowfall makes this ecosystem unusually moist. Hardy trees of the subalpine forest include the Engelmann spruce, subalpine fir, and aspen, with its distinctive white bark. Bristlecone pines, the oldest trees in Colorado (some are 2,000 years old), also live here. Visitors to the subalpine in the spring and summer are delighted by its symphony of wildflowers, including avalanche lilies, Indian paintbrush, golden banner, and columbines. (The columbine is the Colorado state flower.) Elk graze here in the summer but move to lower elevations in winter. Year-round residents include snowshoe hares and weasels that change colors from summer to winter to match the surrounding environment, and black bears that hibernate throughout the long winter months.

Colorado's alpine tundra begins at the treeline, between 11,500 and 12,000 feet, where talus-covered mountains are barefaced. Alpine tundra regions include the highest parts of Rocky Mountain National Park and the Sawatch Range near Leadville and Salida. Trees living directly at treeline are warped by harsh winds and sub-zero temperatures. Ground-covering tundra plants can withstand the Arctic cold above treeline, but are extremely fragile and immediately destroyed upon human contact. The wildflowers at these elevations are brilliantly colored, as their dark pigments actually convert light into heat and help them survive. The few animals that inhabit the tundra include marmots, playful pikas, ptarmigans, and sparrows.

THE LAY OF THE LAND

Colorado's lowest point is 3,387 feet above sea level, where the Arkansas River crosses into Kansas. Its highest point is the second highest mountain in the contiguous 48 states, Mt. Elbert, at 14,433 feet—which makes for an overall difference in elevation of more than 11,000 feet! In between are gently rolling plains, soaring peaks, deep canyons, flat-topped mesas, and rushing rivers.

With more than 50 "Fourteeners" (peaks above 14,000 feet), this state is truly a mountaineer's paradise. Most ranges run primarily from north to south, such as the Front Range, which is easily accessible from Colorado Springs and Denver, and the Sangre de Cristo and Sawatch Ranges framing the western and eastern boundaries of the San Luis Valley. Other ranges are angled differently, from east to west or at a 45-degree angle, such as the San Juan Mountains in southwestern Colorado and the massive Grand Mesa near Grand Junction.

Winding its way through the high peaks of Colorado is the Continental Divide, a high crest of mountains and passes from which the continent's streams drain either to the Atlantic or Pacific Ocean. Coloradans refer to residents living west of the Divide as "west slopers," while those to the east are "front rangers." A sometimes serious rivalry exists between these two groups, especially when it comes to the availability of water resources. Several major rivers headwater at the crest of the Divide. The mighty Colorado River, which begins above Grand Lake in Rocky Mountain National Park, courses through Colorado's western slope into Utah, then heads south into Arizona, where it travels through the Grand Canyon. Further west it is captured behind Hoover Dam near Las Vegas, and then deposits its remaining drops into the Gulf of California.

The fabled Rio Grande begins on the eastern slope of the San Juan Mountains, flowing through southern Colorado and New Mexico, until it becomes the border between Texas and Mexico. In the Sawatch Range, the home of Colorado's highest peaks, the Arkansas River is born, flowing south through river canyons near Salida that are wildly popular with river rafters, and continuing its long journey to the Mississippi River. On the eastern side of the Mosquito Range, the Platte River originates as a rushing mountain river that flows northward through Denver, where it begins to flatten (similar to a plate, for which it is named), and continues its course through the northeastern plains of Colorado and Nebraska as the South and North Platte Rivers.

OUTDOOR ACTIVITIES

The best way to experience Colorado is to take part in any number of outdoor activities. Recreation here holds something for people of all ages and abilities. With more than 23.9 million acres of land preserved and managed by state and federal agencies, there is more than enough room to "get lost" in Colorado's the great outdoors.

Colorado's mountains support more than 20 downhill ski resorts. Scores of cross-country centers and miles of backcountry trails are available for all types of winter recreation. If you've been scared off by the notoriously exorbitant cost of a ski vacation, rest easy. While it's true that some ski areas are extremely pricey, others cater to budget and beginner skiers, particularly pleasing for families. Besides, there are plenty of other things to do in Colorado during the winter—snowshoeing, ice skating, dipping in hot springs—that don't require a high-priced lift ticket.

River rafting on high mountain streams is Colorado's second-most popular activity (behind skiing). Any type of river trip is possible, from calm and relaxed floats to white-knuckle adrenaline rushes on boiling rapids. The river rafting season usually begins in May, when the mountain snowmelt turns calm rivers into raging torrents, and peaks in June and July. River outfitters rent equipment, lead float trips, and give you important lessons and instructions to help you enjoy your water ride.

Fishing is one of Colorado's favorite pastimes. Opportunities range from fly-fishing in cold streams and rivers to dropping a line from a boat, canoe, or shore. The regulations in each part of the state vary greatly; contact the Division of Wildlife (see "Resources" at the end of this chapter) to get up-to-date information. Before heading out to enjoy your day, pick up a fishing license, required for those over age 15, $18.25 for five days. Consider also purchasing an optional wilderness license ($1); your contribution will help fund search-and-rescue operations in the state.

Exploring Colorado on foot is the best way to experience its splendor. You can take short walks along bike paths or nature trails in urban areas, seek out longer day hikes in one of several national forests or national parks, or plan an overnight or multi-day excursion through an untouched wilderness. Bicycling, on both dirt trails and roadways, is also extremely popular. Bike trails lace the entire state, in urban areas, in rural towns, and through a network of mountain trails fanning out into the backcountry.

Understandably, one of Colorado's most popular outdoor activities is scenic driving, simply taking the time to travel through the state and stop along the way. Many interstate travelers, anxious to reach their destination in a hurry, miss out on much of Colorado's scenery, history, and wildlife. In 1991, the governor of Colorado instituted a Scenic Historic Byways program, which now recognizes 21 scenic routes throughout the state. Several state parks and wildlife areas display outdoor signs that identify wildlife in the area and provide wildlife-watching tips. The Colorado Historical Society's interpretive signs, found at most major rest areas and scenic overlooks, offer information about the state's cultural and natural history. Whatever outdoor activity you choose in Colorado, enjoy!

Unicorn/Dick Young

PRACTICAL TIPS

HOW MUCH WILL IT COST?

Your trip to Colorado can be as expensive or as inexpensive as you want—it really depends on the condition of your pocketbook. I tend to be a budget traveler, so I have passed on several money-saving recommendations to you in the food and lodging sections of each chapter. But if I have come across a place where spending a little extra money is definitely worth it, I let you know.

Parts of Colorado are less expensive than others. Take, for example, Fort Morgan, Alamosa, or La Junta, where prices are generally a quarter of what they would be in Denver, Durango, or Estes Park. These out-of-the-way destinations offer completely different visitor experiences than their well-known counterparts, and I strongly urge you to take advantage of them. You won't soon forget a journey out to the Pawnee Grasslands, the San Luis Valley, or the Santa Fe Trail region.

You will also see a huge difference in lodging rates according to the high tourist season in each destination. Ski resorts such as Aspen, Steamboat Springs, and Telluride are astronomically expensive during the winter (late December to late March) and the summer (late May to late September). But during spring and fall their prices drop 10 to 20 percent, if not more, a bonus for travelers who like to visit a place when it is less crowded. Other destinations, such as the San Luis Valley, Upper Rio Grande Valley, and Rocky Mountain National Park, are nearly deserted during the winter, and prices are lowered at these times to attract visitors.

Let's say you've purchased your airline ticket, rented a car, and are ready to hit the road. If you like to camp and buy your food at a local market instead of eating every meal out, you should budget $10 to $20 per person, per day. If you don't like to camp, expect to spend $50 to $75 per person, per day (prices based on double occupancy at budget accommodations and two to three moderately priced meals). The amount of money you spend on gas depends on your vehicle, and airfare and rental fees are also variable. Add another $10 per day to visit museums, parks, and attractions, and then budget how much you can spend to buy some souvenirs or presents for those friends and family members you've left behind.

WHEN TO GO

Colorado is a wonderful place to visit at any time of year, but you should schedule your trip according to your interests. If you like to downhill ski, you'll want to come sometime between Thanksgiving weekend and the end of April, although the ski season has been known to last until the Fourth of July at higher elevations! Keep in mind that winter is also the most treacherous time to drive in Colorado, as winter storms can close passes and highways. Even in early and late summer, rain-and snowstorms at higher elevations can make driving extremely dangerous. You should also know that many campgrounds and RV parks close during the winter.

When the snow begins to melt in the high country (usually by mid-May), the dirt roads and trails in the mountains become one large and messy pile of mud. The high country is often inaccessible for driving, hiking, or mountain biking until things dry out, usually by mid-June. Summer and autumn are ideal for hiking and backpacking in the higher elevations in Colorado.

Outdoor festivals take place every weekend during the summer throughout Colorado. I have given you approximate dates (such as mid-June or late September) for some of the larger events, so you can plan your visit to a certain destination accordingly. You might want to make plans to attend a certain festival or delay your visit until after its conclusion if you like to avoid such events. During the more popular festivals, it can be tough (and sometimes downright impossible) to book a room in a place overrun with festival goers.

If you are a warm-weather traveler and like to beat the crowds, plan your trip before Memorial Day or after Labor Day. During these months, the weather is still pleasant for sightseeing, and many families can't travel because the kids are in school. You might have your chosen destination all to yourself.

CLIMATE

The most important thing to know about Colorado's weather is that it is exceptionally fickle. The extreme differences in elevation in the state means weather patterns vary considerably from one place to the next. For example, eastern Colorado can be locked in a torrential downpour while western Colorado remains dry as a bone. This wide range of climatic variation can occur even in a space of less than 30 miles. To make things even more exciting, on any given day a region might see a variance of 50+ degrees in a 12-hour period, with sub-zero temperatures in the morning soaring to 50 degrees Fahrenheit by 2:00 p.m.

The climate is greatly affected by the position of mountain ranges in the central and western parts of the state, where mountains can either shield from harsh weather or trap a valley within it. Mountain valleys tend to be much colder than the mountains themselves in the winter months because cold air from higher elevations sinks to the valley floor. The mountains west of the Continental Divide receive their moisture from storms that begin as Pacific air masses, while the mountains east of the Divide tend to be hit by storms originating in the Gulf of Mexico.

Although Colorado's weather is variable, the one thing you can always depend on is that bad weather never sticks around for long. A bitter winter snowstorm will almost always be followed by a sunny day that quickly melts the snow at lower elevations. This pattern can make winter in Colorado downright enjoyable. During the spring and fall,

COLORADO'S CLIMATE

Average daily high and low temperatures in degrees Fahrenheit, plus monthly precipitation in inches:

	Colorado Springs	Denver	Grand Junction	Telluride
Jan.	41/16 .30	43/17 .47	36/15 .59	37/6 1.4
March	49/24 .88	51/26 1.1	54/31 .82	42/13 1.6
May	69/42 2.3	69/44 2.4	75/48 .76	62/30 1.7
July	85/57 2.9	87/59 1.7	92/64 .62	77/41 2.5
Sept.	75/61 1.3	77/48 1.1	81/53 .89	69/34 2.1
Nov.	50/25 .47	52/26 .69	51/28 .63	46/15 1.5

the state is usually blessed with long periods of dry, pleasant weather often punctuated by sudden snowstorms. The summer months are hot in the lower elevations (average temperatures are around 80 degrees, but have been known to climb into the 100s for days at a time), but thunderstorms regularly cool things off in the late afternoon.

You should always be prepared for changes in weather conditions and expect precipitation at any time, even on clear and sunny days. When exploring the high country, be sure to summit heights above timberline before noon, and hightail it back down to the trees as soon as possible. The last place you want to be during an afternoon light-ning storm is at the top of a mountain. Always bring rough weather gear, such as a raincoat, heavy pants, a hat, and gloves when exploring the high country to protect yourself from hypothermia during a sudden storm. And because the sun shines brightly in Colorado all year-round, always wear sunscreen and a hat, especially at higher elevations.

TRANSPORTATION

If you are going to fly to Colorado, you can choose one of several airports for your destination, depending on where you'd like to start your vacation. Denver International Airport (DIA) is the largest airport in the state, larger than the Dallas-Ft. Worth and Chicago O'Hare Airports—combined. The airline runways are designed in a pinwheel shape to help combat delays in landing and takeoff. Situated a half-hour east of metropolitan Denver, the newly completed airport cost $5 billion. It features a unique peaked roof that resembles a series of white tents, and inside, local and national artists have created a multitude of murals, paintings, sculpture, and mosaics (the bill for the art alone was $7.5 million). The concourses are filled with retail shops and restau-rants rivaling those found in any American mall.

DIA is the first stop for most major flights into Colorado, which gives you some flexibility in planning your trip. You can fly directly into Denver, rent a car, and begin your trip there, or take a connecting flight to another Colorado airport. You have your pick among the Colorado Springs airport (just an hour south of Denver along the Front Range), or the major Western Slope airports of Grand Junction, Aspen, or Durango (this is especially helpful if you want to spend most of your time in the western part of the state).

Many rental car companies are located at DIA. Be sure to compare prices of national companies with those of locally owned companies for the best deal. Each rental agency has fleets of minivans and four-wheel drive vehicles, the most popular rentals in the state. I also recommend checking out U.S. Rent-a-Car, (303) 341-0111, located outside the airport, although there is a service charge if you take one of their vehicles out of state. Many travelers, especially Europeans, like to rent recreational vehicles to undertake their road trip in comfort. Nolan's RV and Marine rents RVs by the day, week, or month. The business is located at 6935 Federal Boulevard in Denver, (303) 429-6114.

Once you're on the road in the vehicle of your choice, you will find driving around Colorado an extremely pleasurable experience. All driving to and from these destinations can be easily accomplished by any type of vehicle. However, some destinations have options for scenic drives that follow some pretty rough roads, unsuitable for two-wheel drive vehicles and RVs. You can rent a four-wheel drive at the outset (a smart idea if you plan to be driving during the winter months) or when you reach a certain destination, as many towns have companies that rent vehicles for such a purpose. I have provided you with this type of information when available.

When driving through Colorado, you should always check road conditions by calling the Colorado Department of Transportation Road Conditions Hotline, (303) 639-1111 or 639-1234. Or call the local sheriff's department for an up-to-date report before leaving.

While train travel is not the most convenient method of getting around Colorado, there is one train trip I highly recommend. You can take an Amtrak train from Union Station in Denver to the resort town of Glenwood Springs (see the Roaring Fork Valley chapter), on a gorgeous trip through the Rocky Mountains and the incomparable Glenwood Canyon. This is a great way to see the scenery without having to drive. For more information, call Amtrak at (800) 872-7245 or (303) 534-2812.

CAMPING, LODGING, AND DINING

Should you choose to camp during your stay in Colorado, thousands of camping opportunities await you. You won't spend more than $10 per night to camp at a public site, or more than $20 per night at a private site. Some camping sites are accessible from the highway, others are tucked along a remote county or forest road, and still others can be reached only by foot.

Most private campgrounds cater to RVs, providing long pull-through sites, electricity, and water. Some even have swimming pools, hot tubs, horseback rides, and fishing access right from your campsite. You should call ahead to make reservations at a private RV park, especially during the summer months. Many private campgrounds are closed during the late fall, winter, and early spring.

Public sites usually don't offer the same services as private campgrounds, but most do have water and restroom facilities. The more popular national parks, such as Mesa Verde and Rocky Mountain National Park, have several large campgrounds with hundreds of sites open year-round. The options within national forests tend to be fairly rustic and accommodate fewer people. If you are traveling through Bureau of Land Management land, you can usually just pull off the road and pick your site—it's all public land, all available for camping.

Even if you plan on camping most of the time during your trip to Colorado, there will still be some nights when you just need a full-size bed. You don't necessarily have to pay an arm and a leg to find a decent place for the night. Unless they are the only accommodations in town, I have avoided recommending chain hotels and motels. There are many more personable places to stay that offer the same degree of quality. If you are traveling on a limited budget, you might want to take advantage of cozy bed and breakfasts that offer lower rates if you have to walk down the hall to use the bathroom (remember, the rate also includes breakfast). Motor motels and rustic cabins, also very affordable, usually have small kitchenettes.

Historic hotels, inns, and rustic lodges tend to be slightly more expensive, but their rates vary according to season. Often these types of accommodations include a full breakfast, with some providing other meals, as well. The only catch about staying in such places is that they often have strict reservation policies, requiring at least 30 days' notice for cancellation. The rooms are usually nonsmoking, and children and pets are not always welcome. The amenities of such accommodations are truly special, because the innkeepers will often provide fresh flowers, robes, reading material, and other personal touches usually unheard of in the hotel/motel industry.

On the upper end of the lodging scale are those legendary places you should know about just in case you receive a windfall and want to spend it all in one night. These accommodations may be a resplendent historic hotel, a bed and breakfast with a special suite, or a condominium at a ski resort. The hosts will do their best to treat you like a king or queen.

The dining recommendations in this book vary widely and should satisfy the requirements for any type of meal. Because your vacation will be spent doing a variety of things, you will want to have a variety of meals, with different prices, tastes, and ambience. You might want to grab a bagel before hiking or search out the best diner in town for a steaming platter of eggs, hash browns, and toast for under $3. Lunch might find you eating a burger or diving into a substantial salad while sitting on a sunny patio people-watching, while dinner can range from a hearty ethnic meal to a feast of prime rib with a bottle of wine. The dining possibilities in each destination are usually diverse enough to allow you to choose from the frugal to the extravagant.

RECOMMENDED READING

A wealth of knowledge exists in numerous books written on many different Colorado subjects. I have recommended a few—actually only a fraction of my favorites—to enhance your trip to this state. Most of these books are still in print and can be found at most major bookstores. If you have trouble locating one, contact the bookstore at the Colorado Historical Society, 1300 Broadway, Denver, CO 80203, (303) 866-3682, which has the most extensive selection of books about Colorado in the state.

The Colorado Book, edited by Eleanor Gehres et al., is a compendium of fiction, nonfiction, history, art, poetry, and music, all about Colorado. This indispensable volume does a nice job of assembling the best of the best in Colorado writings. To step into the shoes of earlier Colorado travelers, find a copy of Isabella Bird's A Lady's Life in the Rocky Mountains. This intrepid Englishwoman thrived on adventure travel and made several trips abroad—by herself—during her exciting life. She trekked through Colorado during the late 1870s, when she stayed, among other places, in Estes Park, and climbed Longs Peak in a pair of borrowed boots many sizes too large. Bird's insights into Colorado during this period are priceless.

The Colorado Wildlife Viewing Guide, by Mary Taylor Gray, is a well-organized and carefully researched guide with suggestions on what types of wildlife to look for in national parks, wildlife refuges, national forests, and state wildlife areas, as well as in lesser-known county and municipal parks. Gray's maps and place descriptions are excellent. The Denver Museum of Natural History published a companion book to its ecological diorama exhibits titled Explore Colorado: A

Naturalist's Notebook. It is filled with stunning color photographs by John Fielder, a premier nature photographer, as well as photos of the actual dioramas that look surprisingly real. Interspersed throughout the text are delightful illustrations of the flora and fauna of Colorado. Wildflower enthusiasts will want to use the two volumes of *Colorado Wildflowers*, by G.K. Guennel, as their bible; the books include full-page glossy photos of wonderfully diverse specimens.

Enos Mills, Colorado's most well-known naturalist, lived in the Estes Park region for many years and championed the designation of Rocky Mountain National Park in 1915. He wrote prolifically about the nature and beauty of the Rockies, excerpts of which have been compiled in *Radiant Days: Writings by Enos Mills*, edited by John Dotson.

Of the many books on Colorado history, I would first recommend *A Colorado History*, by Carl Ubbelohde, Maxine Benson, and Duane Smith, as the most comprehensive and informative. Many well-written regional histories provide fascinating insights into the early years of a place, such as *Pikes Peak*, by the late Frank Waters, one of the Southwest's most distinguished authors. Another classic, this one about the rich history of northeast Colorado, is *The South Platte Trail*, by Nell Brown Propst, a wonderful writer who has lived for many years in northeastern Colorado on a successful cattle ranch. In *Bent's Fort*, David Lavender captures the essence of the cultural and economic interaction of fur traders, merchants from Missouri, Plains Indians, and Mexicans who met at the isolated fort on the Arkansas River in 1834.

Volumes have been written about Colorado's mining camps, but there are several books that stand above the rest. *The Life of an Ordinary Woman*, by Anne Ellis, is a touching diary written by a woman who lived in several Colorado mining camps. Ellis compellingly describes, with stark realism, the everyday issues faced by women in these harsh places, and tells with humor and insight how they coped. For an informative guide with directions to many of Colorado's most famous ghost towns, pick up *Ghost Towns and Mining Camps of Colorado*, by Muriel Sibell Wolle.

For information on hikes within the state, one of the best guides available is *100 Hikes in Colorado*, by Scott S. Warren. Mountain bike enthusiasts will find many challenging rides described in *Bicycling the Colorado Rockies*, by Vici De Haan, an experienced cyclist who knows every region of the state. And should you be traveling with children, I highly recommend a book written by two intrepid moms, Marty Meitus and Patty Thorn, called *Places to go with Children in Colorado*. The authors impart several fresh ideas that make traveling fun for children and recommend many "child-friendly" places throughout the state.

For more suggestions on camping and other rustic accommodations, turn to *Colorado RV Parks* and *Colorado Cabins, Cottages, and Lodges*, both written by Hilton and Jenny Fitt-Peaster, who know the cabins and RV parks like they were in their own backyard. And *Absolutely Every Bed and Breakfast in Colorado (Almost)*, edited by Toni Knapp, gives helpful summaries of 356 bed and breakfasts within the state.

RESOURCES

Bed & Breakfast Innkeepers of Colorado: P.O. Box 38416, Colorado Springs, CO 80937-8416.

BLM Wild Hot Line: (800) 354-4595; call this number for ideas on where to go in Colorado to watch wildlife.

Bureau of Land Management: 2850 Youngfield, Lakewood, CO 80215, (303) 239-3600.

Colorado Association of Campgrounds, Cabins, and Lodges: 5101 Pennsylvania Avenue, Boulder, CO 80303, (303) 499-9343.

Colorado Bicycle Program: 4201 East Arkansas Avenue, Room 225, Denver, CO 80222; (303) 757-9982.

Colorado Cross Country Ski Association: Box 1292, Kremmling, CO 80459, (800) 869-4560.

Colorado Department for Local Affairs (manages the State Tourism Board): 1313 Sherman Street, Denver, CO 80203, (303) 866-2771.

Colorado Department of Transportation: Road Conditions, 4201 East Arkansas, Denver, CO 80222, (303) 639-1111 or 639-1234.

Colorado Division of Parks and Outdoor Recreation: 1313 Sherman Street, Suite 618, Denver, CO 80203, (303) 866-3437.

Colorado Division of Wildlife: 6060 Broadway, Denver, CO 80216. General information, (303) 297-1192; fishing information, (303) 291-7533; up-to-date fishing reports, (303) 291-7534; camping information, (303) 291-7532.

Colorado Dude & Guest Ranch Association: P.O. Box 300, Tabernash, CO 80478, (970) 887-3128.

Colorado Mountain Club: 710 Tenth Street, Golden, CO 80401, (303) 279-5643.

Colorado Ski Country USA: 1560 Broadway, Denver, CO 80203, (303) 837-0793.

Denver Metro Convention and Visitors Bureau: 225 West Colfax Avenue, Denver, CO 80202, (303) 892-1112.
National Park Service: 12795 West Alameda Parkway, Lakewood, CO 80225, (303) 969-2000.
United States Forest Service, mailing address: P.O. Box 25127, Lakewood, CO 80225; street address: 740 Simms, Lakewood, CO 80225, (303) 275-5360.

Unicorn/Ann Trulove

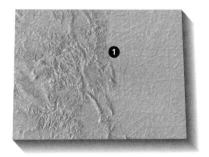

1
DENVER

In November 1858, the confluence of Cherry Creek and the South Platte River, formerly an Indian camping ground, erupted into a brawling boom town swarming with gold seekers, confident men, and whiskey-fueled fighters. The banks of the waterways would forever be changed by the discovery of precious metals in the mountains to the west. Promoters and businessmen flooded into Denver, carefully plotting ways to make the settlement bigger and better. At the eastern fringe of the Rocky Mountains, Denver is now the largest city in the Rocky Mountain West. Its importance as a center for commerce, industry, and trade in the West is due, in part, to the tireless efforts of those first promoters.

Although dubbed the "Queen City of the Plains," Denver's connection to the mountains stretching across its western horizon cannot be overstated. The mountains are a haven and escape for many Denverites, and their proximity to the sprawling metropolis make this city one of the best places to live in the country. The 1990s have heralded phenomenal growth for Denver and its many suburbs. Some estimates claim the population increases by as many as 2,000 new residents a week, with more than 2 million people now living in the metropolitan area. Denver now boasts a state-of-the-art airport and a municipal library, world-class museums, four professional sports teams, and an eclectic entertainment scene. The city is a major visitor destination in itself, and many people like to spend a few days exploring it before heading into other parts of Colorado. ◼

DENVER

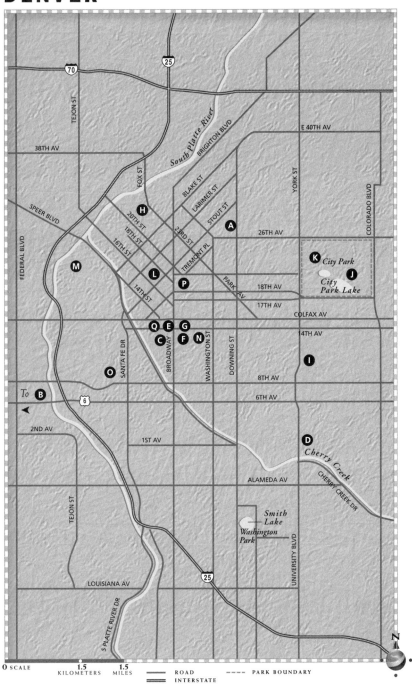

O SCALE   1.5 KILOMETERS   1.5 MILES   —— ROAD   ----- PARK BOUNDARY   ═══ INTERSTATE

Sightseeing Highlights

Ⓐ Black American West Museum

Ⓑ Buffalo Bill Memorial Museum and Grave

Ⓒ Byers-Evans House and Denver History Museum

Ⓓ Cherry Creek

Ⓔ Civic Center Cultural Complex

Ⓕ Colorado History Museum

Ⓖ Colorado State Capitol

Ⓗ Coors Field

Ⓘ Denver Art Museum

Ⓘ Denver Botanic Gardens

Ⓙ Denver Museum of Natural History/Planetarium/IMAX Theater

Ⓒ Denver Public Library

Ⓚ Denver Zoo

Ⓛ Downtown

Ⓜ Elitch Gardens Amusement Park

Ⓝ Molly Brown House

Ⓞ Museo de las Americas

Ⓟ Museum of Western Art

Ⓠ United States Mint

Note: Items with the same letter are in the same area.

A PERFECT DAY IN DENVER

Spend the day exploring Denver's downtown. Museum buffs have their pick of three excellent regional venues: Denver Art Museum, Museum of Western Art, and the Colorado Historical Society. In the evening, treat yourself to one of the city's excellent restaurants, and then check out the local listings for concerts, plays, movies, or special events in the metro area.

SIGHTSEEING HIGHLIGHTS

✪✪✪ **Civic Center Cultural Complex**—Situated around a graceful park in the heart of downtown Denver, this complex includes several of the city's most important cultural attractions. To the east is the classical **Colorado State Capitol**, with dramatic murals in the entrance, gilded stairways, and an eye-catching gold dome. A stunning 360-degree view of the mountains, plains, and the city can be enjoyed on the upper rotunda of the building. Free tours are given on weekdays from 9:00 a.m. to 3:00 p.m. Location: Between Sherman and Lincoln on Colfax (15th Avenue). Phone: (303) 866-2604. (½ hour)

Bordering the eastern section of the complex is the **Colorado History Museum**, highlighting Colorado's multifarious history through permanent and changing exhibits. The museum tells the stories of explorers, mountain men, Native Americans, pioneers, and the diverse ethnic groups who have lived within the borders of present-day Colorado. A public library, bookstore, educational programs, and the office of Archaeology and Historic Preservation round out the public services of this facility. Admission: $3 for adults, $2.50 for seniors and students, and $1.50 for children 6–16. You can also purchase a combination ticket here to visit the Byers Evans House and Denver History Museum, $5 for adults, $4 for seniors and students, and $2 for children. Hours: Monday through Saturday 10:00 a.m. to 4:30 p.m., Sunday 12:00 p.m. to 4:30 p.m. Address: 1300 Broadway. Phone: (303) 866-3682. (2 hours)

Directly west of the Colorado History Museum is the **Denver Public Library**, completed in 1995, designed by world-renowned architect Michael Graves. The addition to Denver's historic Central Library, designed by architect Burnham Hoyt, resembles a medieval city, with its contrasting shapes, heights, and colors. The $75 million expansion made this public library the largest between Chicago and Los Angeles.

The library boasts 5 million items and 47 miles of shelving. Wood-paneled walls, intriguing murals in the spacious atrium, and a limestone floor with actual fossils all embellish this stunning piece of architecture. On the fifth floor are the Western History and Genealogy Collections, including the Gates Western History Reading Room. In the center of this reading room is a dramatic wooden derrick, harkening back to Colorado's mining and oil drilling days. Western art graces the walls, including the dramatic landscape painting "Estes Park" by Albert Bierstadt. Hours: Monday, Tuesday, and Wednesday 10:00 a.m. to 9:00 p.m., Thursday, Friday, and Saturday 10:00 a.m. to 5:30 p.m., and Sunday 1:00 p.m. to 5:00 p.m. Phone: (303) 640-6200. (½ hour)

Connected by a small walking plaza to the west of the Denver Public Library is the **Denver Art Museum**. The strengths of this municipal museum are its American Indian, Pre-Columbian, Spanish Colonial, and Western American collections. The museum also presents several changing exhibits annually. Admission: $3 for adults, $1.50 for seniors and students; free on Saturdays. Hours: Tuesday through Saturday 10:00 a.m. to 5:00 p.m., Sunday 12:00 p.m. to 5:00 p.m. Address: 100 West 14th Avenue (14th and Bannock). Phone: (303) 640-2793. (2 hours)

On the southwestern fringe of the Civic Center Cultural Complex beyond the Denver Art Museum is the **Byers-Evans House and Denver History Museum**, operated by the Colorado Historical Society. Housed in the former home of two prominent Denver families and filled with Victorian furnishings, this facility also includes an innovative interactive computer program that provides interesting facts about Denver's history. Admission: $3 adults, $2.50 seniors or students, and $1.50 for children 6–16. Hours: Tuesday through Saturday 10:00 a.m. to 4:00 p.m., Sunday 1:00 p.m. to 4:00 p.m. Address: 1310 Bannock Street. Phone: (303) 620-4933. (1 hour)

★★★ **Denver Museum of Natural History**—In addition to many unique exhibits, dioramas, and interactive programs on Colorado's diverse natural history, this museum has a fascinating permanent dinosaur exhibit called "Prehistoric Journey." Visitors are transported to the age of the dinosaurs through a state-of-the-art eco-environment that simulates an ecosystem of billions of years ago. Several dinosaur skeletons in the museum's voluminous collection have been painstakingly reassembled, and the informative exhibits tell you just about everything you need to know about dinosaurs.

The **Planetarium** and **IMAX** theater are also part of the Denver Museum of Natural History complex. The Planetarium presents laser shows and multimedia attractions, while the IMAX theater projects films on a screen 4½ stories high and five stories wide, immersing the audience in stunning cinematography. Show times start at 11:00 a.m. and run every hour. On Wednesday, Thursday, and Sunday shows run until 7:00 p.m.; on Friday and Saturday until 9:00 p.m. Museum admission: Adults, $4.50, children 4–12, $2.50, seniors, $2. IMAX admission: Adults, $5, children and seniors, $4. Planetarium admission: Adults, $3.50, children and seniors, $2.50. Combination tickets to these attractions can also be purchased at lower prices. Hours: Open daily 9:00 a.m. to 5:00 p.m. Phone: (303) 322-7009. IMAX information: (303) 370-6300. (2–3 hours)

✮✮✮ **The Denver Zoo**—More than 3,500 animals live in Denver's city zoo, located next to the Denver Museum of Natural History in City Park. Tropical Discovery is a simulated rainforest habitat with highlights such as vibrant and colorful fish swimming in aquariums and a collection of exotic snakes living in the ruins of a temple wall. In the Northern Shores exhibit you can see polar bears powerfully swimming underwater and sea lions and seals playfully coursing through outdoor pools. Admission: $6 for adults, $4 for children 4–12 and seniors. Hours: Open daily 10:00 a.m. to 5:00 p.m. Address: East 23rd Street and Steele, between York Street and Colorado Boulevard in City Park. Phone: (303) 331-4110. (2–3 hours)

✮✮ **Denver Botanic Gardens**—In the midst of a bustling city, the Denver Botanic Gardens provide a quiet oasis of trees, plants, flowers, and birds. The alpine garden has a wide assemblage of mountain flora from around the world. Nearby, the Japanese garden has a serene goldfish pond and small tea house imported from Japan. The facility also offers horticulture programs, a public garden, a complete botanical library, and a gift shop. Several unique festivals and special events occur here during the warmer months. Admission: $4. Hours: Open daily 9:00 a.m. to 5:00 p.m. Address: 1005 York Street, at the eastern end of Cheesman Park. Phone: (303) 331-4010. (1½ hours)

✮✮ **Downtown Denver**—The historic heart of Denver has been the focus of a vigilant rejuvenation in recent years. Many renovated warehouses and office buildings now accommodate restaurants, bars, galleries, lofts, and specialty stores. The urban improvements were spurred by the opening of **Coors Field,** at 20th and Blake, the home of the Colorado Rockies, Denver's major league baseball team. Designed as a tribute to old-time downtown baseball parks, Coors Field has natural grass and the 48,000 seats are arranged so that fans sit close to the action. Tickets are often available for many of the games. For more information, call (800) 388-7625.

For more than 100 years, **Elitch Gardens Amusement Park** resided in a quiet and shady oasis in North Denver. In 1995, the facility moved into the Platte River Valley, a downtown urban area. Along with the move to a new location came improved versions of the rides, such as the "Twister," a wooden roller coaster, and the "Colorado River" water ride. All of the old favorites are here too, as well as a 350-foot-high observation tower. Admission: $20 for adults, $16 for children 5 years old to 52" tall. Hours: 10:00 a.m. to 10:00 p.m. during the summer. Address: I-25 and Speer. Phone: (303) 595-4386. (3 hours)

✯ **Black American West Museum**—This heritage center, situated in the historic Five Points neighborhood, chronicles the migrations of African-American cowboys, soldiers, and pioneers who came to the West and to Colorado after the Civil War. Many people consider this museum the best source of information on African-Americans in the West. Admission: $2 for adults, $1.50 for seniors, 75 cents for youths 12–17, and 50 cents for children. Hours: Wednesday through Friday 10:00 a.m. to 2:00 p.m., Saturday 10:00 a.m. to 5:00 p.m., Sunday 2:00 p.m. to 5:00 p.m. Address: 3091 California Street, at the northeast end of the lightrail system. Phone: (303) 292-2566. (1 hour)

✯ **Buffalo Bill Memorial Museum and Grave**—Buffalo Bill (William F. Cody), arguably the most famous man of his time, died at his sister's home in Denver in 1915. Thousands of people filed past his body on display in the state capitol. Even though Buffalo Bill wished to be buried in the town of Cody, Wyoming, his wife instructed Denver officials to bury him on top of Lookout Mountain, just west of town. The Buffalo Bill Memorial Museum at the gravesite displays rare memorabilia from this showman, army scout, and frontier legend. The views from Lookout Mountain are the finest from outside of the metro area. Admission: $2 for adults, $1 for children 6–15. Winter hours: Tuesday through Sunday 9:00 a.m. to 4:00 p.m. Summer hours: May through October, open daily 9:00 a.m. to 5:00 p.m. Address and directions: 987½ Lookout Mountain

Road. Take Interstate 70 west of Denver to exit 256 and follow the signs up Lookout Mountain. Phone: (303) 526-0747. (1 hour)

✵ **Cherry Creek**—For a fun afternoon of window shopping or spending money with wild abandon, head to Cherry Creek, southeast of downtown. The **Cherry Creek Shopping Mall** features well-known retailers such as Neiman Marcus, Saks Fifth Avenue, and Williams and Sonoma, in addition to hundreds of specialty stores.

Just north of the mall is **Cherry Creek North,** a delightful area with restaurants, boutiques, and great coffee shops. The multistoried **Tattered Cover Bookstore**, on the corner of Steele and First Avenue, (303) 322-7727, is one of Denver's most treasured institutions. The wood shelves are stocked with every conceivable type of printed material. Scattered throughout the maze of bookshelves are plush loveseats and overstuffed chairs, perfect for spending a quiet afternoon browsing through books, magazines, and newspapers. The coffee shop on the first floor will tempt you with delectable pastries and desserts. (2 hours)

✵ **Molly Brown House**—The fabulously wealthy Molly Brown never cared that Denver's snobbish high society found her gauche and uncultured. After she survived the disastrous Titanic shipwreck, she became known as the "Unsinkable Molly Brown" and even became the subject of a Broadway play of the same name. Historic Denver, a preservation agency, has restored her luxurious mansion into a Victorian museum, with guided tours and afternoon teas. Admission: $5 for adults, $1.50 for children 6–12. Hours: Tuesday through Saturday 10:00 a.m. to 4:00 p.m., Sunday 12:00 p.m. to 4:00 p.m.; also open Mondays June through August. Address: 1340 Pennsylvania. Phone: (303) 832-4092. (1 hour)

✵ **Museo de las Americas**—Hispanic art, culture, and history are exhibited in this museum on Santa Fe Drive, the nucleus of Denver's Hispanic community. The museum presents changing displays throughout the year, all focusing on Latin America and the American Southwest. Admission: $3 for adults, $2 for students and seniors. Hours: Tuesday through Saturday 10:00 a.m. to 5:00 p.m. Address: 861 Santa Fe Drive. Phone: (303) 571-4401. (1 hour)

✵ **Museum of Western Art**—If you are a fan of Western art, don't miss this collection—the third largest of its kind in the country. The museum is located in the Navarre Building, a former bordello and gambling hall connected by an underground tunnel to the Brown Palace Hotel across the street. Admission: $3 for adults, $2 for seniors and students. Hours: Tuesday through Saturday 10:00 a.m. to 4:30 p.m. Address: 1727 Tremont Place. Phone: (303) 296-1880. (1 hour)

✯ **United States Mint**—The basement of this formidable building has the second largest storehouse of gold in the country; only Fort Knox's is bigger. You can visit the mint and see how it forges the nation's coins. There are also several excellent displays on the history of the U.S. Mint and Treasury. Free tours of the facility are offered on weekdays. Hours: Monday through Friday 8:00 a.m. to 2:45 p.m., with tours leaving every 20 minutes. Closed the last week of June to July 4. Address: West Colfax and Cherokee. Phone: (303) 844-3582. (1 hour)

FITNESS AND RECREATION

More than 130 miles of bike paths lace the metro area, connecting Denver to many outlying suburbs. One of the more popular paths, the **Cherry Creek Trail,** can be accessed behind the Cherry Creek Shopping Center. If taken north 5 miles, the trail ends up in **Confluence Park**, in Lower Downtown Denver. Eight miles south on the trail is the **Cherry Creek Reservoir**, a popular recreation spot for volleyball, windsurfing, waterskiing, and jetskiing.

Denverites love their many well-kept neighborhood parks, such as **Washington Park** in south Denver, and **Cheesman Park**, in the Capitol Hill neighborhood southeast of downtown. Both have loops for jogging, walking, roller blading, and biking, and acres of fields for playing soccer, volleyball, or the recently popular ultimate frisbee. Several nearby state parks are also excellent places to enjoy beautiful scenery, a picnic, or a short hike, such as **Castlewood Canyon State Park** and **Roxborough State Park**, both south of Denver.

FOOD

The cuisine of Denver is superb—from tantalizing Colorado specialties to a wide variety of ethnic cuisines. However, with more than 2,000 restaurants in the metro area, recommending one can be difficult! I have given you just a sampling of my favorite restaurants, places

DENVER

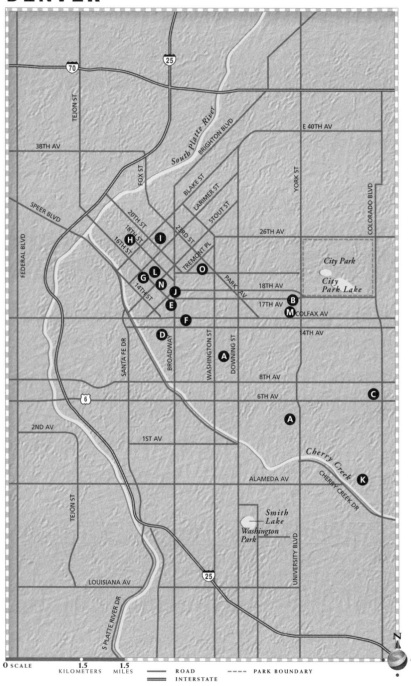

Map labels:
- TEJON ST
- 38TH AV
- SPEER BLVD
- FEDERAL BLVD
- FOX ST
- South Platte River
- BRIGHTON BLVD
- BLAKE ST
- LARIMER ST
- STOUT ST
- 20TH ST
- 23RD ST
- 18TH ST
- 16TH ST
- TREMONT PL
- 14TH ST
- SANTA FE DR
- BROADWAY
- WASHINGTON ST
- DOWNING ST
- PARK AV
- YORK ST
- COLORADO BLVD
- E 40TH AV
- 26TH AV
- City Park
- City Park Lake
- 18TH AV
- 17TH AV
- COLFAX AV
- 14TH AV
- 8TH AV
- 6TH AV
- 4TH AV
- 2ND AV
- 1ST AV
- ALAMEDA AV
- Cherry Creek
- CHERRY CREEK DR
- Smith Lake
- Washington Park
- UNIVERSITY BLVD
- LOUISIANA AV
- S PLATTE RIVER DR
- TEJON ST

Interstate/road markers: 70, 25, 6, 25

N

O SCALE
1.5 KILOMETERS
1.5 MILES

—— ROAD
===== PARK BOUNDARY
▭▭▭ INTERSTATE

Food

(A) Alfalfa's Market

(B) Mike Berardi's

(C) Chipotle's

(D) Dozen's

(E) Duffy's Shamrock Restaurant and Bar

(F) Golden Tempura Bowl

(G) Little Russian Café

(H) McCormick's/Cruise Room

(I) Mori Japanese Restaurant

(J) Palace Arms

(K) Rick's Bluewater Grill

(L) Zenith American Grill

Lodging

(J) Brown Palace Hotel

(M) Castle Marne

(N) Comfort Inn

(H) Oxford Hotel

(O) Queen Anne Inn

Note: Items with the same letter are located in the same place.

I like to go when treating myself or friends. Dinner entrees at these restaurants usually fall within the $11 to $22 range.

At **Mike Berardi's**, 2115 East 17th Avenue, (303) 399-8800, expect a sumptuous meal accompanied by an excellent wine, with choices such as pasta with shellfish, stuffed chicken, veal Parmesan, and traditional favorites such as lasagna or spaghetti with homemade sausage. Opera singers perform on weekend evenings, making an evening here truly special. Open Monday through Friday for lunch 11:30 a.m. to 2:00 p.m., nightly for dinner 5:30 p.m. to 10:00 p.m., and until 11:00 p.m. on Friday and Saturday.

For traditional Japanese delicacies, visit **Mori Japanese Restaurant**, 2019 Market, (303) 298-1864, in the backyard of Coors Field. The extensive menu features only the freshest sushi and sashimi, as well as mouth-watering seafood soups, teriyaki, and tempura dishes. Open daily 11:30 a.m. to 2:30 p.m. and 5:00 p.m. to 10:00 p.m. For freshly prepared seafood, such as grilled salmon, or a tasty plate of fish and chips, try **Rick's Bluewater Grill**, 80 South Madison, (303) 399-4448. Hours: Monday through Thursday 11:00 a.m. to 10:00 p.m., Friday 11:00 a.m. to 11:00 p.m., Saturday 5:00 p.m. to 11:00 p.m., and Sunday 5:00 p.m. to 10:00 p.m.

The **Zenith American Grill**, 1750 Lawrence Street, (303) 820-2800, describes its cuisine as "New Western." Entrees include Colorado lamb chops with goat cheese and a pinot noir sauce, or macadamia nut–crusted sea bass with a Thai red curry. Open Monday through Thursday 11:00 a.m. to 10:00 p.m., Friday 11:00 a.m. to 11:00 p.m., Saturday 5:00 p.m. to 11:00 p.m., and Sunday 5:00 p.m. to 10:00 p.m. If you'd really like to treat yourself to an elegant meal, visit the legendary **Palace Arms**, in the Brown Palace Hotel, 321 17th Street, (303) 297-3111, across from the Museum of Western Art. The restaurant specializes in pheasant and other wild game entrees. Open from 11:30 a.m. to 2:00 p.m. and 6:00 p.m. to 10:00 p.m., with a special Sunday brunch served 10:00 a.m. to 2:30 p.m.

One of Denver's best ethnic restaurants is tucked behind the fashionable boutiques of Larimer Square. The **Little Russian Café**, 1424 ½ Larimer Street, (303) 595-8600, specializes in hearty Russian fare guaranteed to stick to your ribs and soothe you with its warm and subtle flavors. The potatoes, borscht, goulash, and several meat dishes are all excellent, and should be washed down with a shot of flavored Vodka. Open 11:00 a.m. to 2:30 p.m. and 5:30 p.m. to 10:30 p.m. Monday through Thursday, and until 11:30 p.m. on Friday and Saturday.

If you would rather avoid expensive places, don't worry, you will still be able to find a decent meal—and take advantage of some of the best deals in town. **Alfalfa's Market**, 900 East 11th Avenue, (303) 832-7701, or 201 University Boulevard, (303) 320-0700, is a natural and gourmet foods grocery store, with a deli, salad bar, and healthy and satisfying hot meals (eggplant lasagna, pasta, roasted chicken) available at relatively inexpensive prices. Open 7:30 a.m. to 10:00 p.m. Monday through Saturday, and 7:30 a.m. to 9:30 p.m. on Sunday. **The Golden Tempura Bowl**, 406 East Colfax Avenue, (303) 832-8440, is a must for those who like the convenience and price of fast food, but want something a little different. Teriyaki, tempura, and curry bowls are dished out here quickly, all under $5. Open daily 11:00 a.m. to 9:00 p.m. For another great deal in fast, healthy, and inexpensive food, try **Chipotle's**, 745 Colorado Boulevard, (303) 333-2121, and ask for one of their chicken fajita burritos—a blend of rice, beans, seasoned chicken, and your choice of salsa—$4.95. Open daily 11:00 a.m. to 10:00 p.m.

For a large plate of comfort food, such as hot roast beef, mashed potatoes, gravy, and green beans, or sirloin beef tips smothered in stew, head over to the businessperson's pub, **Duffy's Shamrock Restaurant and Bar**, 1635 Court Place, (303) 534-4935. Your meal will be served in a matter of seconds (only a slight exaggeration), with prices ranging from $3 to $7. Open for breakfast, lunch, dinner, and drinks, from 7:00 a.m. to 2:00 a.m. Monday through Friday, 8:00 a.m. to 2:00 a.m. Saturday, and 11:00 a.m. to 2:00 a.m. Sunday. **Dozen's**, 236 West 13th Avenue, is a great place for breakfast, brunch, or lunch (open 6:00 a.m. to 2:00 p.m.), and conveniently located near the attractions of the Civic Center Cultural Complex. The menu includes fluffy omelets, egg and vegetable skillets, and a range of healthy sandwiches for under $7.

LODGING

Historic hotels, Victorian bed and breakfasts, and more modern accommodations proliferate in downtown Denver. The elegant **Brown Palace Hotel**, 321 17th Street, at Tremont Place, (800) 321-2599 or (303) 297-3111, is the grande dame of all Denver hotels, built in 1893 to attract a first-class clientele. Its distinctive triangular Renaissance structure sits prominently among Denver's skyscrapers. The hotel's galleried atrium lobby is adorned with tapestries, a terrazzo floor, and onyx arches. The rooms feature either Victorian or art deco furnishings. Rates for a double begin at $180. Across the street is the budget-minded **Comfort Inn**,

401 17th Street, (303) 296-0400, which is linked to the luxury hotel by a pedestrian skywalk. Rates are from $69 to $85.

The **Oxford Hotel**, 1600 17th Street, (800) 228-5838 or (303) 628-5400, is another of Denver's historic and elegant hotels ($75–$175). It is within a stone's throw of Coors Field and the booming restaurant, bar, and gallery scene in Lower Downtown. The hotel restaurant and pub, **McCormick's**, specializes in seafood, and its quirky art deco martini bar, the **Cruise Room**, is one of Denver's most popular night spots.

Located near many cultural attractions in downtown Denver is the **Queen Anne Inn**, 2147 Tremont Place, (303) 296-6666, a well-known bed and breakfast inn housed in two shingled Victorian structures. The rooms, nonsmoking and spacious, start at $75. Another well-appointed bed and breakfast near the downtown area is the **Castle Marne**, 1572 Race Street, (303) 331-0621 or (800) 926-2763. With amenities such as robes, Jacuzzis, and fresh flowers, this is a great place to be pampered. Rates, including a full breakfast with homemade breads and muffins, start at $85.

NIGHTLIFE

As in many big cities, the nightlife found in Denver will satisfy just about any taste. When you get to town, pick up a copy of *Westword*, Denver's independent weekly newspaper, or Friday's entertainment section in either the *Denver Post* or *Rocky Mountain News* for a listing of weekly plays, concerts, lectures, dance performances, and gallery offerings. The **Ticket Bus**, on the corner of the 16th Street Mall and Curtis Street, has a current calendar of events and tickets for dozens of attractions in the region.

Several art deco movie theaters have been converted into concert venues offering a great variety of live music, from salsa, country, big band, and alternative to plain old rock 'n' roll. The **Bluebird Theater**, 3317 East Colfax Avenue, (303) 322-2308, the **Ogden Theatre**, 935 East Colfax Avenue, (303) 831-9448, and the **Paramount Theatre**, 1631 Glenarm Place, (303) 534-8336, always have something interesting going on, such as comedy acts, cult movies, or concerts.

There are 11 microbreweries clustered in downtown Denver. While each brews distinctive beers, one stands above the rest. The **Wynkoop Brewing Company**, 1634 18th Street (18th and Wynkoop) across from Union Station, (303) 297-2700, is in an 1880s warehouse along one of Denver's earliest commercial streets. The establishment has grown to three levels, with a long-running comedy act in the basement, a restaurant and old-fashioned bar on the first level, and a sea of pool tables upstairs. Another popular brewpub, **Rock Bottom**, 1001 16th Street Mall, (303) 534-7616, is a haven for young professionals, the hot spot in town to see and be seen.

The **Denver Center for the Performing Arts**, at 13th and Curtis, is the city's first-class entertainment complex, with nine separate venues. The circular Boettcher Concert Hall is home to the Colorado Symphony Orchestra, and the Temple Hoyne Buell Theatre hosts traveling shows and nationally acclaimed performances. The smaller theaters feature everything from dramatic stage plays to musicals. To hear about current attractions, call (303) 893-3272. For tickets, call the box office at (303) 893-4100.

In addition to the big-name acts, independent theaters present everything from avant-garde productions to traditional comedies and dramas. **Jack's Theater**, 1553 Platte, (303) 433-8082, and the **Avenue Theater**, 2119 East 17th Avenue (next to Mike Berardi's restaurant), (303) 321-5925, are just two of the many playhouses in the metro area. The very popular **Chicken Lips Comedy Theater**, 17th and Market, (303) 534-4440, stages improvisational comedy.

Last, but certainly not least, Denver is the proud home of four professional sports teams. During your stay, you can catch a variety of games, including basketball (the **Nuggets**), baseball (the **Rockies**), football (the **Broncos**), and hockey (the **Avalanche**). To inquire about tickets for any of these sports, contact the **Ticket Connection**, (303) 758-1999, or look in the Easy Reference Guide of any Denver phone book.

SIDETRIP: BOULDER

Located about 45 miles northwest of Denver on U.S. Highway 36, Boulder is one of Colorado's most handsome towns. The **University of Colorado** campus sprawls just south of downtown Boulder along Broadway. The collegiate atmosphere is enriched by ivy-covered red sandstone buildings adorning campus. After exploring campus and "the Hill" just across the street, amble a few more blocks down North Broadway to the **Pearl Street Mall and Historic District** to absorb some of Boulder's relaxed atmosphere. The interesting boutiques, galleries, street performers, and excellent restaurants lining this walking mall are popular with CU students, Boulder residents, and visitors. (2 hours)

BOULDER

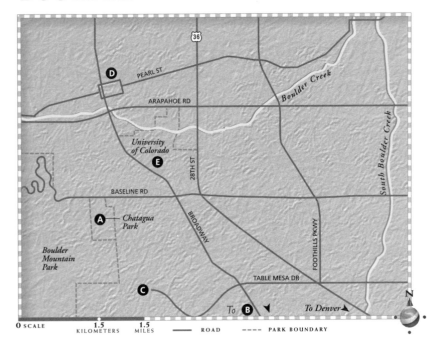

Sightseeing Highlights

A Chautauqua Park and Auditorium

B Eldorado Canyon

C National Center for Atmospheric Research

D Pearl Street and Historic District

E University of Colorado

Boulderites are diehard sports enthusiasts, and everywhere you look people are out walking, jogging, roller blading, or biking. There are wonderful hikes in the many open-space parks surrounding the town. One of the more popular is the **Mesa Trail**, which links several parks along the Flatirons, a series of uplifted sandstone slabs that are prominent landmarks seen when driving from Denver to Boulder on Highway 36. You can hike portions of the trail from **Eldorado Canyon**, the **National Center for Atmospheric Research** (see below), and **Chautauqua Park and Auditorium**. (2–3 hours)

Situated dramatically below the Flatirons is the National Center for Atmospheric Research (NCAR), a center for weather and climate research. This buff-colored building blends beautifully into the natural landscape. Acclaimed architect I. M. Pei designed this distinctive structure, inspired by Anasazi cliff dwellings at Mesa Verde. Inside, you can wander through several interesting scientific weather displays and observe the super-computers busily computing in the lower level of the building. The open space area behind NCAR, a great place for a picnic, has several connecting hiking trails. Free admission. The building is open to the public from 8:00 a.m. to 5:00 p.m. on weekdays, and 9:00 a.m. to 3:00 p.m. on weekends and holidays. Address: 1850 Table Mesa Drive. Located at the west end of Table Mesa Drive in South Boulder. Phone: (303) 497-1174. (½ hour)

Unicorn/Robert Hitchman

SIDETRIP: GEORGETOWN/SILVER PLUME

For an entertaining day trip from Denver, head to these historic Victorian towns 45 miles west of Denver on Interstate 70. Rich gold deposits lured many eager prospectors to this valley, but the silver mines of Georgetown and Silver Plume turned out to be the choice prize of this region. Both towns peaked in the 1870s, when their solid and forward-thinking citizens built churches, hotels, homes, a city park, flagstone sidewalks, and a large school building to demonstrate the permanence of their settlements. Much of the early architecture of these towns has been lovingly preserved, and today Georgetown and Silver Plume comprise a National Register Historic District.

When the Colorado & Southern Railroad steamed through the valley in 1885, these isolated towns finally were connected to the burgeoning settlement of Denver and beyond. But the Colorado & Southern struggled mightily to build their rails a minuscule distance between Georgetown and Silver Plume. In just 2 miles, the train had to scale an elevation of 600 feet, causing it to twist and turn over trestles, loops, and curves totaling over 4½ miles of track.

In 1939, after declining mining activity and the effects of the Depression, the Colorado & Southern Railroad rails were sold for scrap. The Colorado Historical Society purchased the property in the 1950s, but didn't restore the route to its former glory until 1975. Renamed the **Georgetown Loop**, the narrow-gauge train ride includes a visit to the historic **Lebanon Silver Mine**. Admission: For the round-trip tour, which can start from either Georgetown or Silver Plume, $10.95 for adults, $6.50 for children 4–15. The Lebanon Silver Mine Tour, accessible only from the train ride, costs $4 for adults, and $2 for children. Hours: Daily from Memorial Day through October 1, with trains departing approximately every hour and 20 minutes. Location: Old Georgetown Station is located at 11th and Rose Streets. Phone: (970) 569-2403; Denver line, (303) 670-1686; or (800) 691-4FUN. (2½ hours)

A herd of 150 to 200 bighorn sheep can often be seen grazing on ridges high above Georgetown. The Colorado Division of Wildlife constructed the **Georgetown Bighorn Sheep Viewing Site** east of Georgetown, with viewing scopes and interpretive signs about the herd. Volunteers staff the viewing station at certain times to answer questions about the wildlife. (½ hour)

The streets of Georgetown and Silver Plume can accurately be described as whimsical and otherworldly. Spend some time wandering

GEORGETOWN/SILVER PLUME

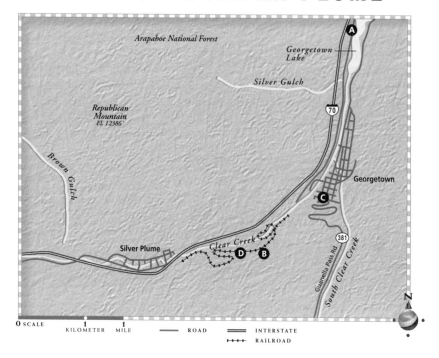

Sightseeing Highlights

A Georgetown Bighorn Sheep Viewing Site

B Georgetown Loop

C Hamill House

D Lebanon Silver Mine

the streets, poking into galleries, specialty shops, and bookstores. The **Hamill House**, a restored structure in Georgetown dating to 1867, has an interesting past as the former home of one of the richest men in Clear Creek County, William Arthur Hamill. Operated today by the Georgetown Society, a dedicated agency that preserves many of the town's historic structures, the home is filled with 1880s furnishings and artifacts. Admission: $2.50 for adults, $1.50 for seniors, $1 for children. Hours: June through September, daily 10:00 a.m. to 5:00 p.m., October through May, Saturday and Sunday 12:00 p.m. to 4:00 p.m. Address: 3rd and Argentine Streets. Phone: (970) 569-2840. (½ hour)

2

PAWNEE GRASSLANDS

While Colorado's soaring mountains and ski resorts are well known to people across the globe, the high plains grasslands that blanket the eastern one-third of the state are often overlooked. This common oversight is unfortunate, as Colorado's plains have much to offer in the way of ample sightseeing, unpretentious beauty, and comfortable hospitality. People who see the plains as an unchanging, flat landscape are missing out on the diverse nature of this expansive region, with its rolling hills, canyons, and plenitude of wildlife.

The Pawnee Grasslands are an isolated patchwork of public and private lands in northeastern Colorado, accessible from Fort Collins to the west, Sterling to the east, and Fort Morgan to the south. Gravel county roads form a grid across the landscape, and most are navigable by any type of vehicle. When the roads get wet or muddy, however, they are usually impassable. Before visiting the area, inquire about road conditions at the Pawnee National Grasslands headquarters in Greeley, 666 "O" Street, (970) 353-5004. Start with a full tank of gas and plenty of water and food, especially if you plan to stay overnight, because this is remote country. And please, stay only on designated roads in the grasslands and never trespass on private land. ◣

PAWNEE GRASSLANDS

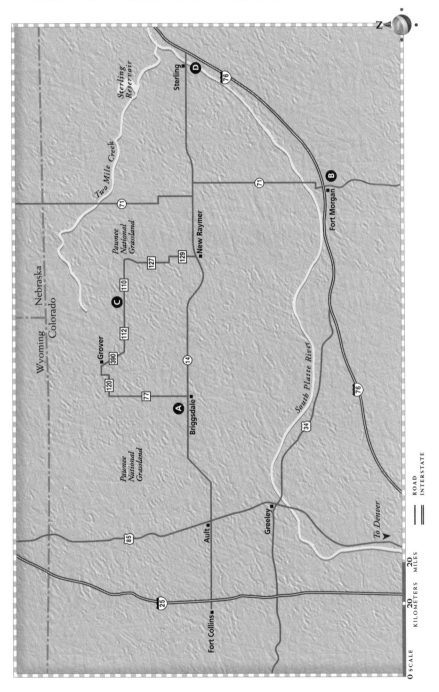

N

Sterling Reservoir

Two Mile Creek

Sterling **D** 76

71 **B**
Fort Morgan

Nebraska
Colorado
Wyoming

Pawnee National Grassland

New Raymer

127
129

110 **C**

112

Grover
390

120

77 14

A Briggsdale

Pawnee National Grassland

South Platte River

34

76

85

Ault

Greeley

To Denver

25

Fort Collins

ROAD
INTERSTATE

0 SCALE
20 KILOMETERS
20 MILES

Sightseeing Highlights

- **Ⓐ** Crow Valley Recreation Area

- **Ⓑ** Fort Morgan Museum

- **Ⓑ** Rainbow Bridge

- **Ⓑ** Riverside Park

- **Ⓒ** Pawnee Buttes

- **Ⓓ** Overland Museum

Note: Items with the same letter are located in the same area.

A PERFECT DAY IN THE PAWNEE GRASSLANDS

Journey across Colorado's northeastern plains to visit Pawnee Buttes, two striking bluffs rising from this vast landscape. Take advantage of the hikes, mountain bike rides, or scenic drives all possible in the Pawnee National Grasslands. Along the way, stop to stretch your legs in shady places like the small town of Grover or the Crow Valley Recreation Area.

GRASSLANDS WEATHER, ECOLOGY, AND HISTORY

Plains weather is always unpredictable. A sweltering, sunny summer day can suddenly turn stormy and cool with a spectacular show of thunder and lightning. The temperatures from September to early November are usually pleasant, and heavy rainfall from April to June carpets the prairie with wildflowers. The grasslands can even be delightful on a mild winter day.

Dominated by short grasses such as buffalo and blue grama, grasslands are punctuated by stands of big cottonwood trees growing along creeks and streams. Birds of prey soar overhead in the wide sky, swift foxes dart through the shrubs, and prairie dogs poke their heads out of their burrows. Owls, ferrets, badgers, gophers, and rattlesnakes also live in underground caves and passages, allowing them to escape from summer's unrelenting heat.

The nutritional grasses of these vast high plains once supported millions of bison. Plains Indians laying claim to these premier hunting grounds include the Comanche, Lakota, Cheyenne, and Arapaho tribes. It is puzzling that these grasslands are named for the Pawnee Indians, as this area was not part of their traditional homeland. The Pawnee lived near the Loop River in present-day Nebraska, and if these longstanding enemies of the Lakota, Cheyenne, and Arapaho ventured onto these plains to hunt bison, they did so at their peril. Many great battles occurred on these plains because of Pawnee encroachments.

The grasslands receive only about 14 inches of precipitation annually, most of it falling during the spring months. Drought-resistant vegetation and animals flourish here, practicing unique adaptations that capture every last drop of moisture. If you visit the grasslands during a wet year, you might be fooled into thinking that this is fertile agricultural land.

Thousands of optimistic homesteaders moved here during a rash of wet years during the 1880s. The country hummed with several farming settlements, all visited by the railroad. The craze back then was something called "dry farming," a practice that didn't require extensive irrigation ditches to support wheat, hay, or alfalfa crops. Farmers dug deep furrows in their fields and rested them every other year to attract whatever moisture was lingering in the air. However, they disturbed the surface of the ground so much that all the topsoil blew away during the Dust Bowl of the 1930s. During these years, the land was devastated by drought, strong winds, and hard winters, forcing most luckless and bankrupt farmers off their lands.

Only a few families managed to eke out a living in the years following the Depression. Shortly thereafter, the Soil Conservation Service purchased large parcels of the prairie and began to teach farming and irrigating practices better suited to the high plains environment. Today, a handful of cattle ranchers lease grazing land from the United States Department of Agriculture through the Pawnee National Grasslands. Skeletons of homes, barns, and cemeteries dot the landscape, reminders of the earlier agricultural bust. Large portions of the natural grassland environment have been disturbed by plowing and overgrazing. A very few sections remain unspoiled, such as near the Pawnee Buttes, where native grasses and plants can still be seen.

SIGHTSEEING HIGHLIGHTS

✯✯✯ **Pawnee Buttes**—These two sedimentary buttes have resisted the erosional forces of wind and water for millions of years and are well-known sentinels of the northeastern plains. Plains Indian tribes often gathered at the buttes, in the midst of their vast bison hunting grounds. The plains rise gently at this spot, revealing an expansive view of the prairie and the Rocky Mountains to the west. Far off in the distance, you can see Longs Peak, a landmark visible throughout the northeastern plains. In *Centennial*, James Michener's epic book about Colorado, the buttes are known as Rattlesnake Buttes, for good reason. Keep an eye out for these creatures sunning on the rocks.

Thirty million years ago this area supported large populations of ancestral mammals. Paleontologists began excavating fossilized bones here in the 1870s, discovering many skeletons resembling modern-day rhinoceroses, horses, camels, and turtles. The Denver Museum of Natural History displays several mammal skeletons excavated from the buttes. Discoveries of ancestral horse skeletons from this location contributed significantly to understanding how the horse evolved into its modern form.

The 3-mile round-trip hiking trail to the buttes wends through swaying grasses, yucca plants, and prickly pear cacti, ending at the base of the west butte. The small ridge near the buttes is a nesting place for eagles, hawks, and falcons. Access to the cliffs is closed during springtime to protect the young broods living in the nests. (2½ hours)

✯✯ **Crow Valley Recreation Area**—Just a quarter-mile north of Briggsdale on Highway 14, this quiet and shady area has a developed campground, picnic area, and baseball diamond. Also on the grounds is the Steward J. Adams Educational Site, a center for studying grasslands ecology.

The Audubon Society often takes birdwatching groups to the grasslands and has prepared a 36-mile self-guided tour. The tour begins at the Crow Valley Recreation Area and winds through the western section of the grasslands. There is also a special 12-mile loop for mountain bikes. To receive a map of the tour or information about the area, contact the Pawnee National Grasslands in Greeley, 666 "O" Street, (970) 353-5004. (1–2 hours)

During your visit you will see a host of birds, such as golden eagles, ferruginous hawks, prairie falcons, and burrowing owls. The mountain plover is the unofficial mascot of the grasslands, recently added to the state's endangered species list. These birds lay their eggs in the grass. Listen for the singing of the western meadow lark and the lark bunting, Colorado's state bird. (½ day)

✫ **Fort Morgan**—Established in 1864, Fort Morgan protected travelers from Indian attacks on the South Platte River Trail into Denver. In later years, the settlement evolved into a thriving agricultural center. Just after the turn of the century, the Great Western Sugar Company built a sugar beet processing factory in town that supported hundreds of farmers in the area. Sugar beet farming attracted diverse ethnic groups, such as Volga Germans (German-speaking people from the Volga River Valley in Russia) and Japanese, who started out working as field laborers and later bought their own farms. Many descendants of these ethnic groups still remain in the area. Hispanics also came north from southern Colorado and northern New Mexico to work the fields, although fewer of them stayed as permanent residents. Located across from Riverside Park on Highway 52, Fort Morgan's historic sugar beet processing factory continues to convert northeastern Colorado's sugar beet harvest into refined white sugar.

The **Fort Morgan Museum** features an extensive Native American artifact collection, exclusively from northeastern Colorado, encompassing over 13,000 years. The museum also proudly displays some belongings of its native son, Glenn Miller, in addition to first-rate exhibits on regional history. Inquire here about a walking tour of historic Fort Morgan and its National Register properties, and driving tours to nearby wildlife areas. Admission is free. Hours: Monday through Friday 10:00 a.m. to 5:00 p.m., Tuesday, Wednesday, and Thursday evenings 6:00 to 8:00, and Saturday 11:00 a.m. to 5:00 p.m. Address: 414 Main. Phone: (970) 867-6331. (1 hour)

Riverside Park is located on Highway 52, the southern portal of the Pawnee Pioneer Trail Byway. One of the main features of the park is **Rainbow Bridge**, a National Historic Civil Engineering Landmark with a unique patented rainbow arch design. When built in 1922, the bridge was the longest rainbow arch in the world. Riverside Park is a 240-acre wildlife preserve, established to protect the riparian ecosystem of the South Platte. (1 hour)

✫ **Sterling**—After the discovery of gold in the mountains west of Denver in 1859, many opportunists packed up and rushed to present-day Colorado in hope of striking it rich—either by mining, farming, or raising cattle to feed residents in the new settlements. A large number of the travelers came by the great Oregon Trail, which began in Independence, Missouri, and followed the Platte River through Nebraska. Those destined for the new settlements journeyed to the confluence of the South Platte and Platte Rivers, today just east of the Colorado/Nebraska border, and then veered southwest to follow the South Platte all the way into Denver. This cutoff became known as the South Platte Trail, and it brought thousands of settlers into fledgling Colorado Territory, established in 1861.

Sterling's history is filled with rich tales of the trail and hardships encountered by many who undertook the long journey. Several ranches and stage stops along the river provided voyagers with a meal and a place to sleep. The **Overland Museum** displays early trail artifacts and items from the first settlers of this area. The museum also has excellent replicas of extinct animal fossils similar to those found near the Pawnee Buttes. Pioneer farm machinery, a Concord stage, native grasses, and wildflowers grace the exterior of the building. Admission is free. Hours: Open April 1 through November 1, Monday through Saturday 9:00 a.m. to 5:00 p.m., Sundays and holidays 10:00 a.m. to 5:00 p.m. Other times of the year, Tuesday through Saturday 10:00 a.m. to 4:00 p.m. Located at Centennial Square, on Highway 6, just off Interstate 76. Phone: (970) 522-3895. (1 hour)

FITNESS AND RECREATION

Jackson Lake State Park, northwest of Fort Morgan on State Highway 144, offers boating, camping, fishing, and wildlife viewing. Species seen here include doves, pheasants, pelicans, beavers, badgers, and waterfowl. **Riverside Park** is a great place to take a jog or walk, enjoy a picnic, or swim in the public pool. The park also has fishing ponds and extensive nature paths. It is located north of the intersection of Highways 52 and 6 in Fort Morgan.

FOOD

While in Grover, you just might crave an authentic milkshake, and lucky for you, the **Grover Market Basket**, (970) 895-2215, on the corner of Custer and Chatoga Avenues, serves the thickest one in town. You'll also find daily hot dinner specials, such as top sirloin, shrimp, or T-bone steak ($5.25), chicken fried steak ($4.95), or a burrito plate

PAWNEE GRASSLANDS

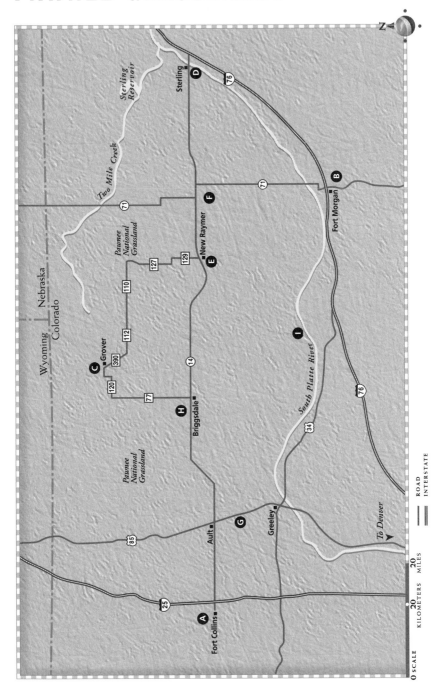

Food

- **Ⓐ** Bisetti's
- **Ⓐ** CooperSmith's
- **Ⓑ** Country Steak-Out
- **Ⓒ** Grover Market Basket
- **Ⓑ** Memories Restaurant
- **Ⓓ** Momma Conde's
- **Ⓔ** Pawnee Station
- **Ⓓ** T.J. Bummer's

Lodging

- **Ⓑ** Central Motel
- **Ⓕ** Elk Echo Ranch
- **Ⓓ** Fountain Lodge
- **Ⓑ** Madison Motel
- **Ⓐ** Mulberry Inn
- **Ⓓ** Oakwood Inn
- **Ⓒ** Plover Inn
- **Ⓖ** Victorian Veranda Bed and Breakfast
- **Ⓐ** West Mulberry Street Bed and Breakfast Inn

Camping

- **Ⓗ** Steward J. Adams Campground
- **Ⓓ** Buffalo Hills Camper Park
- **Ⓘ** Jackson Lake State Park
- **Ⓐ** Pioneer Mobile Home Park
- **Ⓑ** Riverside Park
- **Ⓑ** Wayward Wind Campground

Note: Items with the same letter are located in the same area.

($3.95), which include dessert. Another restaurant found in the grass-lands is **Pawnee Station**, (970) 437-5726, on Highway 14 in New Raymer, open during the spring, summer, and fall from 7:00 a.m. to 7:00 p.m. and during the winter from 7:00 a.m. to 6:00 p.m., Monday through Saturday. They have full breakfasts, hamburgers, steaks, and daily specials for under $5.

In Sterling, the smoke-free **T.J. Bummer's**, 203 Broadway, (970) 522-8397, serves hearty burgers, steaks, and chicken dishes ranging from $3 to $12. Open Monday through Saturday from 5:30 p.m. to 9:00 p.m., and Sunday 5:30 p.m. to 8:00 p.m. Locals rave about **Momma Conde's** homemade Mexican food, with *huevos rancheros*, *chimichangas*, and *sopaipillas* that melt in your mouth, all under $7 for dinner. Located at 20944 Highway 6, (970) 522-2830. Open daily from 6:00 a.m. to 9:00 p.m.

In Fort Morgan, the **Country Steak-Out**, 19592 East 8th Avenue, (970) 867-7887, serves a mean chicken-fried steak, with din-ners starting at $6 and going up to $20 for prime rib or lobster. Open Tuesday through Saturday 11:00 a.m. to 9:00 p.m., and for Sunday brunch 11:00 a.m. to 2:00 p.m. **Memories Restaurant**, in the Park Terrace Inn, 725 Main, (970) 867-8205, is open daily, from 6:30 a.m. to 9:30 p.m. The large menu has Italian and Mexican entrees as well as superb steaks. Lunch and dinner range from $3.50 to $10.25.

There are numerous restaurants in Fort Collins. A fine Italian restaurant is **Bisetti's**, 120 South College Avenue, (970) 493-0086, which specializes in homemade pasta and seafood dishes ranging from $7 to $15. Open for lunch Monday through Friday 11:00 a.m. to 2:00 p.m., and dinner Sunday through Thursday 5:00 p.m. to 9:00 p.m., and Friday and Saturday 5:00 p.m. to 10:00 p.m. **CooperSmith's**, 5 Old Town Square, (970) 498-0483, is a traditional English-style pub and restaurant. The in-house brewery features a wide variety of well-crafted selections, and several dishes ($5–$13) are made using beer recipes. Next door is **CooperSmith's Billiards**, with professional billiard tables, serving pizzas from a wood-burning oven. Open Sunday through Thursday 11:00 a.m. to 11:30 p.m., and Friday and Saturday until 1:30 a.m. The billiards room is open daily until 1:30 a.m.

LODGING

Lodging within the remote grasslands country is hard to come by, which is why the **Elk Echo Ranch**, 47490 Weld County Road 155,

(970) 735-2426, is so unique. The ranch is located 5 miles north of the intersection of County Road 155 and Highway 14, 4 miles east of Stoneham. It sits on a majestic 1,000 acres and has its own elk and buffalo herds. Call ahead for reservations and rates. In the town of Grover, the **Plover Inn**, (970) 895-2275, is a bed and breakfast in a restored historic hotel. Its four suites are named for prairie songbirds. Open from May to October, with rates from $60 to $90.

The nearby towns of Sterling, Fort Morgan, Eaton, and Fort Collins all have a variety of lodging options. In Sterling, the **Fountain Lodge**, 619 North 3rd, (970) 522-1821, is an eccentric motor court, with lighted fountains shimmering in the courtyard. The modern **Oakwood Inn**, 810 Division Avenue, (970) 522-1416, has rooms beginning at $37.

In Fort Morgan, the **Madison Motel**, 14378 U.S. Highway 34, (970) 867-8208, has rooms with two queen-size beds starting at $44. They also have suites with king- or queen-size beds starting at $52. The **Central Motel**, a true mom-and-pop operation, is clean and hospitable, at 201 West Platte Avenue, (970) 867-2401. Rates start at $37.

The **Victorian Veranda Bed and Breakfast**, 515 Cheyenne Avenue, (970) 454-3890, is in the quiet town of Eaton, just south of Ault, which is the eastern portal of the Pawnee Pioneer Trails Scenic Byway. This relaxing and affordable inn ($45–$55) is a treat for travelers, especially if you book the room with a private whirlpool.

As the largest town near the Pawnee Grasslands, Fort Collins offers the most choices for lodging. The **Mulberry Inn**, 4333 East Mulberry Street, east of I-25 at exit 269A, (970) 493-9000, has rooms starting around $50, some with a balcony. Near Colorado State University is the **West Mulberry Street Bed and Breakfast Inn**, 616 West Mulberry Street, (970) 221-1917. This turn-of-the-century Four Square home is filled with period furnishings. Year-round rates start at $75 for a double with a private bathroom and include a full breakfast of quiche, omelets, crepes, or homemade baked goods.

CAMPING

The only standard campground in this area is the **Steward J. Adams Campground**, in the Crow Valley Recreation Area just north of Briggsdale. Managed by the Pawnee National Grasslands, it is shaded by numerous tall cottonwoods that line Crow Creek.

More than 200 camping spots can be found in **Jackson Lake State Park** for trailers, RVs, or tents. Facilities include running water, showers, and toilets. The park is northwest of Fort Morgan on Highway 144, near the town of Orchard. For more information, call (970) 645-2577. Free camping is available at Fort Morgan's **Riverside Park.**

RV camping can be found at **Pioneer Mobile Home Park**, 300 East Harmony Road, I-25 exit 265; the park is 4½ miles west on Harmony Road, near downtown Fort Collins, (970) 226-3325. In Sterling, the **Buffalo Hills Camper Park**, 22018 Highway 6 East, (970) 522-2233 or (800) 569-1824, is a full-service camping spot with hookups, picnic tables, and group camping. Fort Morgan also has its own camping park, the **Wayward Wind Campground**, near I-76 off exit 75A, (970) 867-8948.

Scenic Route: Pawnee Pioneer Trails

This driving tour starts in the agricultural town of Ault on Highway 85, 14 miles east of Fort Collins. This route has been designated the **Pawnee Pioneer Trails Byway** by Colorado's Scenic and Historic Byway Commission. You will see blue columbine signs along the way that mark the byway route.

Drive east on Highway 14 through a long stretch of irrigated farmlands. As you continue to head east, look for a change in the passing landscape. Suddenly you leave the green fields behind and enter the golden grasses of the natural prairie at the border of Pawnee National Grasslands, about 13 miles east of Ault. Next you come upon the hamlet of Briggsdale, once a successful farming center but today a mere fraction of its former size. Many artifacts of a bygone era have been preserved in the **Briggsdale Museum**, in a former one-room schoolhouse, open only by appointment. If you'd like to see it, stop by the **Briggsdale Market**, or call ahead, (970) 656-3436.

PAWNEE PIONEER TRAILS BYWAY

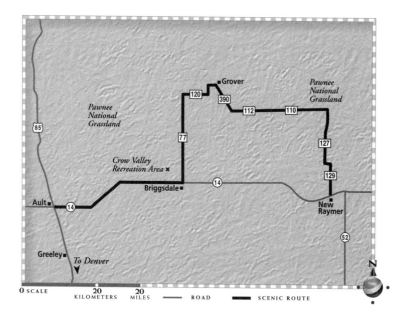

At Briggsdale, take County Road 77 north past the **Crow Valley Recreation Area** and continue north about 15 more miles until you reach County Road 120. Take this road east to the pleasant town of **Grover**. Grover sits in a naturally irrigated pocket on the grasslands, and its residents have enjoyed relative prosperity from ranching over the years. The **Grover History Museum** is in the former railroad depot. Across the way is a grain elevator on the National Register of Historic Places. You can just imagine the railcars pulling in at the depot and men loading grain from the high elevator. The museum has many unique artifacts donated by the community, a display about the Pawnee Buttes, and an historic fire engine. It's usually open during the summer on Sundays from 1:00 p.m. to 4:00 p.m. Otherwise, the museum members will be glad to show it if you call ahead, (970) 895-2349. The museum is free, but donations are appreciated.

From Grover, continue on County Road 120 until it deadends into County Road 390. This flat, wide road is the former route of the Chicago, Burlington, and Quincy Railroad, the lifeline of the prairie settlements. Continue on this stretch until you come to County Road 112, then turn east. Approximately 2 miles down the road, you will see a weathered wooden gate marking the lonely, windswept **Sligo Cemetery**. The struggles of homesteaders in Sligo, a community that once numbered 100 people, are poignantly remembered in this cemetery. Many young people who died from illnesses or injuries are buried here.

After visiting the cemetery (be sure to close the gate behind you), continue another 5 miles on County Road 112 until you intersect County Road 107, where you will head south and east to County Road 685, which takes you on top of a broad ridge and to the **Pawnee Buttes Trail Head**. Once you've seen the buttes, return to County Road 112, and head south and east, roughly following County Roads 110, 110.5, and 115. Don't worry about the changing road numbers—just continue to head east until you come to the intersection of County Road 127. Drive south, and then transfer over to County Road 129, which takes you into the tiny town of **New Raymer** on State Highway 14. From New Raymer, it's 27 miles south to Fort Morgan, 25 miles east to Sterling, 50 miles west to Ault, and 65 miles west to Fort Collins. There's a gas station in New Raymer in case you are running low. ◼

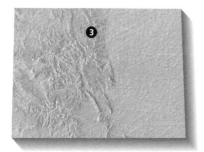

3

ROCKY MOUNTAIN NATIONAL PARK

The dedication of Rocky Mountain National Park on September 4, 1915, officially preserved the alpine ecology, wildlife, and vegetation of a spectacular portion of the Central Rocky Mountains. The many individuals who had tirelessly lobbied for national park status savored their victory. At last, the glorious Rockies were protected from the logging, grazing, and development that had threatened them.

In the mid-1970s, more than 90 percent of Rocky Mountain National Park was designated as Wilderness Area, ensuring that no roads, structures, or other human comforts would be constructed. At the same time, park administrators confronted the problem of overwhelming public interest in the park—it was being "loved to death." While the park remains popular with visitors, there are still many areas where people can appreciate the vast beauty of these mountains in silence and solitude.

Access to Rocky Mountain National Park is through two gateway communities: Estes Park on the eastern side (65 miles from Denver on Highway 36), and Grand Lake on the western side (a little more than 100 miles from Denver on Highways 40 and 34). These communities are connected by Trail Ridge Road, or Highway 34, which traverses the width of the park. The eastern side of the park receives twice as many visitors as the western because it is closer to several large communities along the Front Range, including Denver, Boulder, Fort Collins, and Loveland. While facilities within the park are limited, the towns of Grand Lake and Estes Park cater to visitors. The park entrance fee is $5 per vehicle, good for seven days. ◪

ROCKY MOUNTAIN NATIONAL PARK

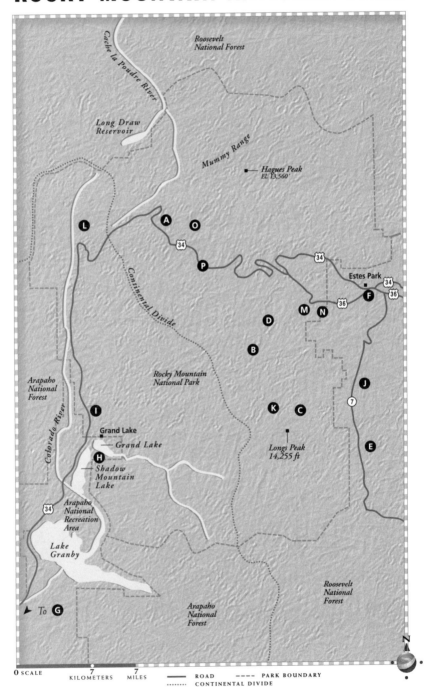

Roosevelt National Forest

Cache la Poudre River

Long Draw Reservoir

Mummy Range

Hagues Peak
EL 13,560'

Continental Divide

Arapaho National Forest

Colorado River

Rocky Mountain National Park

Estes Park

Longs Peak
14,255 ft

Grand Lake

Grand Lake

Shadow Mountain Lake

Arapaho National Recreation Area

Lake Granby

To G

Arapaho National Forest

Roosevelt National Forest

N

0 SCALE
KILOMETERS   MILES
7   7

ROAD
PARK BOUNDARY
CONTINENTAL DIVIDE

Sightseeing Highlights

(A) Alpine Visitor Center

(B) Bear Lake Trailhead

(C) Chasm Lake

(D) Cub Lake

(E) Enos Mills Museum

(F) Estes Park Area Historical Museum

(G) Farr (Granby) Pump Plant

(H) Grand Lake

(I) Kawuneeche Visitor Center

(J) Lily Lake Visitor Center

(K) Longs Peak

(L) Lulu City Trail

(M) Moraine Park Museum

(N) Park Headquarters

(F) Stanley Hotel

(O) Toll Memorial

(P) Trail Ridge Road

Note: Items with the same letter are located in the same area.

A PERFECT DAY IN ROCKY MOUNTAIN NATIONAL PARK

Explore the western, or Grand Lake, side of the park. Stop in at Kawuneeche Visitor Center to get oriented, and then take a two- to three-hour hike on the Lulu City Trail, or any other trail that suits your tastes. Afterwards, drive over Trail Ridge Road, stopping at several places along the way to experience the alpine tundra environment.

NATURAL FEATURES OF ROCKY MOUNTAIN NATIONAL PARK

The Continental Divide, the "Backbone of the Nation," winds through the western portion of Rocky Mountain National Park. From this spine, alpine streams flow either east toward the Atlantic Ocean or west toward the Pacific Ocean. Major rivers cascading to the east are the St. Vrain, Big Thompson, and Cache La Poudre, while to the west the mighty Colorado River springs forth from an unassuming place north of Grand Lake.

Powerful mountain-building forces lifted ancient rocks to form these mountains approximately 70 million years ago. Arctic glaciers sculpted away the ancient bedrock, forming mountains, canyons, and U-shaped valleys. Several active glaciers remain on the north-facing slopes of some mountains in the park.

Three different life zones are preserved in the park: the montane zone, with vegetation such as Ponderosa pine, Douglas fir, lodgepole pine, and quaking aspen; the subalpine zone, with Englemann spruce, alpine fir, and the gnarled limber pine; and the alpine zone, beginning at treeline, or 10,500 feet, with hardy ground-covering vegetation. An array of wildflowers flourish throughout the elevations, such as the Rocky Mountain iris, Indian paintbrush, alpine forget-me-not, sunflowers, blue columbine, and arctic gentian.

The autumn elk mating season at Rocky Mountain National Park is legendary. Each evening at dusk, the bulls vie for prominence by battling and bugling, which is a thrilling combination of loud whistles and grunts. A large herd resides in the higher reaches of the park during the summer, but comes down to the lower elevations in the fall. Mule deer are usually seen browsing meadow grasses along park roads, but moose, coyote, and bear are harder to spot.

Native bighorn sheep herds were practically devastated at the turn of the century because of disease. The herd has since grown back, thanks to several protectionist measures taken by the National Park Service and the United States Forest Service in adjoining parcels of Arapaho National Forest.

SIGHTSEEING HIGHLIGHTS

★★★ **Hiking**—Hiking trails in Rocky Mountain National Park vary widely in terrain and scenery. Some follow lazy meadow streams, others cross rushing waterfalls or follow narrow footpaths along canyon walls, and still others take you to elevations so high you feel like you're on top of the world. With more than 355 miles of hiking trails, there is a wide range of options to suit any taste. You can wander down a short 1-mile path through a wooded forest, or take a five-day expedition through the park boundaries.

Trails beginning from the **Bear Lake Trailhead**, on the east side of the park, are by far the most popular. A shuttle bus will take you from the Glacier Basin parking area on Bear Lake Road to the trailhead. The trails here will be crowded during the summer, especially on weekends, while many other trails in the park are virtually empty.

One of the finest hikes found in the eastern portion of the park travels to **Chasm Lake**, roughly 11 miles round-trip. The trailhead is found at the Longs Peak Ranger Station, 9 miles south of Estes Park on Highway 7. This trail can be snow-covered until late June, and patches of snow stick around here all summer. There are no really steep sections, but the hike does climb from 9,400 feet to 11,850 feet. A shorter and more moderate hike to **Cub Lake** begins at Moraine Park. The lake is usually layered with a delicate pattern of green water lilies. You will also see a series of beaver ponds along the way. The trailhead is just past the Moraine Park campground. The hike is 4½ miles round-trip and gains about 750 feet in elevation.

On the west side of the park, the **Lulu City Trail** follows the Colorado River. Lulu City was a booming gold rush town in 1880. Miners never found a large cache of minerals here, so the town eventually died. The 6-mile round-trip hike is fairly level; it begins at the Colorado River Trailhead. For more information on hikes, visit Park Headquarters on the east side of the park or the Kawuneeche Visitor Center on the west.

★★★ **Trail Ridge Road**—Trail Ridge Road is the highest continuously paved road in the United States, with a total length of 48 miles between the eastern and western portals of Rocky Mountain National Park. Even though it climbs to 12,183 feet in elevation, the road never exceeds a 7 percent grade. Construction crews began laboring on the road in 1931, continued through the harsh winter of 1932, and finally opened the road in 1933. The road became an instant success, capitalizing on the American craze for auto touring. Thousands of visitors swarmed to "the playground of the Rockies" to experience elevations of 12,000 feet from the comfort of their own cars.

The road stays open from Memorial Day until the first heavy snowfall, usually mid-September or October. Inclement weather can close the road during the middle of the summer and make driving conditions treacherous in a matter of minutes. Numerous scenic overlooks and trails exist along the roadway. Bighorn sheep and elk herds are often seen grazing on the exposed hillsides. Dramatic views seen from this staggering elevation include deep canyons, pristine snowfields, and towering cliffs of the Continental Divide. Definitely get out of the car and experience the extraordinary tundra environment. A 1-mile round-trip hike to the **Toll Memorial**, a monument to an early superintendent of Rocky, departs from the Rock Cut Trailhead about 6 miles east of the Alpine Visitor Center. The Park Service has placed several interpretive signs along the trail that explain features in the landscape. When hiking, stay only on established trails to avoid damaging the fragile tundra vegetation. (2 hours to drive Trail Ridge, one way)

★★ **Enos Mills Museum**—Enos Mills first visited this region during the summer of 1884, at the age of 14. He fell in love with the Central Rockies at first sight and returned every summer thereafter to work as a hiking guide up Longs Peak. Later in life, he purchased the Longs Peak Inn, where he catered to visitors for many years. Mills became a devoted disciple of naturalists such as John Muir, Ralph Waldo Emerson, and Henry David Thoreau. He also authored his own books describing the glorious wilderness of the Rockies, its flora and fauna, and his many exciting adventures exploring the region. His efforts in promoting the area for National Park designation earned him the title of "Father of Rocky Mountain National Park."

The one-room log cabin where Mills lived for many summers is now a museum. Mills' elderly daughter, Edna, continues to show groups to the cabin, telling of her father's life and work in this area. Other relatives also show the museum. Donations are requested. Hours: Memorial Day to Labor Day 10:00 a.m. to 5:00 p.m., and by special appointment during the winter. Located 8 miles south of Estes Park on Highway 7. Phone: (970) 586-4706. (1 hour)

★★ Rocky Mountain National Park Activities and Visitor Centers—When you enter the park, stop at one of the visitor centers to learn about the many programs, such as short ranger-led nature walks, campfire programs, and longer hikes to more isolated destinations. Several activities are designed just for kids. Rangers at **Park Headquarters**, (970) 586-2371, on the eastern side of the park, issue backcountry permits and give advice on activities suited to your tastes and length of visit. Summer hours are 8:00 a.m. to 9:00 p.m. The **Kawuneeche Visitor Center**, (970) 627-3471, on the western side of the park, has several excellent exhibits on wildlife, vegetation, and history of the park. Especially helpful are the displays recommending activities according to length of stay. Rangers here also issue backcountry permits. Summer hours are 7:00 a.m. to 7:00 p.m. During the winter, Kawuneeche and Park Headquarters both stay open daily 8:00 a.m. to 5:00 p.m. Park Headquarters hosts a Saturday evening program throughout the winter in its auditorium. Other programs resume in late June. (½–1 hour)

Several seasonal visitor centers are open from 9:00 a.m. to 5:00 p.m. during the summer. The **Moraine Park Museum** is located 2½ miles southwest of Park Headquarters on the east side. The Denver Museum of Natural History has designed several interesting and interactive exhibits here about the geology and natural history of the park. The **Alpine Visitor Center** sits atop Fall River Pass on Trail Ridge Road. Its exhibits focus on the ecosystem of arctic tundra. South of Estes Park on Highway 7 is the **Lily Lake Visitor Center**, providing nature walks, ranger-led activities, and information on area resources.

★ Estes Park—When Joel Estes first gazed upon the high mountain valley known today as Estes Park, he expressed wonder and joy at the beautiful sight before him. The Estes family journeyed to Colorado in 1859 searching for prime cattle-grazing lands. In 1860, Estes brought his family to this mountain valley to settle. Subsisting mainly on wild game, Estes and his sons sold surplus meat in Denver. Still, the family had a tough time surviving in their mountain paradise during the interminable winters.

Shortly thereafter, Estes Park and Longs Peak came to be highly regarded by pleasure travelers for mountain sightseeing, hunting, and fishing. Several individuals with an eye for promotion shaped the region into a first-rate visitor destination. The inventor of the Stanley Steamer automobile, F. O. Stanley, came to Estes Park because of an illness, but found his health improved radically in the pure mountain air. He opened the acclaimed **Stanley Hotel** in June 1909, which remains an imposing Estes Park landmark. Do you remember the creepy movie based on the Stephen King novel *The Shining?* The exterior of this hotel was featured in the movie, but its history couldn't be further from that of the fictional hotel.

Summer brings a host of festivals to Estes Park, with special **Sunday Concerts** sponsored by the Stanley Hotel, the **Scandinavian Mid-Summer Festival**, and the **Estes Park Music Festival** on Monday evenings in midsummer. Elkhorn Avenue is bursting with art galleries and specialty shops. For more information on concerts and galleries, contact the Estes Park Visitor Center, (800) 443-7837 or (970) 586-4431.

For a taste of history, visit the **Estes Park Area Historical Museum**. Exhibits portray the history of Estes Park as a resort, with displays geared toward children. Admission: $2.50 for adults, $1 for children, or $10 for families. Hours: May through September, Monday through Saturday 10:00 a.m. to 5:00 p.m., Sunday 1:00 p.m. to 5:00 p.m. During the months of March, April, October, and December, the museum is also open on weekends and by appointment. Address: 200 4th Street. Phone: (970) 586-6256.

✭ **Farr (Granby) Pump Plant**—The Colorado–Big Thompson Water Diversion Project is a massive irrigation system that diverts water from the Colorado River through an underground tunnel beneath the Continental Divide. The water is then pumped to farms, ranches, and municipalities in northern Colorado. When engineers promoted the idea of a tunnel in the 1930s, environmentalists heatedly argued against it, claiming that water diversion was contrary to the conservation and preservation ideals of national parks. But agricultural interests reigned, and the government decided to siphon waters meant for the western slope of the Continental Divide to the eastern side instead.

The system is designed to deliver up to 310,000 acre feet of water annually to municipal, industrial, and agricultural users on the eastern slope. Water is stored in Lake Granby, and then funneled through the Alva Adams Tunnel beneath the Continental Divide at Longs Peak. Engineers tried especially to hide the results of construction. The project involves five reservoirs, two pump plants, and endless miles of canals and pipelines. This operating plant provides a fascinating look into this immense project. Free public tours are offered daily on the hour, from Memorial Day to Labor Day, 9:00 a.m. to 4:00 p.m., except at noon. The plant is located 10 miles north of Granby on Highway 34, on County Road 64.

✻ **Grand Lake**—Established in the 1870s, Grand Lake provided supplies to fledgling silver camps in the central Rocky Mountains. After the mining fizzled, Grand Lake, similar to Estes Park, became a resort. Located on Colorado's largest natural lake, the small village of Grand Lake is still popular with visitors, offering motor boating, sailing, fishing, and windsurfing on Grand Lake and Lake Granby. Every Fourth of July the town sponsors a spectacular fireworks display over Grand Lake.

✻ **Longs Peak**—Named for Stephen H. Long, the military explorer who sighted this imposing mountain near present-day Fort Morgan in 1820, Longs Peak is the highest mountain, at 14,255 feet, within the boundaries of Rocky Mountain National Park. This enormous landform can be seen from many high points on the northern plains.

The trail to the flat-topped summit of Longs Peak is no ordinary walk in the woods. It is perhaps one of the hardest of Colorado's Fourteeners to climb. Yet many people attempt to scale the peak without adequate preparation. The 16-mile round-trip hike starts at the Longs Peak Ranger Station south of Estes Park, beginning at 9,300 feet and climbing 4,855 feet to the summit. Hikers fit for a strenuous journey and accustomed to the altitude will certainly revel in this challenge, but others might wish to enjoy the beauty of Rocky Mountain National Park on a more moderate trail (see "Hiking," above, and "Fitness and Recreation," below). If you do attempt the climb, be sure to start at dawn, reach the summit, and then make it below treeline by noon to avoid any afternoon thunder and lightning storms on top of the peak.

FITNESS AND RECREATION

Rocky Mountain National Park offers a host of outdoor activities. Hiking is by far the preferred recreational pursuit here in the summertime, in addition to horseback or road bike rides on **Bear Lake Road, Trail Ridge Road,** or the **Horseshoe Park/Estes Park Loop.** Bicyclists pay a $3 fee to enter the park, good for seven days. Backpackers relish the remote backcountry areas of the park, with numerous opportunities to "get lost" for a certain amount of time. Fly-fishing on the Big Thompson River is one of the most popular recreational pursuits in the area. For information on good fishing spots, or any other type of recreation in the area, visit Colorado Wilderness Sports, 358 East Elkhorn Avenue, Estes Park, (970) 586-6548.

Technical rock climbing is a popular sport here, but only experienced mountaineers should attempt it. Several climbing schools in the area offer instruction. For more information contact the **American Climbing Guides Association**, Estes Park, (970) 586-0571, or the **Colorado Mountain School**, Estes Park, (970) 586-5758.

Winter in the park is a treat because you see more wildlife than people. Rangers often lead special cross-country skiing tours on the weekends. The **Grand Lake Touring Center**, (970) 627-8008, features more than 18 miles of groomed trails.

FOOD

Pippi's Place, a bakery and coffeehouse in Estes Park, 361 South St. Vrain Avenue, (970) 586-9299, is the perfect place to go for a hearty breakfast before hitting the trail. It serves breakfast and lunch daily from 6:00 a.m. to 4:00 p.m. during the spring, summer, and fall, and 7:00 a.m. to 4:00 p.m. Monday through Saturday, during the winter. The menu includes waffles, croissants, sandwiches, and soups for $5 to $7.

A lively place to quaff some homemade beers and enjoy a burger or pizza for under $10 is the **Estes Park Brewery**, 470 Prospect Village Drive, (970) 586-5421. It's open 11:00 a.m. to 6:00 p.m. (weekdays) or 8:00 p.m. (weekends) during the winter, and until 10:00 p.m. or midnight during the summer. The **Dunraven Inn**, 2470 Highway 66, (970) 586-6409, serves affordable Italian entrees such as manicotti, lasagna, ravioli, shrimp scampi, lobster, or steak, ranging from $7.50 to $20. Open for dinner during the winter, weekdays 5:00 p.m. to 9:00 p.m., and until 10:30 p.m. on weekends. During the summer, lunch and dinner are served 11:00 a.m. to 10:30 p.m. For an elegant meal, try the **Black Canyon Inn**, 800 MacGregor Avenue (Devil's Gulch Road), (970) 586-9344. The specialties of the house ($15–$20) are freshly and creatively prepared, with seafood, wild game, poultry, veal, and pasta. Open for lunch 11:30 a.m. to 2:00 p.m., and for dinner 5:00 p.m. to 9:00 p.m., Wednesday through Sunday.

In Grand Lake, the **Chuck Hole**, 1119 Grand Avenue, (970) 627-3509, is the place to go for a breakfast platter of eggs, hash browns, or pancakes. Open daily from 7:00 a.m. to 2:00 p.m., with prices ranging from $3.25 to $5.50. The **Mountain Inn**, 612 Grand Avenue, (970) 627-3385, serves family-style meals, with large platters for two to three people. They also have a good children's menu. Dinners range from $3.99 for some of their Mexican entrees to $15.30 for a New York strip steak. Open during the summer daily from 11:00 a.m. to 10:00 p.m., and during the winter for dinner nightly and lunch on Saturday, Sunday, and Monday.

Northern Exposure, 916 Grand Avenue, (970) 627-3543, serves lunch and dinner in a relaxed atmosphere. Specializing in burgers, nachos, and soups, prices here are in the $5 to $10 range. They are open for lunch and dinner and have a relaxed and lively bar. The **Rapids Restaurant**, 209 Rapids Lane, (970) 627-3707, in a rustic log cabin, is a nice place to go for a romantic dinner, with entrees such as prime rib, pasta, and poultry, ranging from $11 to $20. Open nightly during the summer, 5:00 p.m. to 9:30 p.m., and until 10:00 p.m. on Friday and Saturday. The restaurant is closed the month of November, and Monday and Tuesday evenings from October until the last weekend in May.

LODGING

Families often prefer to spend vacations at one of the many dude ranches surrounding Rocky Mountain National Park, with horseback rides, swimming pools, hikes, and other Western-style activities. If this interests you, contact the **Colorado Dude & Guest Ranch Association**, P.O. Box 300, Tabernash, CO 80478, (970) 887-3128, for a list of ranches in this area.

Both Estes Park and Grand Lake have a wide variety of lodging, with numerous motor courts, bed and breakfasts, and historic cabins. Most accommodations stay open year-round, but some close after October and don't re-open until May.

In Estes Park, the **Baldpate Inn**, 4900 South Highway 7, (970) 586-6151, is a rustic and comfortable lodge, cleverly named after a key collection featured in the novel *Seven Keys to Baldpate*, written by Earl D. Biggers in 1917. The plot of this mystery involves seven people who each believe they hold the only key to an isolated mountain hotel. Rates range from $65 to $125, open from May to October. For budget-minded travelers, the **Trapper's Motor Inn**, 553 West Elkhorn Avenue, (970) 586-2833, is your best bet for clean and well-kept rooms, at $39.

Allenspark is a small community 13 miles south of Estes Park on

ROCKY MOUNTAIN NATIONAL PARK

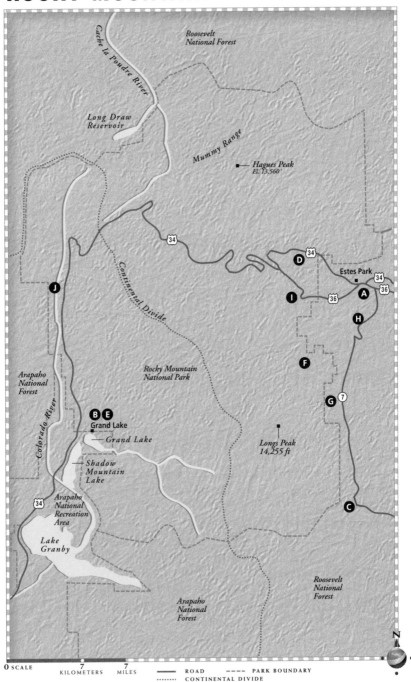

Roosevelt National Forest

Cache la Poudre River

Long Draw Reservoir

Mummy Range

Hagues Peak
El. 13,560'

34

34

D

Estes Park

34

36

I

36

A

H

Continental Divide

F

Arapaho National Forest

Rocky Mountain National Park

G 7

Colorado River

B **E**
Grand Lake

Grand Lake

Longs Peak
14,255 ft

Shadow Mountain Lake

34

Arapaho National Recreation Area

C

Lake Granby

Roosevelt National Forest

Arapaho National Forest

N

0 SCALE   7   7
        KILOMETERS   MILES   ——— ROAD   - - - - PARK BOUNDARY
                                    ·········· CONTINENTAL DIVIDE

Food

Ⓐ Black Canyon Inn

Ⓑ Chuck Hole

Ⓐ Dunraven Inn

Ⓐ Estes Park Brewery

Ⓑ Mountain Inn

Ⓑ Northern Exposure

Ⓐ Pippi's Place

Ⓑ Rapids Restaurant

Lodging

Ⓒ Allenspark Lodge and Cabins

Ⓐ Baldpate Inn

Ⓑ Daven Haven Lodge

Ⓑ Lemmon Lodge Cabins

Ⓑ Soda Springs Ranch

Ⓐ Trapper's Motor Inn

Camping

Ⓓ Aspenglen Campground

Ⓔ Elk Creek Campground

Ⓕ Glacier Basin Campground

Ⓖ Longs Peak Campground

Ⓗ Mary's Lake Campground

Ⓘ Moraine Park Campground

Ⓙ Timber Creek Campground

Note: Items with the same letter are located in the same area.

Highway 7. If you'd like to avoid the crowds that descend on Estes Park during the summer, stay at the **Allenspark Lodge and Cabins**, 184 Main, (970) 747-2552 or (800) 206-2552. This romantic and cozy bed and breakfast has a hot tub, game room, and library, with nearby hiking and skiing trails. A continental-plus breakfast is included in the rate, starting at $45 for rooms with a shared bathroom. Lunch and dinner are also served in the dining room.

In Grand Lake, the **Lemmon Lodge Cabins**, 1224 Lake Avenue, (970) 727-3314, are open from May to October. Clustered on the shore of Grand Lake, the cabins enjoy a magnificent view and direct lake access. The 24 units vary in price and style, sleeping from four to 12 people. Rates start at $80. The **Daven Haven Lodge**, 604 Marina Avenue, (970) 627-8144 or (800) 426-2755, stays open year-round. The cabins here cater to families, sleeping up to nine, and range from $60 to $115. The **Soda Springs Ranch**, 9921 Highway 34, (970) 627-8125, has one-, two-, and three-bedroom condos ranging from $85 to $170. Open year-round, the ranch is 4 miles south of Grand Lake.

CAMPING

Camping within the park fills up quickly from mid-June to mid-August. On the Estes Park side, the **Moraine Park Campground** and the **Glacier Basin Campground** can accommodate RVs or tents for $10 per night. To make advance reservations for these two campgrounds, call (800) 365-CAMP. Other campgrounds in the park do not require reservations, but fill up quickly on a first-come, first-served basis. **Longs Peak** and **Aspenglen**, on the east side of the park, are for tents only, for $8 per night. And on the west side, the **Timber Creek Campground** is for RVs or tents, $8 per night.

Backcountry camping is allowed within the park, and permits are issued from May to mid-August for $10. Contact the **Back Country Office**, (970) 586-1242, for more information. You'll have to give them an idea of where you'll be camping, and permits are only issued for a maximum of seven nights. Fires are allowed only at sites with fire rings.

For private RV campgrounds, in Grand Lake try the **Elk Creek Campground**, 143 County Road 48, north of Grand Lake on Highway 34, at the west entrance to Rocky Mountain National Park, (970) 627-8502 or (800) ELK-CREEK. In Estes Park **Mary's Lake Campground**, 2120 Mary's Lake Road, (970) 586-4411 or (800) 445-MARY, has a playground on the shores of Mary's Lake, campfire pits, and picnic tables.

4

STEAMBOAT SPRINGS

The Yampa River courses through the sparsely populated heart of northwestern Colorado. The Yamparika Utes freely hunted and fished up this river, which they knew as Bear River. (Both the river and the Utes are named after the yampa plant, an onionlike root that grows here.) Homesteaders who settled here in the late 1870s established cattle and sheep ranches, many of which are still in operation.

A strong Western lifestyle prevails in northwestern Colorado, where hardy people ably support themselves from the land and their animals. Coal mining is also influential. In fact, more than one-third of Colorado's power is generated from coal-fueled plants in Moffat and Routt Counties. In the 1980s, Steamboat Springs vaulted to international resort status when downhill skiers discovered its first-class ski area.

Just east of Steamboat Springs is the Continental Divide, with passages over Muddy Pass at 8,772 feet and Rabbit Ears Pass at 9,426 feet. Prominent mountains form a barrier to the east, while to the south, high tablelands created by lava beds and glaciers (known as the Flat Tops) stretch out a hundred miles. Originating in the Flat Tops, the Yampa River provides a rich habitat for a variety of plants and animals. Beavers, Canadian geese, bald eagles, great blue herons, and the greater sandhill crane all live along the river. Gigantic herds of deer, elk, and antelope roam the high mountain valley, as do bighorn sheep, moose, and a fairly large herd of wild mustangs in Sandwash Creek Basin near Craig. ◼

STEAMBOAT SPRINGS AREA

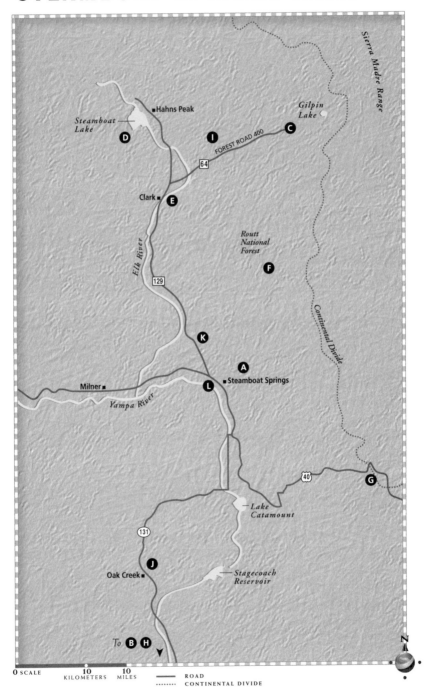

Sierra Madre Range

Hahns Peak

Steamboat Lake

D

Gilpin Lake

I

FOREST ROAD 400

C

64

Clark

E

Elk River

Routt National Forest

F

129

Continental Divide

K

A

Steamboat Springs

Milner

L

Yampa River

40

G

Lake Catamount

131

Stagecoach Reservoir

J

Oak Creek

To B H

N

| 0 SCALE | 10 KILOMETERS | 10 MILES | ——— ROAD |
| | | | ········· CONTINENTAL DIVIDE |

Sightseeing Highlights

A Fish Creek Falls

B Flat Tops Wilderness Area

C Gilpin Lake Trail

C Gold Creek Lake Trail

D Hahn's Peak/Steamboat Lake
Recreation Area

E Home Ranch Resort

A Long Lake

F Mt. Zirkel Wilderness

G Rabbit Ears Pass

C Three Island Lake Trail

H Trappers Lake

I Vista Verde Guest Ranch

Food

J Chelsea's

Lodging

K Elk Run Estates

Camping

B Flat Tops Wilderness Area

L Ski Town KOA Campground

J Stagecoach State Park

D Steamboat Lake State Park

Note: Items with the same letter are located in the same area.

A PERFECT DAY IN STEAMBOAT SPRINGS

Start the morning off at first light with a hot-air balloon ride. You will linger above the town of Steamboat, enjoying spectacular views of the Continental Divide, the Flat Tops, and the Snowy Range in Wyoming. Once you're back on the ground, sip the customary champagne toast and then set off to explore the town of Steamboat, with its many hot springs, shops, and galleries. In the evening, journey to Strawberry Hot Springs to enjoy a quiet evening under the stars in a bubbling mineral bath.

SIGHTSEEING HIGHLIGHTS

★★★ **Flat Tops Wilderness Area**—South of Steamboat Springs, accessible from the town of Yampa, is an exceptionally wild and scenic area known as the Flat Tops. The Flat Tops Trail Scenic and Historic Byway starts in Yampa, travels through two national forests (Routt and White River), and ends in the town of Meeker. It takes approximately 2½ hours to travel the byway between Yampa and Meeker, not including stops along the way. Although half of this 82-mile drive is unpaved, it is still adequate for two-wheel drive vehicles, except when wet. The road closes to cars in the winter, when it becomes a favored spot for cross-country skiers.

The Utes used a series of ancient trails across the Flat Tops when traveling between their winter grounds in the White River Valley and summer grounds in the Yampa River Valley. Beginning in the 1820s, fur trappers were lured here by huge beaver populations on the Yampa River. Each summer, the Utes and mountain men journeyed to a predetermined place for a rendezvous, where agents from the fur companies swapped traps, gunpowder, bullets, utensils, and other supplies for large quantities of beaver pelts.

On the west end of the Flat Tops are lands formerly within the White River Indian Agency, set aside for the Utes after white settlers encroached on their lands in the central mountains of Colorado. Nathan Meeker, an unyielding man appointed as Indian agent, attempted to convert the Utes to white ways by teaching them farming. He was murdered during an uprising at the agency in 1879. As a result, the Utes at White River Agency were removed from Colorado to the Uintah-Ouray Reservation in northeastern Utah.

United States Forest Service architect Arthur Carhart visited these mountains in the early 1900s to make recommendations for development around the serene **Trappers Lake**. But after viewing the splendid natural environment of the lake, he realized that constructing roads and homes for people to enjoy it in comfort would destroy the very wilderness that made the area so special. His defiant stand against development helped pave the way for further legislation, resulting in the 1964 Wilderness Act, which protected unspoiled sections of nature. The Flat Tops became a Wilderness Area in 1975. From the eastern portal of the byway at Yampa, the access road (Forest Road 205) to Trappers Lake is approximately 40 miles. From there, the lake is another 7 to 8 miles. For additional information, contact the Routt National Forest ranger office in Yampa, 300 Roselawn, (970) 638-4516. (Full day)

★★★ **Mt. Zirkel Wilderness**—Straddling the Park Range of the Continental Divide northeast of Steamboat, the Mt. Zirkel Wilderness embraces numerous alpine lakes, tundra, forests, and the Elk and Encampment Rivers. **Mt. Zirkel**, elevation 12,180 feet, in the northern reaches of the wilderness boundary, can be reached in a long, exhilarating day hike for experienced hikers. Drive 2 miles from the center of Steamboat Springs on Highway 40 to County Road 129 (the road to Steamboat Lake and Hahn's Peak). At County Road 64 (Forest Road 400), turn right. The road will parallel the Elk River for approximately 30 to 45 minutes, until you reach the parking area and trailhead at Slavonia. You can also hike to several tranquil mountain lakes from branching forks at this trailhead, such as the **Gold Creek Lake Trail**, **Three Island Lake Trail**, or the **Gilpin Lake Trail**, which terminates at the Continental Divide. Before exploring the wilderness, stop in at the Hahn's Peak Ranger District office, 57 10th Street, for a topographical map of the area. (½–full day)

★★★ **Steamboat Ski Area/Winter Sports**—Steamboat residents are delighted to boast that more than 35 of their youngsters have made it to the Winter Olympics, a record that beats any other ski town in the country. Winter sports are a passion here, beginning when early day residents used skis for transportation during the winter months. And it isn't just downhill skiing that steals the spotlight, as snowboarding, ski jumping, freestyle and cross-country skiing have all been mastered by local athletes.

Steamboat Ski Area is an exceptional mountain for intermediate skiers, but there is also plenty here for beginning and advanced skiers. This is where the term "champagne powder" originated to describe the light and fluffy snow that usually blankets these mountains by December or January. The area offers special kids and preteen programs, all types of ski lessons, and the Billy Kidd Center of Performance Skiing, which specializes in coaching intermediate and advanced skiers. Snowboarding, once the sport of an elite group of grunge kids, has now hit the mainstream, as seen in the types (and ages) of people showing off at Steamboat's special snowboarder's park.

One of the more entertaining times to visit Steamboat is mid-January, when cowboys from the National Western Stock Show in Denver converge on the mountain to display their skiing finesse (or lack thereof). The ski area is generally open by Thanksgiving weekend, with lift tickets in the $39 to $44 range for adults, $25 for children. For more information on the ski area, call the Steamboat Ski & Resort Company, (970) 879-6111.

Cross-country skiers at the **Steamboat Ski Touring Center** appreciate the 20 miles of groomed trails that meander along Fish Creek near the alpine ski area. Admission is $10 for a full day, and $8 for a half-day, beginning after 1:00 p.m. Rental equipment and lessons are available. Phone: (970) 879-8180. Several guest ranches in the surrounding region specialize in cross-country skiing, with rentals, lessons, and special group programs. The **Home Ranch Resort** is north of Steamboat Springs in the small town of Clark, (970) 879-9044, and the **Vista Verde Guest Ranch** is in a secluded location outside of town, (800) 526-7433.

Carl Howelsen brought competitive and recreational ski jumping to Steamboat Springs, and taught many local kids how to ski jump during the long winter months. The jumping hills at **Howelsen Park**, used by Olympic ski jumpers and national competitors, are the largest and most complete in the United States. The ski area has novice slopes open for nighttime skiing until 10:00 p.m., an outdoor ice-skating rink, a bobsled course, and approximately 7 miles of groomed cross-country ski trails. The facility transforms during the summer into an area for mountain biking, with roller skating and in-line blading on the rink. Admission to the ski slope: $8 for adults and $4 for children. Ice-skating: $4 for adults, $2.50 for children 13 and under; $3 for skate rentals. Bobsledding: $8 per person, per ride. Take Highway 40 into Steamboat, turn left at 5th Street, and drive two blocks across the bridge. Take a right in front of the rodeo stands. For general information, call (970) 879-4300. (Full day)

Rabbit Ears Pass is a paradise for backcountry Nordic skiers. The summit of the pass is actually a long meadow, interspersed with evergreens and gentle hills. Many consider this the best place to cross-country ski in Colorado, for its solitude, scenery, and voluminous snow. Several trails, for all abilities, begin at a trailhead near the high point of the pass, about 25 miles southeast of Steamboat Springs on Highway 40. (½–full day)

✸✸ **Fish Creek Falls**—East of Steamboat is Fish Creek Falls, a natural waterfall spilling into a steep canyon within Routt National Forest. At the turn of the century, local families made day trips to the falls, where they would picnic amongst the rocks and catch large volumes of fish for winter's supply. In the 1930s, the Civilian Conservation Corps improved the area, constructing a road, picnic facilities, and a trail to the falls.

While many people visit the 238-foot falls, located a short way up a wheelchair accessible walking trail, fewer continue along the trail destined for **Long Lake**, 7 miles up the steep Fish Creek Canyon. This can be an invigorating day hike or overnight trip. To reach the parking area for Fish Creek Falls, take South Lincoln Street (Highway 40) to 3rd Street, and turn east. When you reach Oak Street (it turns into Fish Creek Falls Road), turn right and drive about 3 miles until you see the parking lot. For more information on hiking up Fish Creek, stop by the Hahn's Peak Ranger District office, 57 10th Street, or call (970) 879-1870. (1 hour–full day)

✸✸ **Hahn's Peak/Steamboat Lake Recreation Area**—The Hahn's Peak Mining District first attracted prospectors in search of gold in 1865. The low-grade ore here never kept things hopping, although a short revival did occur in 1872, when operations consisted of hydraulic mining, a practice that used up a staggering amount of water to recover a small amount of gold. The **Hahn's Peak Schoolhouse,** on the National Register of Historic Places, displays artifacts from the earliest settlement in northwest Colorado. The museum is free, but they do accept donations. Open daily from June through October. Call ahead for hours, (970) 879-6781.

At the foot of Hahn's Peak, **Steamboat Lake** is a peaceful recreation spot developed in 1967 by a dam of Willow Creek. Although this is a reservoir, a natural ecosystem has developed here, similar to those of other alpine lakes. The water is used as backup storage for the

Colorado Ute Power Plant near Craig, should the Yampa River run low. It has never been needed for its intended purpose, and many visitors come here to enjoy its peaceful scenery, camping, swimming, and fishing. To get to the lake, drive 2 miles west from the center of Steamboat Springs on Highway 40 to County Road 129. Turn right and drive 26 miles to the park entrance. The fee is $3 for a daily pass. The day-use area is generally open from 5:00 a.m. to 10:00 p.m. For more information, call (970) 879-3922. (½ day)

☆☆ **Steamboat Springs Swimming Pool**—You will need a soak in these soothing hot springs after a hard day of outdoor activity, be it skiing, hiking, mountain biking, or even wildlife viewing. The Steamboat Sanitarium Association, incorporated near the turn of the century, officially inaugurated a longstanding local tradition of frequenting the mineral springs gurgling throughout town. Heart Spring feeds these four outdoor mineral pools, each from 99 to 102 degrees Fahrenheit. You can also get a massage here, dry out in a sauna, or swim in the lap pool. Admission: $5 for adults, $2 for children; an enclosed water slide is open daily; ten rides cost $3.50 in addition to pool admission. Hours: 8:00 a.m. to 9:45 p.m. weekends, 5:30 a.m. to 9:45 p.m. weekdays. Address: 136 Lincoln Avenue. Phone: (970) 879-1828. (2 hours)

☆ **Strawberry Park Hot Springs**—One of the more well-known hot springs in Colorado, Strawberry Park Hot Springs is located 8 miles north of Steamboat Springs. The springs are a popular destination for mountain bikers, cross-country skiers, snowshoers, or even the less intrepid who drive up the gravel access road 7 miles to Hot Springs Creek. Especially inviting during the chilly winter months, these 100-degree Fahrenheit waters do the trick in warming up cold toes and fingers. Another great time to partake is by moonlight, when you can stargaze while you luxuriate. To reach the springs, take 7th Street to Park Road, turn north, and drive 7 miles to Hot Springs Creek. Admission: $5 for adults until 5:00 p.m., when the price goes up to $7, $2 for children under 12. Hours: 10:00 a.m. to midnight (no admission after 11:00 p.m.). Minors are not allowed in the springs after dark. Phone: (970) 879-0342. (2 hours)

☆ **Tread of the Pioneers Museum**—Established in a historic home built in 1900, the historical ski collection displayed here demonstrates the love of this sport in Steamboat Springs. Donated artifacts tell an engaging history of the town, established by a pioneer family in 1875. Admission: $2.50 for adults, $2 for teens, $1 for children 6–12. Hours: Vary during the year, but the museum is open 11:00 a.m. to 5:00 p.m., Monday through Saturday during ski season and daily during the summer. Address: 8th and Oak Streets. Phone: (970) 879-2214. (½ hour)

✯ **Walking Tour of the Hot Springs of Steamboat**—Numerous hot mineral springs rise to the surface in the immediate area of Steamboat Springs. The town is named for a particularly noisy spring that sounded like steamboats chugging up the Mississippi. **Soda Spring** and **Hot Sulphur Spring** are just across from the library, while **Steamboat Spring**, **Black Sulphur Spring**, and **Narcissus Spring** are all found across the bridge from the park on the south side of the Yampa River. The Chamber of Commerce has prepared a 2-mile walking tour of these springs and others in the nearby area. For more information, stop by the offices at 1255 South Lincoln Avenue, open during the summer, Monday through Saturday 8:00 a.m. to 7:00 p.m., and Sunday 8:00 a.m. to 5:00 p.m. The chamber is open shorter hours during the winter, so call ahead to make sure they are open. Phone: (970) 879-0880. (2 hours)

✯ **Routt County Rodeos**—The residents of northwestern Colorado take their horse riding and cattle roping skills seriously. On summer weekends, rodeos bring out the best in local, and sometimes national, competition. County fairs take place during the late summer. If you're here at that time, be sure to go, as they feature a rodeo, live entertainment, kid's activities, and livestock judging. (2 hours)

FITNESS AND RECREATION

Winter sports are the premier recreational attraction here, but summer also brings a host of exciting outdoor activities. You can ride the wild Yampa River on the flotation device of your choice, or hike, backpack, and camp in the millions of acres of remote public lands surrounding Steamboat.

Mountain bike riders of all abilities will delight in the rides possible on the slopes of **Steamboat Ski Area**, from easy jaunts on relatively flat terrain to goose-pimple rides down precipitous mountain slopes. For an intermediate ride, the **Spring Creek Trail** is perfect; advanced riders will be challenged by the dirt paths on the **Rabbit Ears**

Continental Divide Trail. Stop in the **Ski Haus**, 1450 South Lincoln Avenue, (970) 879-0385, to rent a bike or ask for information on trails. The **Yampa River Core Trail** is a 4-mile path linking downtown Steamboat with the ski area. The trail is paved and has an adjoining gravel path to accommodate all types of activities. You can walk up **Mt. Werner**, the Steamboat ski hill, where you will be rewarded by majestic views of the Yampa River Valley, Continental Divide, and Flat Tops. Or, take the **Silver Bullet Gondola**, which runs from mid-June through late September, from 10:00 a.m. to 4:00 p.m. daily, $11 for adults, $6 for children under 13 and seniors.

Consider taking a hot-air balloon trip for the most panoramic view of the stunning scenery of northwestern Colorado. You will rise 2,000 to 3,000 feet above the ground in a colorful balloon that holds four to six people. Two companies that offer balloon flights are **Balloons Over Steamboat**, (970) 879-3298, or **Pegasus Balloon Tours**, (970) 879-9191 or (800) 748-2487. The trips cost $80 for a half-hour and $150 for an hour, and children can fly for half price. Balloons fly year-round, starting at 7:00 a.m. or earlier in the summer, and at 9:00 a.m. during the winter, weather permitting. Both companies ask you to make reservations at least one day in advance.

FOOD

Winona's Restaurant, 617 Lincoln Avenue, (970) 879-2483, is especially known for breakfast (served all day) with omelets, waffles, and French toast. They also serve light lunch and dinner entrees such as salads and pasta dishes, all under $10. Open 7:00 a.m. to 9:00 p.m. For a more substantial meal, head over to the **Old Town Pub**, 600 Lincoln Avenue, (970) 879-2101, where you can feast on T-bone steak, prime rib, baby-back ribs, pasta, chicken sandwiches, or burgers from $6.50 to $17.95. Open from 11:00 a.m. to 10:00 p.m.

If you'd like to share a pizza with some friends, **Cugino's Pizzeria**, 825 Oak Street, (970) 879-5805, is the place to go. Large pizzas range in price from $8.50 to $21.25. They are open from 11:00 a.m. to 10:00 p.m. Cugino's will also deliver from 5:00 p.m. to 9:30 p.m.

To really treat yourself, visit **L'apogee**, 911 Lincoln Avenue, (970) 879-1919, an elegant French restaurant that often features fresh seafood, veal, and beef entrees ($21–$26). They serve dinner from 5:30 to 10:00 p.m. nightly. Another favorite Steamboat restaurant is **La Montana**, 2500 Village Drive, (970) 879-5800, which serves tasty new Southwestern and Mexican dishes, with dinner entrees ranging from $11 to $20.

The brewery located near the ski area, **Heavenly Daze**, Ski Time Square, (970) 879-8080, is beginning to make a name for itself with its raspberry wheat beer. They also serve pub food, with a large selection of burgers and pasta (under $10). Open from 11:00 a.m. until 10:00 p.m., with a top-floor nightclub that has live music and stays open until 2:00 a.m. Another excellent microbrewery downtown is the **Steamboat Brewery & Tavern**, 5th Street and Lincoln Avenue, (970) 879-2233, where you can relax with a homemade beer and well-prepared meal, or munch on a great assortment of appetizers (under $10). Lunch from 11:30 a.m. to 5:00 p.m., dinner from 5:00 p.m. to 10:00 p.m., pizza until 2:00 a.m.

The town of Oak Creek, about 20 miles south of Steamboat on Highway 131, is a funky collection of buildings, shops, and restaurants. The town is the home of one of the best restaurants in this region, **Chelsea's**, (970) 736-8538, which specializes in Szechuan Chinese cuisine, as spicy as you can stand it. The chef prepares succulent dishes such as Peking duck ($24 for two people) or crispy chicken ($14.95 for two), if you call ahead two days in advance. They also feature wonderful shrimp dishes for around $8.95, soups, egg rolls, and fried rice ($4.95). Open for dinner Tuesday through Sunday 5:00 p.m. to 10:00 p.m.

LODGING

During the winter, lodging prices in Steamboat are as steep as the surrounding mountains. The high rates are generally halved during the summer. I have recommended some of the better deals in town based on their high-season rates. For inexpensive and very rustic lodging, head up to **Strawberry Park Hot Springs Cabins and Campground**, 44200 Routt County Road 36, (970) 879-0342, where cabins rent for under $20 and you can pitch a tent for about $5 per night. An unique performing arts camp north of Steamboat, the **Perry-Mansfield Dance Camp**, 40755 Routt County Road 36, (970) 879-7125, has six cabins starting at $70 that sleep up to ten people and are available year-round. During the summer, the "campers" give theater and dance performances. Directions are similar for both the hot springs cabins and the camp: Head north on 7th Street until you reach Missouri Avenue, and turn right. When you reach Park Road (County Road 36), head north and follow the signs to either location.

STEAMBOAT SPRINGS

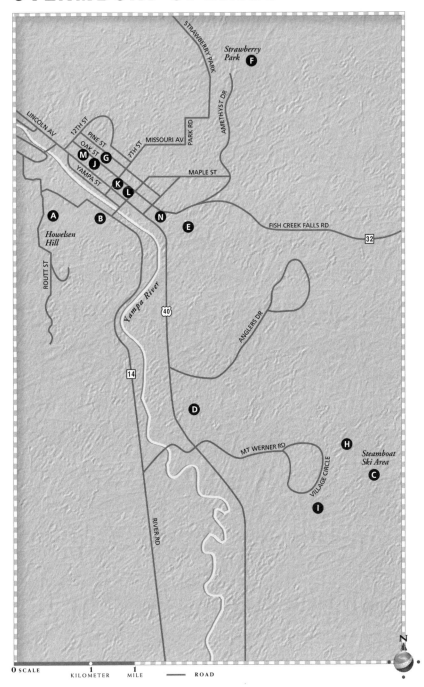

Strawberry Park **F**

STRAWBERRY PARK

AMETHYST DR

PARK RD

LINCOLN AV

12TH ST

PINE ST

OAK ST

7TH ST

MISSOURI AV

M **G**

J

YAMPA ST

MAPLE ST

K

L

A **B** **N**

E

FISH CREEK FALLS RD

32

Howelsen
Hill

ROUTT ST

Yampa River

40

14

ANGLERS DR

D

MT WERNER RD

H

Steamboat
Ski Area

VILLAGE CIRCLE

C

I

RIVER RD

N

0 SCALE   1   1 ———— ROAD
KILOMETER   MILE

Sightseeing Highlights

A Howelson Park

B Routt County Rodeo

C Steamboat Ski Area

D Steamboat Ski Touring Center

E Steamboat Springs Swimming Pool

F Strawberry Park Hot Springs

G Tread of the Pioneers Museum

Food

G Cugino's Pizzeria

H Heavenly Daze

I La Montana

J L'apogee

K Old Town Pub

L Steamboat Brewery & Tavern

K Winona's Restaurant

Lodging

M Clermont Inn

F Perry-Mansfield Dance Camp

N Rabbit Ears Motel

F Strawberry Park Hot Springs
Cabins and Campground

Note: Items with the same letter are located in the same area.

One of the best lodging deals in town is the **Clermont Inn**, 917 Lincoln Avenue, (970) 879-3083. This motor inn has 22 rooms that share tubs and showers for $85, including a full breakfast, a hot tub, and ski lockers. The famous marquee of the **Rabbit Ears Motel**, 201 Lincoln Avenue, across from the Steamboat Hot Springs, (800) 828-7701 or (970) 879-1150, has welcomed people for decades. A double here starts at $106.

Steamboat Central Reservations, (800) 922-2722, department 300, can book you a hotel, motel, condominium, or house for your stay. The high-season rates (mid-December to January 1) begin at $42 (for a motel) and can go up to $200 to $300 (for one- or two-bedroom condos). Ask about ski packages with free lift tickets for children.

Located 5 miles north of Steamboat is the **Elk River Estates**, on County Road 129, (970) 879-7556. Year-round rates are $45 (including a full breakfast) for a double with a private bath. The home is heated during the winter by a wood-burning fireplace and electric heat. The owner likes to include guided ski services or trips to Strawberry Park Hot Springs.

CAMPING

Most campgrounds in the **Flat Tops Wilderness** have fishing access, restrooms, and trash receptacles. Several are located on the base of Forest Road 205, at Trappers Lake. Look for **Bucks, Trapline, Cutthroat**, and **Shepherds Rim**.

Two state parks near Steamboat have ample spaces for RVs or tents, such as **Steamboat Lake**, north of town about 30 miles, and **Stagecoach**, south of town on Highway 131, just east of the town of Oak Creek. Both parks have nightly camping fees of $6.

Ski Town KOA Campground, 2 miles west of Steamboat Springs on Highway 40, (970) 879-0273, has spaces for RVs and tents, is open year-round, and has a general store, laundromat, and pool.

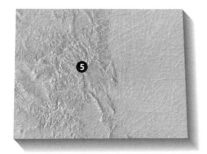

5
LEADVILLE

After the discovery of gold in the Rocky Mountains in 1858, prospectors scoured every gully and hill in the region searching for the "Mother Lode." In 1860, a group struck paydirt southwest of present-day Leadville in California Gulch. This rush didn't last long, however, because of a perplexing black dirt that clung to the gold and made separation of the ore almost impossible. By the mid-1860s, all but a few persistent prospectors had abandoned the settlement.

Finally a miner had the black dirt assayed; it turned out to be lead carbonate—chock-full of profitable silver. The second rush to California Gulch began in 1877 and attracted 20,000 people by the end of the decade. Leadville exploded as a maze of ramshackle tents, half-finished buildings, hotels, saloons, and bordellos. The town has since weathered many busts, but mining has persisted as its mainstay industry for well over a century.

In some of the most violent upheavals of the continent, geologic forces lifted this land 2 miles above sea level. Pressures deep within the earth forced mineral-rich liquids into great fissures, accumulating in veins that eventually reached the earth's surface, only to be hacked, drilled, or blasted out by invasive mining methods.

To the west of Leadville is the imperial Sawatch Range, birthplace of the Arkansas River and home to Colorado's highest mountains. To the east are the lower, but no less magnificent, peaks of the Mosquito Range. In this lofty valley began the odyssey of Leadville, Colorado's most memorable mining town. ◼

LEADVILLE AREA

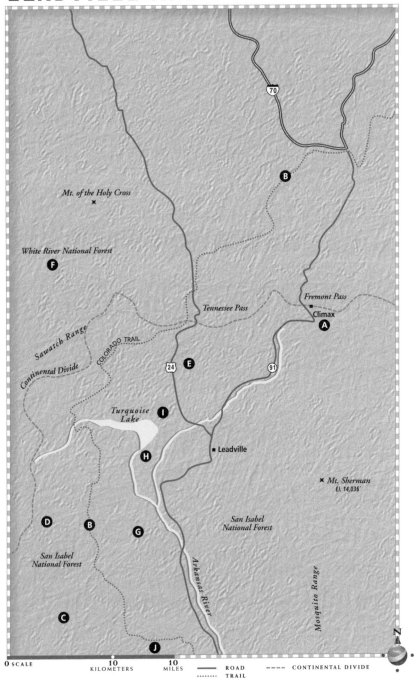

Mt. of the Holy Cross ×

White River National Forest

F

B

Fremont Pass

Tennessee Pass

Climax ■

A

Sawatch Range

Continental Divide

COLORADO TRAIL

24 **E**

91

Turquoise Lake

I

H

■ Leadville

× Mt. Sherman
El. 14,036´

D

B

G

San Isabel National Forest

San Isabel National Forest

Mosquito Range

Arkansas River

C

J

N

0 SCALE
10 KILOMETERS
10 MILES

——— ROAD

········· TRAIL

––––– CONTINENTAL DIVIDE

Sightseeing Highlights

A Climax Molybdenum Mine

B Colorado Trail

C Mt. Elbert

D Mt. Massive

E Ski Cooper/Camp Hale

F Tenth Mountain Division Hut System

Camping

G Elbert Creek Campground

G Half Moon Campground

H Sugar Loafin' Campground

I Turquoise Reservoir

J Twin Lakes

Note: Items with the same letter are located in the same place or area.

A PERFECT DAY IN LEADVILLE

Leadville's charm is in its rich history. Many historic buildings and houses, built with the most luxurious appointments at the height of mining activity, have been restored to their original splendor. Spend the morning exploring Leadville's historical attractions, such as the National Mining Hall of Fame & Museum, the Tabor Opera House, or the Healy House. Then take a scenic drive through the "Route of the Silver Kings," to get a taste of the frenzied mining activity that took place in these hills.

SIGHTSEEING HIGHLIGHTS

★★★ **Hiking near Leadville**—The possibilities for hiking in the crisp mountain air of this region are endless. In the Sawatch Range, Colorado's two highest Fourteeners present formidable hiking challenges: **Mt. Massive**, (round-trip of 14 miles to an elevation of 14,421 feet) and **Mt. Elbert**, (round-trip of 9 miles to an elevation of 14,433 feet). Both begin just above the Halfmoon Campground in the San Isabel National Forest. You can get to the trailheads by driving south on Highway 24 to Malta. Head west (right) on Highway 300 at Malta until you reach road 160, which takes you to road 110, along Halfmoon Creek and to the campground. While it is possible to hike either Elbert or Massive in one day, be prepared for a lengthy and strenuous journey that will last from dawn to dusk.

The **Colorado Trail** skirts Leadville to the west, along its 500-mile journey between Denver and Durango. The trail can be accessed at the summit of Tennessee Pass or in the San Isabel Forest near the town of Twin Lakes. For more information on these or any other hikes in the region, contact the **Leadville Ranger District**, San Isabel National Forest, 2015 North Poplar Street, (719) 486-0749.

Another stunning place to hike and camp in posh accommodations along the way, is on the 350 miles of backcountry trails comprising the **Tenth Mountain Division Hut System**. The "huts" are actually large and comfortable log cabins that can sleep up to 16 people. Situated in the pristine wilderness, they include wood burning stoves used for cooking and heating, and solar-powered electricity. They stretch along backcountry trails between Vail, Leadville, and Aspen in the White River National Forest. The difficulty of the terrain varies, and trips can be geared toward your ability level. In addition to hiking, year-round activities on the trails include mountain biking, backcountry skiing, and snowshoeing. You have to make advance reservations to use the huts, which run $20 to $25 per person, per night. A detailed map of the back country is a necessity. For more information, call the Tenth Mountain Division Hut Association in Aspen at (970) 925-4554. (Full day–several days)

★★★ **National Mining Hall of Fame & Museum**—Leadville is the home of the nation's mining museum, authorized through an act of Congress and presidential approval in 1988. During a period of 130 years, mineral production in the Leadville region has grossed approximately $2 billion. It is fitting that this nonprofit museum, dedicated to the science, industry, and history of mining, is located here.

Exhibits include many priceless minerals, some loaned by the Smithsonian and the Harvard Mineralogical Museum, in addition to the Bowman Gold Collection of specimens found only within Colorado. Two full-size replicas of underground mines—hard rock and coal—illustrate day-to-day experiences in the lives of miners. Admission: $3.50 for adults, $3 for seniors, $2 for children 6–12. Hours: October through April, Monday through Friday 10:00 a.m. to 2:00 p.m.; May through September, daily 9:00 a.m. to 5:00 p.m. Address: 120 West 9th Street. Phone: (719) 486-1229. (2 hours)

★★★ **"The Route of the Silver Kings"**—Situated east of Leadville is the Leadville Mining District, a 20-square-mile cradle that once held minerals such as gold, silver, lead, zinc, copper, and iron. The district is littered with abandoned and dilapidated structures from previous mining operations, all reminders of the potent effects of mining on the landscape. Forgotten head frames, chutes, dumps, cables, and cars lie dormant throughout the area.

You may be tempted to explore these old structures and mineshafts—don't. They are unstable and extremely dangerous. It's best to stay on the road and view them from a distance. The roads of the mining district, accessible from both 7th Street and 5th Street, can be driven by any type of car. This is a great place for a mountain bike ride or leisurely walk. The **Leadville Chamber of Commerce**, on the corner of 9th and Harrison, sells booklets ($2) about the mines of the district and the men who worked them—some made colossal fortunes, while others lost their last dollar. Winter hours: Daily 10:00 a.m. to 5:00 p.m. Summer hours: Daily 9:00 a.m. to 5:00 p.m. Phone: (719) 486-3900. (2 hours)

★★★ **Tabor Opera House**—Horace A. Tabor, Leadville's first mayor and later a United States senator, built this distinguished and elegant opera house in 1879. The famous author Oscar Wilde visited Leadville on April 14, 1882, and delivered a lecture on the "Ethics of Art" to a full audience in the Tabor Opera House. Many audience members admitted no understanding or interest in this subject, but still had a hearty good time at the lecture. Afterwards, they escorted Wilde to the Matchless Mine for a private tour, then served him a balanced meal of whiskey, whiskey, and more whiskey. When Wilde wrote about his Leadville visit in later years, he was most impressed with the sign above the piano in a local saloon that read: "Please do not shoot the pianist. He is doing his best."

Wilde was just one celebrity of many who visited Leadville to entertain, or be entertained in, its rowdy atmosphere. Presiding over the merriment, the Tabor Opera House brought culture and refinement to the young town, and was a great asset to the mining camp. Tabor lost the house in 1893 with the crash of the silver market. It changed hands several times, until it was saved by a dedicated resident in 1955. This venerable structure has been restored and still contains many original furnishings and decor. Memorabilia from its notable events is on display, and it continues as a venue for films, lectures, theater, and exhibits. Admission: $4 for adults, $2 for children 6–12. Hours: June through October, Sunday through Friday 9:00 a.m. to 5:30 p.m., November through May by appointment. Address: 306–310 Harrison Avenue. Phone: (719) 486-1147. (1 hour)

✮✮ **Climax Molybdenum Mine**—A huge stock of molybdenum, a mineral used to harden steel, once existed at the summit of Fremont Pass. The sprawling complex constructed by the Climax Mining Company became one of the world's largest underground mines. By the mid-1950s, molybdenum mining had taken over as the dominant industry in Lake County. Highly prized during World Wars I and II, the mineral aided the fabrication of stainless steel, aircraft, and automobiles, and in later years, spacecraft.

The company developed a town, also called Climax, at the 11,318-foot summit of Fremont Pass, which achieved the distinction of being the highest town in the United States until it closed in 1963. The town housed the miners and families and provided a variety of services, such as a school, hospital, and even its own ski area. When mining operations encroached on the townsite in the early 1960s, the company moved the town to Leadville. In 1982, full-scale mining stopped, with only a small workforce remaining to manage environmental reclamation of former mine sites. Interpretive signs at the summit explain the significance of the mineral and give some history on the mining operations and former town. To visit the site, drive north of Leadville on Highway 91 about 12 miles. (1 hour)

✮✮ **Healy House and Dexter Cabin**—These two examples of 1880s architecture in Leadville provide an interesting contrast. The three-storied Healy House has a favored view of the Continental

Divide on top of Harrison Avenue. August Meyer, who built the house, was one of the first men to own a smelter in Leadville. Meyer went to great lengths to please his new bride, Emma, filling the home with only the finest Victorian furnishings. The house is named Healy after a later owner who donated the home to the town of Leadville in the mid-1900s.

Next door to the Healy House is a curious two-room log structure, the Dexter Cabin, that at first glance appears to be a rudely constructed miner's cabin. It actually belonged to a learned and wealthy man, James Dexter, who had an elegant home for his family in Denver, but used this cabin when on business in Leadville. Decorations of his "bachelor" digs (often used for late-night poker parties) included English wall coverings and a matched black walnut and white oak floor. A Persian rug and zinc-lined bathtub completed the lavish appointments.

Both the Healy House and Dexter Cabin are operated by the Colorado Historical Society, which offers tours conducted by guides in period costume. Admission: $3 for adults, $2.50 for seniors, and $2 for children 6–12. Hours: Memorial Day to Labor Day 10:00 a.m. to 4:30 p.m., during September on weekends only. Address: 912 Harrison Avenue. Phone: (719) 486-0487. (1 hour)

★★ **Ski Cooper/Camp Hale**—During World War II, the present location of the downhill ski area, Ski Cooper, was the center of active training for United States troops specializing in mountain and winter warfare. Thousands of men, dubbed the "Soldiers of the Summit," formed the famous Tenth Mountain Division, the only division of its kind in the United States. The recruits mastered the arts of alpine skiing, snowshoeing, technical climbing, and alpine survival and rescue skills to be effective against the intrusion of Hitler's army in the mountains of Europe. Serving in Italy in 1944, almost 1,000 men from the Tenth Mountain Division were killed in active fighting and are memorialized today in a granite monument at the entrance of Ski Cooper.

After returning from fighting overseas, many veterans of the Tenth Mountain Division returned to Colorado and pioneered the state's recreational ski industry, at places like Ski Cooper, Vail, and Aspen. Ski Cooper is an affordable and challenging ski area, peaking at an elevation of 11,700 feet above Tennessee Pass. In the Ski Cooper lodge are displays of artifacts from the Tenth Mountain Division. Located 10 miles north of Leadville on Highway 24, the ski season usually begins Thanksgiving weekend and concludes at the end of March. Lift tickets are $23 for adults, and $15 for children, and the area has a ski school, equipment rental, and nursery. Phone: (719) 486-2277. (Full day)

✸ **Matchless Mine Tour**—The final chapter in the odyssey of Horace Tabor and his second wife, the beautiful Elizabeth (better known as "Baby Doe"), is intertwined with the Matchless Mine. When Horace Tabor purchased sole title to this silver claim in 1879, he turned a questionable sale into an overnight success and became known throughout the country as the "Silver King of Colorado." The profits from this mine (over $7 million) kept him rolling in dough through the 1880s. But after the 1893 silver crash, it was worthless, and Tabor lost his entire fortune.

When Tabor died in 1899, he left Baby Doe penniless. Local legend has Horace clutching Baby Doe on his deathbed and whispering these dying words: "Hang on to the Matchless. It will make millions again." Dramatic, isn't it? Well, yes, but Tabor never actually said it. Regardless, Baby Doe did spend the rest of her life and energy holding on to the Matchless. She moved into a shack at the Matchless Mine, sold her jewels, and borrowed money from influential friends to hold on to her "last chance." But the Matchless never again produced anything of value, and Baby Doe never regained her former status. In March 1935, at the age of 80, she froze to death in her cabin.

Thousands of people have visited Baby Doe's lonely shack at the Matchless Mine to steal a quick glimpse of her fateful life. Admission: $2 for adults, children under 12 no charge. Hours: Open daily from early June through Labor Day. Address: 414 East 7th Street. Phone: (719) 486-0371. (½ hour)

✸ **Heritage Museum**—Leadville's municipal museum has mining artifacts, ore samples, and other artifacts donated by early pioneers. One of the most interesting displays in the museum is a quarter-inch scale replica of Leadville's Ice Palace. To raise morale during the interminable winter months of 1895, Leadville businessmen concocted a fantastic Winter Carnival, including the construction of a massive timber palace surrounded by 5,000 tons of ice. It opened on January 1, 1896, to the amazement of the entire world, and included an indoor skating rink, ballroom, taxidermy displays, and intricately carved ice statues. But to everyone's chagrin, unseasonable chinook winds caused an early meltdown by the end of March. Still, the Palace helped raise the spirits of Leadville residents after the dreadful Panic of 1893.

Admission: $2.50 for adults, $1.50 for children. Hours: May through October, daily from 10:00 a.m. to 6:00 p.m. Address: 102 East 9th Street. Phone: (719) 486-1878. (½ hour)

FITNESS AND RECREATION

The **Arkansas Headwaters Recreation Area**, encompassing 150 miles of numerous recreational possibilities, begins north of Leadville. Along this high stretch, the Arkansas is a gentle stream spooling through meadows and forested areas. Fishing is possible at **Turquoise Lake** and at a scenic overlook south of Leadville at the petite **Crystal Lakes**. It isn't until below Granite that the river begins to change, crashing through narrow canyons ideal for white-water rafting. For more information on raft trips in the lower sections of the river, contact **Tenth Mountain Sports**, 322 Harrison Avenue, (800) 892-6371 or (719) 486-2202 (and refer to the Salida chapter).

Lands in the San Isabel National Forest have multitudes of trails for hiking, mountain biking, and backcountry camping. One of the more difficult mountain biking trails in the area ascends to the summit of Mosquito Pass, east of Leadville. Hiking trails around Twin Lakes (see the scenic drive section at the end of this chapter) make for moderate outings. Contact the Leadville Ranger District, San Isabel Forest, 2015 Poplar, (719) 486-0749.

FOOD

For an authentic Leadville experience, stop in at the **Silver Dollar Bar**, 315 Harrison, (719) 486-9914, which has been serving libations since 1879 (during Prohibition, the moonshine was well concealed underneath the bar). An original silver dollar marquee manufactured by silver titan Horace Tabor has an honored place here. If you are craving Chinese food, Mandarin style, visit **Szechuan Taste II**, 500 Harrison Avenue, (719) 486-0484, for a plate of mixed vegetables, sweet and sour chicken, kung pao shrimp, or Szechuan beef, with prices ranging from $4.50 to $6.25. Open daily 11:00 a.m. to 9:30 p.m.

Callaway's Restaurant in the Delaware Hotel, 700 Harrison Ave., (719) 486-1418 or (800) 748-2004, serves innovative pizzas for about $8. Dinner specials include a tenderloin beef for $14.95 and other American continental dishes. The restaurant is open for breakfast

LEADVILLE

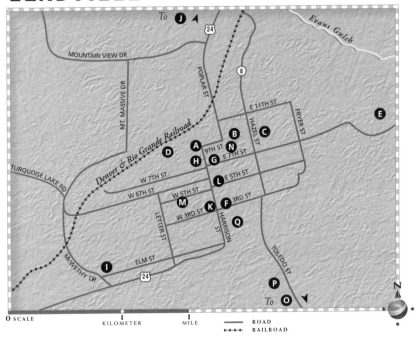

Sights

Ⓐ Dexter Cabin

Ⓐ Healy House

Ⓑ Heritage Museum

Ⓒ Matchless Mine

Ⓓ National Mining Hall of Fame and Museum

Ⓔ Route of the Silver Kings

Ⓕ Tabor Opera House

Food

Ⓖ Callaway's Restaurant

Ⓗ Golden Burro

Ⓘ The Grill

Ⓙ Leadville Prospector

Ⓚ Silver Dollar Bar

Ⓛ Szechuan Taste II

Lodging

Ⓜ Apple Blossom Inn

Ⓖ Delaware Hotel

Ⓝ Leadville Country Inn

Ⓞ Mt. Elbert Lodge

Ⓟ Pan Ark Lodge

Ⓠ Timberline Motel

Note: Items with the same letter are located in the same place.

7:00 a.m. to 10:30 a.m., lunch, 11:30 a.m. to 2:00 p.m., and dinner 5:00 p.m. to 9:00 p.m. The **Leadville Prospector**, 3 miles north of Leadville on Highway 91, (719) 486-3955 or (800) 844-2828, is open for dinner Tuesday through Saturday 5:00 p.m. to 9:00 p.m. during the winter, and on Sunday during the summer. The menu features steaks, seafood, and pasta, with specials such as prime rib, New York strip steak, or a 24-ounce sirloin. All meals include soup and salad.

Delicious and authentic Mexican food is prepared at **The Grill**, 715 Elm, (719) 486-9930, open daily 11:00 a.m. to 10:00 p.m. A la carte items start at $2.25, but the real temptation are the full dinners, such as stuffed sopaipillas smothered in green chile for $10.50. Made with homemade bread, the French toast at the **Golden Burro**, 710 Harrison Avenue, (719) 486-1239, is truly delightful ($3). Breakfast is served all day, in addition to lunch (try a Monte Cristo sandwich with fries, $5.50, or burgers on homemade buns, $4.25) and dinner (entrees include rainbow trout, baked half-chicken, baby-back ribs, or chicken fried steak, from $6.50 to $12.95).

LODGING

Leadville is a popular destination in both the summer and winter, and reservations are often needed during the peak months of December through February, and June through August. Most of the lodging rates I have given you here are for the high season, unless noted. Off-season rates are generally 10 to 20 percent less.

Located near the small community of Twin Lakes is a comfortable country lodge worth looking into for a relaxing getaway. The **Mt. Elbert Lodge**, 10764 Highway 82, (719) 486-0594, is on the road to Aspen, 11 miles west of Twin Lakes. Situated below its towering namesake, you can hike the back route up Mt. Elbert that starts just behind the lodge. Year-round rates for a double with a shared bathroom are $53.

In Leadville, the **Apple Blossom Inn**, 120 West 4th Street, (719) 486-2141 or (800) 982-9279, is housed in a restored Victorian, built by a wealthy banker in 1879. The gigantic feather beds at the inn make for an untroubled night's sleep. Rates, including breakfast, are $59 to $118. Another place to treat yourself is the **Leadville Country Inn**, 127 East 8th Street, (719) 486-2354 or (800) 748-2354, which has a hot tub in the gazebo, a first-class gourmet breakfast, and freshly baked goods. Rates begin at $67 and go up to $117.

The **Delaware Hotel**, 700 Harrison Avenue, (800) 748-2004, built in 1886, has long been a favored stopping place for travelers passing through Leadville. The hotel is restored in high-Victorian splendor, and the owners often feature theme packages, such as mystery weekends or ski weekends including a ticket to Ski Cooper. Rooms have either double or queen-size beds, with some adjoining suites perfect for a family, ranging from $65 to $120.

One of the most affordable lodging options in Leadville is the **Timberline Motel**, 216 Harrison, (719) 486-1876, where doubles begin at $43. Or try the **Pan Ark Lodge**, 5827 Highway 24, 9½ miles south of town, (719) 486-1063 or (800) 443-1063, where rooms begin at $49.

CAMPING

The San Isabel National Forest hosts 500 campsites, such as at **Twin Lakes**, near the town of the same name, **Halfmoon Campground**, and **Elbert Creek Campground**, near the trailheads for Mt. Massive and Mt. Elbert. **Turquoise Reservoir**, west of Leadville on Turquoise Lake Road, is another good camping spot. The San Isabel National Forest Leadville Ranger District can provide you with more information on the numerous campsites near Leadville: 2015 Poplar Street, (719) 486-0749.

Sugar Loafin' Campground, (719) 486-1031, can be found off of Highway 24 south of Leadville at milepost 177. Drive 3 miles down the county road to the site. The campground is open from late May to late September; it has marvelous views of Mt. Elbert and Mt. Massive, large pull-through RV sites, water, and electricity.

Scenic Route: Leadville to Aspen

The 59-mile trip between these two legendary mining towns is steeped in gorgeous scenery and history, and is especially breathtaking during autumn, when the quaking aspens make their annual debut in shades of russet, gold, and orange. The Independence Pass road (Highway 82) is open only during the summer and usually closes by mid-September, after the first heavy snowfall. Perched precariously on the slopes of Independence Mountain, this paved road tests the skills of even the most experienced mountain drivers. If you have a long recreational vehicle, I wouldn't recommend you tempt fate by taking this drive.

Drive south on Highway 24 through Leadville past the remaining buildings of the American Smelting and Refining Company, which closed its doors in 1961. This smelter is only one example of the many refineries that once flourished in Leadville, converting raw carbonate ores into valuable silver. Continuing south on Highway 24, you follow the dips and bends of the Arkansas River until you reach the junction of Highway 82; turn west (right). Approximately 6 miles up

LEADVILLE TO ASPEN OVER INDEPENDENCE PASS

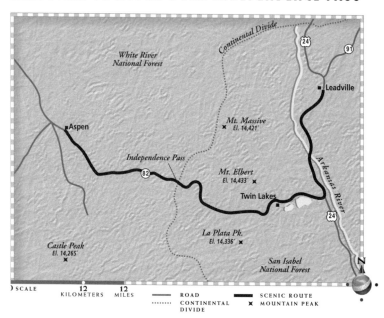

the road is the village of Twin Lakes, a National Historic District, where several Forest Service hiking trails depart into the surrounding wilderness. Twin Lakes began as a mining town and later became a resort destination. Many people came to stay at the famous Interlaken Hotel, built in 1890, on the southern shore of the upper lake. The remains of this once-glamorous hotel can be visited along a hiking trail that loops around the lake.

After leaving Twin Lakes, the road begins to climb towards Independence Pass, scaling to a height of 12,095 feet at the top of the Continental Divide. Hacked out as a toll road between the boom towns of Leadville and Aspen in the 1880s, the road received a lot of use year-round, as sleighs could travel easily over the snow that traps today's automobiles.

Four miles west of the summit of the pass is the ghost town of Independence, where gold was first discovered on July 4, 1879. While Independence did enjoy some prosperity, Aspen eclipsed it in importance during the 1880s. Several lonely buildings remain, and this is a nice spot to pull off for a picnic before reaching Aspen, another 16 miles west. ◧

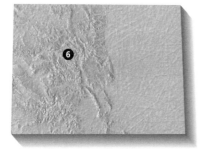

6

ROARING FORK VALLEY

The communities of the Roaring Fork Valley all foster thriving cultural scenes. Dance and musical performances, lectures, art exhibits, and theater can be enjoyed in these towns at any time of the year. While Aspen has the most diverse offerings, other communities such as Glenwood Springs, Carbondale, and Redstone in the Crystal River Valley, hold their own in artistic impression. If you prefer to avoid crowds, don't worry, you will still find plenty of places to appreciate this region without having to fight the masses.

Perhaps you'll catch one of several festivals during your stay. Some of the more popular events include the Glenwood Springs Summer of Jazz, a free jazz concert held every Wednesday night from mid-June to mid-August, at 6:30 p.m. in Two Rivers Park. The Glenwood Springs Strawberry Days, usually held the third weekend of June, is a popular civic fair with live music, artisans, and a town parade. Reservations for hotel rooms fill up quickly during this week.

Snowmass hosts a free Summer of Music Concert Series during weekends in July and August. Aspen also has its fair share of festivals throughout the year. By far the most popular and renowned is the Aspen Music Festival, which actually runs year-round. ◪

ROARING FORK VALLEY

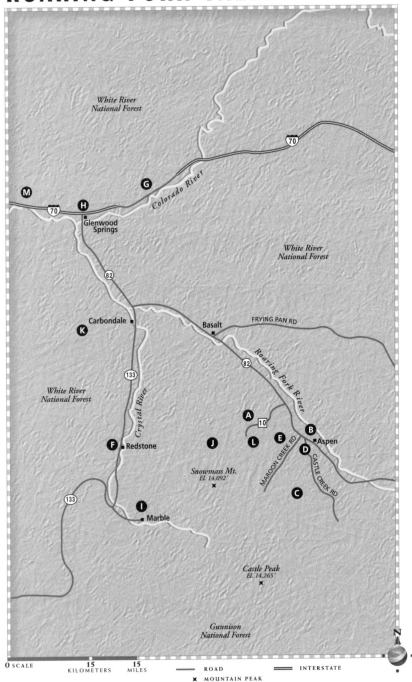

White River
National Forest

70

G

M

70

H

Glenwood
Springs

Colorado River

White River
National Forest

82

Carbondale

Basalt

FRYING PAN RD

K

Roaring Fork River

82

White River
National Forest

133

Crystal River

A

10

J

L

E

B

Aspen

F

Redstone

D

MAROON CREEK RD

CASTLE CREEK RD

C

Snowmass Mt.
El. 14,092'
✕

133

I

Marble

Castle Peak
El. 14,265'
✕

Gunnison
National Forest

N

0 SCALE
15
KILOMETERS
15
MILES
ROAD
INTERSTATE
✕ MOUNTAIN PEAK

Sightseeing Highlights

Ⓐ Anderson Ranch Arts Center

Ⓑ Aspen Center for Environmental Studies

Ⓒ Aspen Highlands

Ⓓ Aspen Mountain

Ⓓ Aspen Mountain Gondola

Ⓑ Aspen Music Festival

Ⓔ Buttermilk/Tiehack

Ⓕ Cleveholm Manor

Ⓖ Glenwood Canyon

Ⓗ Glenwood Hot Springs

Ⓗ Glenwood Springs Center for the Arts

Ⓖ Hanging Lake Trail Head

Ⓘ Marble Museum

Ⓘ Marble National Historic District

Ⓙ Maroon Bells-Snowmass Wilderness

Ⓕ Redstone Historical Museum

Ⓕ The Redstone Inn

Ⓕ Redstone National Historic District

Ⓚ Ski Sunlight

Ⓛ Snowmass

Ⓜ Storm King Mountain Memorials

Ⓗ Yampah Spa and Vapor Caves

Note: Items with the same letter are located in the same area.

A PERFECT DAY IN THE ROARING FORK VALLEY

Start your morning in Aspen, Glenwood Springs, or Carbondale, but spend the rest of the day in Redstone and Marble. In Redstone, tour the opulent Cleveholm Manor, visit the art galleries along Main Street, and walk over to see the coke ovens across the road. Have lunch at The Grill in the Redstone Inn. Then drive to Marble down Highway 133, take a hike up to the historic marble quarry, and see the work of local marble sculptors. Return this evening to where you started and enjoy dinner, live music, or a soak in the Glenwood Hot Springs.

SIGHTSEEING HIGHLIGHTS

★★★ **Aspen Music Festival**—Launched during Aspen's renaissance in the late 1940s, this internationally renowned music festival is connected with the Aspen Music School. This extremely competitive summer school for younger musicians is taught by faculty from major symphonies, orchestras, and universities throughout the world. From June through August, more than 150 public performances are given, 25 percent of which are free. Between November and April, the Winter Music Festival features 15 or more performances from some of the most talented musicians in the country. Reservations are needed for many of the special benefits, but otherwise, you can usually find a ticket for a performance when you get to town. Tickets range in price from $7 to $40 for different shows. The box office is located in the Gondola building at the foot of Aspen Mountain. Phone: (970) 925-3254.

★★★ **Glenwood Hot Springs**—This has always been—and always will be—the most famous attraction in Glenwood Springs. The Utes tell stories about their ancestors using the soothing mineral waters to heal ailments and aches and pains. Miners from nearby coal mines soaked in the hot springs after a hard day's digging. Today's visitors are no different, except now they relax in two huge outdoor pools kept at constant temperatures, while the kids keep busy with the water slide.

The pools rent towels and even swim suits if you've forgotten yours, and the modern locker rooms have showers, hair dryers, and other amenities. You can also use the Hot Springs Athletic Club, with weight machines, aerobics, racquetball, and an indoor Jacuzzi, for an additional fee. Admission to the pool is $6.25 for adults, and $4 for children 3–12; four rides on the water slide costs $2.50, or eight rides for

$3.50. Summer hours: 7:30 a.m. to 10:00 p.m. Winter hours: 9:00 a.m. to 10:00 p.m. You can't miss the springs from exit 116 off Interstate 70. Phone: (800) 537-SWIM or (970) 945-7131. (2 hours)

★★★ **Marble National Historic District**—The marble quarry for which this small town is named once yielded the largest block of marble ever quarried, used for the Tomb of the Unknown Soldier in Arlington National Cemetery. The Colorado Yule Marble Company began extracting marble from this area in 1892, halted in 1942, and reopened again in 1990. Today the marble is hauled by truck to Glenwood Springs and then shipped to points all over the world.

Artisans come here to work on the marble, and you will see many sculptures in town. You can also take a 4-mile hike from town to the original Yule Quarry site. The **Marble Museum**, open daily from May to Labor Day, 2:00 p.m. to 4:00 p.m., is free. Address: 412 West Main Street. Phone: (970) 963-2143 or 963-3035. (2–3 hours)

★★★ **Redstone National Historic District**—In the late 1880s, the Colorado Fuel and Iron Company built Redstone as part of its extensive coal mining operations in this part of the West Elk Mountains. The company's president, John C. Osgood, an industrialist with humanitarian interests, created a unique environment for the miners and their families. Unlike other company coal towns known for their poor living conditions, Osgood built Swiss chalet-style homes for the family men and an inn (today known as **The Redstone Inn**) for the bachelors, all equipped with indoor plumbing and electricity. Osgood believed, correctly as it turned out, that if he provided his workers with clean and modern homes, they would return his investment in productivity. He applied his experiment at Redstone to other areas of his business.

Osgood built his own lavish residence, known as **Cleveholm Manor**, about a mile south of town. This Tudor-style mansion, completed in 1902, still has many of its original furnishings. His wife, known as "Lady Bountiful," was a favorite with Redstone's children. Private tours and lodging are available at the Manor. For more information about tours, call the Redstone Country Store at (970) 963-3408.

Across the road from the inn stands a row of beehive ovens that once burned the high-grade coal extracted from this region into coke, used for making steel. The **Redstone Historical Museum** has exhibits and artifacts from the coal industry in this area. If you'd like to see the museum when you are here, write to P.O. Box 425, Redstone, CO 81623, or call (970) 963-1025. (2 hours)

★★ **Aspen Center for Environmental Studies (ACES)**—If you are looking for something to do in Aspen besides window shopping and people-watching, visit this naturalist center and take advantage of its special programs. Try to see the center's one-hour program on birds of prey, which includes a short slide show and walk through the nature preserve. The naturalists bring certain birds, such as peregrine falcons, owls, and eagles along for you to observe. There is no admission fee, but donations are requested. Hours: Open during the summer Monday through Saturday 9:00 a.m. to 5:00 p.m.; the rest of the year, Monday through Friday 9:00 a.m. to 5:00 p.m. Address: 100 Puppy Smith Street. Phone: (970) 925-5756. (1 hour)

★★ **Glenwood Canyon**—Before the Denver & Rio Grande Railroad blasted a standard-gauge railway through this canyon in 1887, humans had never ventured through it. An automobile road followed in 1902, and the two modes of transportation squeezed on opposite sides of the Colorado River. Traffic accidents on this highway escalated over the years, and Coloradans clamored for a solution.

The challenge to upgrade this two-lane road into four lanes without ruining the surrounding environment took more than 20 years and cost roughly $180 million. Road builders took pains to preserve the magnificence of the canyon by contouring the roadway to the existing canyon walls and avoiding existing boulders and trees. The result, the final link of Interstate 70 from coast to coast, has won numerous engineering and design awards.

Glenwood Canyon also is the center for many recreational activities. An 18-mile recreation path runs east from the Yampah Vapor Caves in Glenwood Canyon to the town of Dotsero. It is completely paved and suited for long bike rides, walks, or Rollerblades. To rent a bike, try **Canyon Bikes**, in the Hotel Colorado, (970) 945-8904. Several rafting companies run trips on the Colorado River from various locations within the canyon. Contact **Whitewater Rafting**, P.O. Box 2462, Glenwood, CO 81602, (970) 945-8477; or **Rock Gardens Rafting**, exit 119 at No Name, (970) 945-6737.

The **Hanging Lake Trail Head**, one of Colorado's most popular hiking trails, can be accessed at the Hanging Lake Rest Area in Glenwood Canyon. Even though traffic on this trail is always heavy, seeing the remarkably beautiful Hanging Lake still makes the trip worthwhile. The hike climbs a steep 900 feet in 1.2 miles. There are plenty of places to rest along the way, but remember to bring some water. (1 hour–½ day)

✯✯ **Maroon Bells–Snowmass Wilderness**—The distinctive Maroon Bells are perhaps the most photographed mountains in Colorado. They are popular among visitors to Aspen, but most people don't venture beyond the actual wilderness boundary. One of the best ways to appreciate the vast Maroon Bells Wilderness is to take a free tour with a naturalist from the **Aspen Center for Environmental Studies**, from mid-June through Labor Day. Tours begin on the hour from 10:00 a.m. to 2:00 p.m. and last about 45 minutes. Afterwards, you can take a longer hike into the wilderness. The White River National Forest can supply you with detailed maps and descriptions of the hiking trails in the area. Contact their headquarters in Glenwood Springs at (970) 945-2521. For more information on the nature tours, contact Aspen Center for Environmental Studies at (970) 925-8484.

Cars are not allowed in the Maroon Bells area, so take one of the Roaring Fork Transit Authority (RFTA) buses from the Ruby Park Transit Center on Durant and Mill Streets. The trip costs $4 for adults, $2 for seniors and children ages 6–16. (3–4 hours)

✯✯ **Skiing in the Roaring Fork Valley**—Before you dig deep into your pocket for the expensive lift ticket at Aspen, look into **Ski Sunlight**, where an adult full-day pass is $28. Sunlight has both downhill and Nordic skiing, a rental shop, and ski school, and is only 10 miles from Glenwood Springs, 10901 County Road 117. Take Grand Avenue south in Glenwood Springs to Four Mile Road. Phone: (800) 445-7931 or (970) 945-7491.

If you are looking for premier skiing at one of Colorado's finest ski areas, you will love Aspen. Where else can you ski the slopes along with the rich and famous? Aspen's four ski mountains give skiers several options. Both **Aspen Mountain** and **Aspen Highlands** appeal to intermediate and advanced skiers, while **Snowmass** and **Buttermilk/ Tiehack** are more popular with those learning to ski. All mountains use the same lift ticket. For more information, call the Aspen Skiing Company at (800) 525-6200 or (970) 925-1220.

The Aspen Center for Environmental Studies gives daily naturalist tours from each ski mountain during the winter, a nice diversion from skiing the bumps. They have a skiing tour for intermediate to advanced skiers and a snowshoe tour, which is just as easy as walking, on top of Aspen Mountain. The skiing tours are free if you have a lift ticket, and the snowshoe tours cost $35 for adults and $15 for kids without a lift ticket; $27 for adults and $10 for kids if you have already purchased a lift ticket. For more information, contact ACES at (970) 925-5756.

For information on backcountry skiing trails and their levels of difficulty, contact the White River National Forest in Glenwood Springs, 900 Grand Avenue, (970) 945-2521. (Full day)

★★ **Yampah Spa and Vapor Caves**—These vapor caves are actually natural underground steam baths, where hot mineral waters keep the floors at a temperature of 125 degrees Fahrenheit. For the ultimate in pampering yourself, get a massage or facial, sink into an herbal Jacuzzi bath, or luxuriate in a variety of body treatments. A single visit to the vapor cave is $7.75, and partial or full massages range from $29 to $68. To really splurge, try the European Body Wrap for $99. Hours: Open daily 9:00 a.m. to 9:00 p.m. Address: 709 East 6th Street. Phone: (970) 945-0667. (1½ hours)

★ **Aspen Mountain Gondola**—The gondola will take you 2 ½ miles to the summit of Aspen Mountain in 18 minutes. The Aspen Center for Environmental Studies runs nature hikes at the summit from mid-June to Labor Day, every hour on the hour from 10:00 a.m. to 2:00 p.m. Special events on the summit run daily throughout the summer, such as Frisbee Golf Days on Thursday and live music on Friday and Saturdays. Tickets for the gondola are free for seniors, $15 for adults, $9 for teenagers 13–19, children 12 and under free when accompanied by an adult. You can also purchase a joint Gondola/Maroon Bells bus tour ticket for only $16.50. Hours: June 16 to September 4, open daily 9:30 a.m. to 4:00 p.m.; late May to mid-June, and through September, open only on weekends. To ride the gondola, go the building at the base of Aspen Mountain. Phone: (970) 925-1220, extension 3598. (2 hours)

★ **Anderson Ranch Arts Center**—Artists come to this ranch for special programs year-round in media such as photography, pottery, painting, and woodworking. You can visit the Dows Gallery to view current exhibits or take a self-guided tour to meet some of the artists. Guided tours are usually offered on Wednesdays at 1:00 p.m. Call before you come to find out about current events. Hours: Monday through Saturday 9:00 a.m. to 5:00 p.m., Sunday noon to 5:00 p.m. Address: 5263 Owl Creek Road, Snowmass Village. Phone: (970) 923-3181. (1½ hours)

✶ **Glenwood Springs Center for the Arts**—This center, adjacent to the Hot Springs Pool, supports the Glenwood Springs art community with poetry readings, dance classes, and gallery exhibits. Hours: Monday through Friday 10:00 a.m. to 4:00 p.m., Saturday and Sunday 12:00 p.m. to 4:00 p.m. If you want to know about current events, call (970) 945-2414.

✶ **Storm King Mountain Memorials**—Fourteen firefighters—both men and women—died while fighting a blaze in South Canyon, west of Glenwood Springs, on Wednesday, July 6, 1994. The deaths of these brave people shocked the nation. They are remembered today at two locations: a memorial at Two Rivers Park, in Glenwood Springs, and a memorial trail at the scene of the fire 2 miles outside of town.

A sculpture cast by artist Joyce Killebrew depicts three firefighters with their equipment. Dedicated on the first anniversary of the tragedy, the sculpture stands in the center of the memorial at Two Rivers Park. To reach Two Rivers Park, take 6th Street west to Devereaux Road, and turn left.

The 1-mile trail at the base of Storm King Mountain leads to an observation point with views of two different memorials placed there to honor the firefighters. The trail takes you through the effects of the fire, where you can observe how a forest naturally regenerates after such an episode. To reach the trail, go west from Glenwood Springs on Interstate 70 to the Canyon Creek exit (#109). Drive east on the frontage road for a half-mile to a parking area, from which you can see the trailhead. (1 hour)

FITNESS AND RECREATION

With scenery this beautiful, it's easy to find a form of outdoor recreation here to suit you. The Crystal River and Dinkle Lake are well-known fishing spots. Trails for hiking and mountain biking are scattered throughout the valley. Contact the White River National Forest in Glenwood Springs, 900 Grand Avenue, (970) 945-2521.

Several outfitters will take you on horseback rides in the White River National Forest, on rafting trips on the Crystal River, or even on a cattle drive. Contact Canyon Creek Outfitters in Glenwood Springs,

ROARING FORK VALLEY

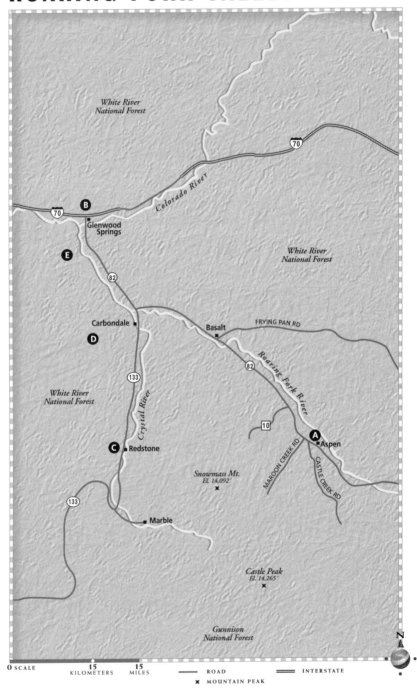

White River
National Forest

70

Colorado River

70

B Glenwood
Springs

E

82

White River
National Forest

Carbondale ■

D

Basalt ■

FRYING PAN RD

82

Roaring Fork River

133

White River
National Forest

Crystal River

10

C ■ Redstone

A ■ Aspen

MAROON CREEK RD

CASTLE CREEK RD

Snowmass Mt.
El. 14,092'
✕

133

■ Marble

Castle Peak
El. 14,265'
✕

Gunnison
National Forest

N

0 SCALE   15   15
KILOMETERS   MILES   ——— ROAD   ⁓⁓⁓ INTERSTATE

✕ MOUNTAIN PEAK

Food

Ⓐ Crystal Palace

Ⓑ Daily Bread Café and Bakery

Ⓑ Fireside

Ⓐ La Cocina

Ⓐ Paradise Bakery

Ⓒ Redstone Inn Grill and Dining Room

Ⓐ Silver City Grille

Lodging

Ⓒ Cleveholm Manor

Ⓑ Hotel Colorado

Ⓐ Little Red Ski Haus

Ⓒ Redstone Inn

Ⓐ St. Moritz

Ⓐ Snowflake Inn

Ⓓ Sunlight Inn

Camping

Ⓔ Hideout Cabins and Campground

Note: Items with the same letter are located in the same area.

(970) 984-2000 or 984-2052. They offer rides lasting from two hours to all day, or a combination trip of horseback riding and rafting.

FOOD

Eateries in Aspen are a dime a dozen. I've given you just a few places in a variety of price ranges. For a great stuffed croissant, muffin, or pastry with a cappuccino, all under $5, try the **Paradise Bakery**, 320 South Galena Street, on the corner of Cooper Avenue, (970) 925-7585. Open daily from 6:30 a.m. to midnight. The **Silver City Grille**, 3085 South Hunter, (970) 925-6698, a small restaurant loved by locals, serves burgers, fries, ribs, fresh fish, and pasta, with prices ranging from $8 to about $15. **La Cocina**, 308 East Hopkins Avenue, (970) 925-9714, serves healthy and tasty Mexican food ranging from $7 to $11 for dinner, featuring several varieties of enchiladas, seafood specials, taco plates, and salads.

For an expensive night out, go to the **Crystal Palace**, 300 East Hyman Avenue, (970) 925-1455. Expect to pay $65 per person, which includes dinner, dessert, and a comedy act that spoofs politics, social events, and famous people, etc. During the summer, the Palace is open Tuesday through Saturday, with dinner starting at 8:00 p.m. In winter, a 7:00 p.m. seating is scheduled Monday through Wednesday, with 6:00 p.m. and 9:15 p.m. seatings on Thursday, and a 7:00 p.m. seating on Friday and Saturday.

When in Glenwood Springs, go to the **Daily Bread Café and Bakery**, 729 Grand Avenue, (970) 945-6253. This Glenwood Springs institution is prized for its healthy menu and delicious bakery sweets. The daily quiche is usually great, as are several of the sandwiches on the low-fat menu. Breakfast: $4 to $6.50; lunch: $5 to $7. Open Monday through Friday 7:00 a.m. to 2:00 p.m., Saturday 8:00 a.m. to 2:00 p.m., and Sunday 8:00 a.m. to noon. The **Fireside**, in West Glenwood at 51701 U.S. 6 and 24, 1 ½ miles from Hotel Colorado, (970-945-6613), serves prime rib, steaks, and seafood. Lunch is usually around $6; dinner, $13. Lunch is served Monday through Friday 11:00 a.m. to 2:00 p.m., and dinner at 4:00 p.m. to 10:00 p.m.; Saturday hours are 4:00 p.m. to 10:00 p.m.; Sunday brunch served 9:00 a.m. to 10:00 p.m.

Redstone has two excellent restaurants in the **Redstone Inn**. **The Grill** is more casual and serves light entrees, soups, and sandwiches for under $10. The **Dining Room** is a classy place and very formal. Each night it features different specials, often offering prime rib, fish, and chicken. Dinners start at $13 and go up to $22. The Grill serves breakfast, lunch, and dinner from 7:00 a.m. to 9:00 p.m.; the Dining Room is open from 5:30 p.m. to 9:00 p.m., and serves a Sunday brunch from 9:00 a.m. to 2:00 p.m.

LODGING

In Aspen, lodging can be just about as fancy, and costly, as you want. The following suggestions are on the inexpensive side and are based on summer rates. During the winter the cost for lodging is at least 20 to 30 percent higher. The **St. Moritz**, 334 West Hyman Avenue, (970) 925-3220, is the cheapest bed in town, next to sleeping on a friend's couch, from $35 to $69. For a step up, try the **Snowflake Inn**, 221 East Hyman Avenue, (970) 925-3221 or (800) 247-2069, $50 to $110 for a one-bedroom, $55 to $159 for a suite. For a unique Victorian bed and breakfast in Aspen, try the **Little Red Ski Haus**, 118 East Cooper, (970) 925-3333, with rates ranging from $52 for rooms with a shared bathroom to $66 for a private bathroom. The lodge has special events year-round, such as picnics, retreats, and cross-country ski trips.

In Glenwood Springs, the classic **Hotel Colorado**, 526 Pine Street, (800) 544-3998 or (970) 945-6511, was built in 1893 and known as the Summer White House for Teddy Roosevelt. It is located on Grand Avenue and 6th Street, directly across from Hot Springs Pool. Year-round rates start at $70 and go up to $275 for the special suites in the bell towers. Twelve miles south of Glenwood Springs is the **Sunlight Inn**, 10252 County Road 117, (970) 945-5225. Eighteen rooms in this rustic Western ranch have private baths, five rooms share three baths, $40 to $75.

Redstone boasts two exceptional places to stay. The **Redstone Inn**, 82 Redstone Boulevard, (970) 963-2526, has a range of prices ($42–$175) depending on the day of the week, season, and type of room. At **Cleveholm Manor**, also known as the Redstone Castle, 58 Redstone Boulevard, (970) 963-3463, the rooms start at $95 for a shared bath and go up to $180 for private suites. See the Redstone section in "Sightseeing Highlights," above, for descriptions of both the Inn and the Castle.

CAMPING

Contact the White River National Forest, 900 Grand Avenue, Glenwood Springs, (970) 945-2521, for ideas on campgrounds and primitive camping within national forest boundaries. The **Hideout Cabins and Campground**, outside of Glenwood Springs at 1293 Road 117, Four Mile Road, (970) 945-5621 or (800) 987-0779, has RV sites and rustic cabins and is open year-round.

NIGHTLIFE

If you are looking for a night on the town, head down the Roaring Fork Valley to Aspen. A number of bands can be found playing in Aspen's nightclubs and saloons just about any night of the week. **The Howling Wolf**, 316 East Hopkins Avenue, (970) 920-7771, is a local hangout that features several excellent local bands, poetry readings, and open-mike nights in a funky coffeehouse atmosphere. The **Hotel Jerome**, 330 East Main Street, (970) 920-1000, is a great place to go for a beer or drink; the hotel's **J-Bar** often has acoustic folk music. **Shooter's Saloon**, 220 South Galena, (970) 925-4567, is the country place in town, with line dancing, two-stepping and live country music. Check out a local newspaper for well-known musical acts booked at the **Double Diamond**, 450 South Galena, (970) 920-6905.

If you'd just like to enjoy a drink in a relaxed setting, go to the **Red Onion**, 420 East Cooper Avenue, (970) 925-9043, or to the **Hunter St. Pub**, downstairs at 308 South Hunter Street, (970) 925-2028. For a late-night meal, several spots stay open, such as the **Alley Café**, 411 East Hopkins Avenue, (970) 544-0825, and **New York Pizza**, overlooking Hyman Avenue Mall, (970) 920-3088. Open daily 11:30 a.m. to 2:30 a.m.

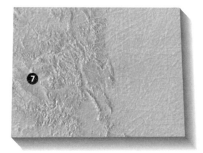

7

GRAND JUNCTION AND THE COLORADO RIVER VALLEY

This part of western Colorado is practically littered with dinosaur fossils. Multitudes of dinosaur bones and tracks remain from the ancient inland seas and giant forests that covered this region millions of years ago. Many fossils discovered in the pastel- and buff-colored shales, silts, and mudstones here have contributed significantly to modern paleontological research. This is a great place to take any child, or adult, who has "dinosaur fever."

Grand Junction is named for its location near the confluence of two great Western rivers: the Gunnison and the Colorado. After the removal of the Utes in the early 1880s, homesteaders flocked to this valley, which is blessed with warm days, cool nights, low precipitation, and plenty of irrigable land. Already the largest town on the Western Slope, Grand Junction has recently experienced phenomenal growth for a city of its size. Its revitalized Main Street walking mall has a variety of outdoor sculpture, unique restaurants, and shops.

Plan on spending at least a day to explore Grand Junction, Fruita, and the fruit stands and vineyards of Palisade. Grand Junction is also a great jumping-off point for several one-day or multi-day excursions. To the east lies the Grand Mesa, and to the west, the mazelike canyons of the Colorado National Monument. Up north, the remote Dinosaur National Monument offers an isolated backcountry experience. ◼

COLORADO RIVER VALLEY

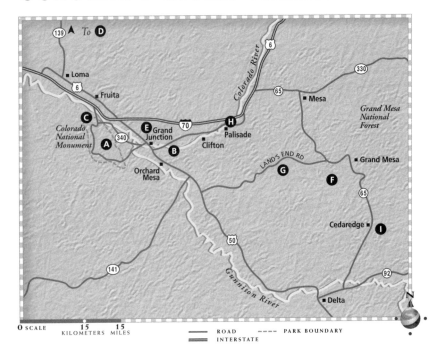

Sightseeing Highlights

A Colorado National Monument

B Cross Orchards Living History Farm

C Devil's Canyon Science & Learning Center

D Dinosaur National Monument

E Dinosaur Valley

F Grand Mesa

G Land's End Observatory

E Museum of Western Colorado

H Palisade Vineyards

I Pioneer Town

Camping

I Aspen Trails Campground

C Fruita Junction RV Park

F Grand Mesa

A Saddlehorn Campground

Note: Items with the same letter are located in the same area.

A PERFECT DAY IN GRAND JUNCTION AND THE COLORADO RIVER VALLEY

Take an hour in the morning to visit one of the Museum of Western Colorado's cultural or natural history sites, then drive to Grand Mesa to spend the rest of the day. Relish the extraordinary views of the landforms and geology of western Colorado and northeastern Utah. Hike on several different trails, including the Crags Crest National Recreation Trail, or fish in one of the 300 lakes that dot the mesa. Afterwards, visit Pioneer Town in Cedaredge.

SIGHTSEEING HIGHLIGHTS

✩✩✩ **Grand Mesa**—Grand Mesa is the world's largest flat-top mountain, with an average elevation of 10,000 feet. More than 300 lakes and reservoirs on the mesa capture rain and snow which flows to nearby communities through hundreds of miles of irrigation ditches. Fishing on Grand Mesa, considered one of Colorado's premier angling sites, has not always been open to the public as it is today. For more than 50 years, private and public interests fought to control fishing rights. Local residents blatantly poached fish from the private fishing holes, which caused the death of one man in the late 1890s. Grand Mesa National Forest eventually won public fishing rights in 1937, after an extensive litigation process. You can drive to the Grand Mesa by three different routes.

Route 1: Drive south from Grand Junction on State Highway 50 to Whitewater. From there, head east on **Land's End Road,** built by the Civilian Conservation Corps in the 1930s. This gravel road is impassable in the winter, and as you near the top, there are many steep switchbacks. If you aren't used to this type of driving, you should take either route 2 or 3.

Route 2: From Whitewater, continue south on Highway 50 to Delta and head east on Highway 92 until you reach Highway 65 to the Grand Mesa. Travel Land's End Road from the eastern side to see the magnificent views from the observatory—it is easier to negotiate than the western section.

Route 3: Head east on Interstate 70 from Grand Junction about 20 miles to Highway 65. Take it south through the beautiful Plateau Canyon, the community of Mesa, and over the Grand Mesa.

Whichever route you take, several locations along the Grand Mesa are worth visiting. The view at the **Land's End Observatory** literally seems like the end of the world. To the west you can see Grand Junction, all the way to the La Sal Mountains of Utah. The northern view reveals the dramatic Book Cliffs running from Colorado to Utah. To the south, the San Juan Mountains tower at the far end of the Uncompahgre River Valley, and the majestic West Elks frame the view to the east. There are numerous hiking trails and fishing ponds all over the mesa.

Pioneer Town, in Cedaredge, is a labor of love of the Surface Creek Historical Society. This remarkable collection of historic structures is outfitted with period artifacts and agricultural implements. Be sure to peek into the Patterson Chapel, modeled after a chapel in New Zealand. The largest arrowhead collection west of the Mississippi is exhibited in the adobe building near the chapel. Admission is $3 for adults, $2 for seniors, and $1.50 for children 8–17. Hours: Open Memorial Day through Labor Day, Monday through Saturday 10:00 a.m. to 4:00 p.m., Sunday 1:00 p.m. to 4:00 p.m. Address: At the Grand Mesa Scenic Byway Visitor Center in Cedaredge. Phone: (970) 835-8231. (3 hours–full day, depending on how many stops you make)

★★★ **Colorado National Monument**—The 32 square miles of Colorado National Monument feature some of Colorado's most exquisite and unspoiled wilderness. Here you will find a maze of colorful sandstone canyons, arches, and monoliths sculpted by the forces of wind and water, resembling the formations of Grand Canyon, Bryce Canyon, Zion, and Canyonlands National Parks.

Part of the geologic province known as the Colorado Plateau, this region receives only 10 to 12 inches of rainfall per year. Drought-resistant plants living here include piñon pine and juniper shrubs, several species of cacti, and the Mormon tea plant, which resembles a cluster of green sticks that can grow up to 2 or 3 feet tall. Reptiles and amphibians flourish here.

Rim Rock Drive is a 23-mile drive through the monument, popular for both automobile and bicycle touring. It has numerous scenic overlooks at which you can stop to savor the views of the landscape. Forty-two miles of trails exist for hiking or horseback riding through the canyons and on the mesa tops. The monument also has several challenging technical rock climbs.

To get to Colorado National Monument from Grand Junction, head west on Grand Avenue, which turns into Highway 340, the entrance road to the monument. Admission is $4 per car. The monument is open year-round, and the visitor center hours are 8:00 a.m. to 8:00 p.m.,

June through Labor Day; 8:00 a.m. to 4:30 p.m. the rest of the year. Phone: (970) 858-3617. (3 hours–3 days)

★★ **Museum of Western Colorado**—This municipal museum operates several sites highlighting the cultural and natural history of the Western Slope, but the main downtown museum should be your first stop. Exhibits here show the importance of mining and agriculture in shaping the settlement of this region. Other sites managed by the museum include the Cross Orchards Historic Site, the Dinosaur Valley Paleontology Center, and four natural resource areas with dinosaur fossils. Ask for more information on the natural resource areas at the main museum, which supplies brochures with guided tours. Admission: $2 for adults, $1 for children 2–12. Hours: Tuesday through Saturday 10:00 a.m. to 4:30 p.m. From Memorial Day through Labor Day, the museum also stays open on Mondays. Address: 248 South Fourth Street. Phone: (970) 242-0971. (1 hour)

The Colorado River Valley, including the towns of Fruita, Palisade, and Clifton, is prime orchard country. Early settlers diverted the Colorado and Gunnison Rivers and planted orchards, quickly establishing a thriving fruit industry. The **Cross Orchards Living History Farm** chronicles the story of a prosperous apple orchard that operated from 1896 to 1923. The old ranch house, packing shed, bunkhouse, carpentry shop, and barn have authentic equipment and artifacts from the early days. An apple grove is cultivated here, and if you visit during the fall harvest, you will be treated to freshly picked apples, cider, and other apple products. Admission is $3 for adults, $2.50 for seniors, and $1.50 for children 2–12. Hours: Open daily 9:00 a.m. to 5:00 p.m. from Memorial Day through Labor Day. During the off-season, the store is open Wednesday through Saturday 10:00 a.m. to 5:00 p.m., but tours of the orchards are not available. Address: 3073 F (Patterson) Road. Phone: (970) 424-9814. (1 hour)

Not just a stuffy museum filled with dinosaur bones, **Dinosaur Valley** demonstrates, through exciting research techniques and exhibits, how dinosaurs still touch our lives today . Dinosaur robots, such as stegosaurs, apatosaurs, and triceratops, are the main attraction here, with dino skeletons, tracks, and other fossils also featured. The front window of the museum contains a paleontology lab where scientists clean and work on specimens from nearby quarries. Admission: $4 for adults, $2.50 for children 2–12. Hours: From Memorial Day to Labor Day, open daily 9:00 a.m. to 5:30 p.m.; otherwise, Tuesday through Saturday 10:00 a.m. to 4:30 p.m. Address: 362 Main. Phone: (970)-242-0971. (1 hour)

✯✯ **Palisade Vineyards**—Vineyards flourished in this fertile river valley prior to Prohibition, when they were replaced with fruit orchards. The cultivation of wine grapes has made a comeback in the Grand Valley, and a wide variety of vintners currently produce reputable wines. Five wineries in the Palisade area operate tasting rooms from which they sell their products. For a brochure about Colorado's vineyards, including the addresses and hours of the tasting rooms, contact the Colorado Wine Industry Development Board, 3168 B ½ Road, Grand Junction, CO 81503. Phone: (970) 523-1232. (2 hours)

✯ **Devil's Canyon Science & Learning Center**—This learning center at Fruita has interactive displays and video presentations about dinosaurs, as well as an earthquake simulation. Dinamation's Dinosaur Discovery Expeditions offers trips with professional paleontologists to hunt dinosaur fossils. For information on the digs, call (800) DIG-DINO. Admission to the learning center is $5 for adults, seniors and children 3–12, $3.50. Hours: Memorial Day to Labor Day 8:30 a.m. to 7:00 p.m.; the rest of the year, 9:00 a.m. to 5:00 p.m. Address: 550 Crossroads Court, 1 mile south of the Fruita exit (# 19) on Interstate 70. Phone: (970) 858-7282. (1–2 hours)

✯ **Dinosaur National Monument**—This remote and isolated monument straddles the Utah/Colorado state line. The Utah side features a working quarry with more than 2,300 visible fossilized bones. While Colorado's portion of the monument doesn't have any dinosaur fossils, it offers solitude, hiking trails, and river rafting on the Green River. To get to Dinosaur National Monument, head east from Grand Junction on Interstate 70 to the small town of Loma. From there turn north on Highway 139 and drive less than two hours to the headquarters of Dinosaur National Monument. The actual entrance to the monument is still about 30 miles from the visitor center. Admission is $5 per vehicle for a week pass. The monument is open year-round. Address: 4545 U.S. Highway 40, Dinosaur, CO 81610. Phone: (970) 374-2216.

FITNESS AND RECREATION

The low elevations and warm weather of this region make it a year-round destination for bicyclists. The **Colorado Plateau Mountain Bike Trail Association (COPMOBA)** is a great source for recommending a good trail. You can contact them by writing to P.O. Box

4603, Grand Junction, CO 81502, or calling (970) 241-9561.
Kokopelli's Trail, an intermediate to advanced mountain bike trail roughly 128 miles long, stretches between Loma (east of Grand Junction) and Moab, Utah. Most of the trail is on unpatrolled Bureau of Land Management land.

Beautiful canyon hiking can be found near Grand Junction in **Rattlesnake, Knowles**, and **Jones Canyons**. For a list of trails, contact the Bureau of Land Management office in Grand Junction, at 2815 H Road, Grand Junction, CO 81506. Phone: (970) 244-3000.

While no one associates skiing with this area of the Western Slope, the **Powderhorn Ski Resort**, on the northern side of the Grand Mesa, is a respectable ski area offering both downhill and Nordic skiing. In addition, the cross-country skiing and snowshoeing on **Grand Mesa** is considered to be some of the best in Colorado.

FOOD

While Grand Junction tends to be a meat and potatoes town, it also has several unique eateries that serve a variety of food.

For a light breakfast, try **Main Street Bagels**, 599 Main Street, (970) 241-2740. Hours: Monday through Saturday 7:00 a.m. to 5:30 p.m., Sunday 8:00 a.m. to 2:00 p.m. Locals come here in the morning to grab a quick cup of coffee and a tasty bagel. You can get a more substantial breakfast or lunch at **Jitters**, 504 Main Street, (970) 245-5194. This tastefully decorated 1950s diner serves waffles, eggs Benedict, muffins, soup, sandwiches, and salads, and has a complete espresso bar.

By far the most inventive restaurant in Grand Junction is **Hawg Heaven Diner**, 2751 Highways 6 and 50, (970) 245-0812. A completely restored 1939 roadside diner from New Jersey sits inside a Harley-Davidson showroom. The windows are even etched with motorcycles. Hours: Monday through Saturday, breakfast served from 7:00 a.m. to 11:00 a.m., and lunch is served until 2:30 p.m. Breakfast runs $3 to $5 and features biscuits and gravy, eggs to order, or a special egg sandwich. Lunch runs about $5. Blue plate specials are served every day, in addition to homemade chicken-fried steak with real mashed potatoes and a half-pound hamburger with all the fixings.

The **Blue Moon Café**, 120 North 7th Street, (970) 242-4506, is a great bar in a relaxed setting, open from 11:00 a.m. to 11:00 p.m. Sunday through Thursday, and until 2:00 a.m. Friday and Saturday. Lunch runs from $4 to $6.25 and dinner from $10 to $16. It's a good

GRAND JUNCTION

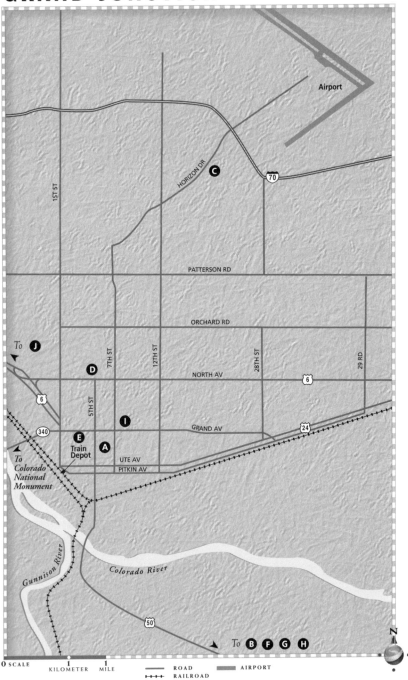

Airport

HORIZON DR

1ST ST

C

70

PATTERSON RD

ORCHARD RD

To **J**

7TH ST

12TH ST

28TH ST

29 RD

D

NORTH AV

6

5TH ST

6

I

GRAND AV

24

340

E

A

Train
Depot

UTE AV

PITKIN AV

To
Colorado
National
Monument

Gunnison River

Colorado River

50

To **B** **F** **G** **H**

N

0 SCALE   1   1
          KILOMETER   MILE   ──── ROAD   ▓▓▓ AIRPORT
          ┝┿┿┥ RAILROAD

Food

Ⓐ Blue Moon Café

Ⓑ The Divot

Ⓒ Good Pastures

Ⓓ Hawg Heaven Diner

Ⓐ Jitters

Ⓐ Main Street Bagels

Ⓔ Rock Slide Brewery and Restaurant

Ⓕ Sylvia's Frog Pond Café

Ⓐ The Winery

Lodging

Ⓖ Cedar's Edge Llama Ranch

Ⓒ Days Inn

Ⓗ Grand Mesa Lodge

Ⓔ Historic Hotel Melrose and International Hostel

Ⓘ Junction Country Inn

Ⓙ Stonehaven Bed and Breakfast

Note: Items with the same letter are located in the same area.

choice for dinner, with 12 beers on tap, including several fine micro-brews. The gyro sandwich is popular, and the menu includes flavorful appetizers like chicken quesadillas. **Good Pastures** is great for families because it offers special kids' meals, great Mexican food, and healthy selections like chicken-vegetable stir fry. It's located in the Days Inn at 733 Horizon Drive, (970) 243-3058, open daily 6:00 a.m. to 9:00 p.m.

A fine restaurant for dinner is **The Winery**, 642 Main Street, (970) 242-4100. The menu features different specials every night, such as steak, pork loin, ahi, or salmon. Hours: Monday through Saturday 4:30 to 10:00 p.m., until 9:00 p.m. on Sunday.

Colorado is wild about microbreweries, and Grand Junction is no exception. The **Rock Slide Brewery and Restaurant**, 401 Main Street, (970) 245-2111, serves its own flavorful brews and standard brewpub fare of pizzas and burgers. Its terrific happy hour deals attract a crowd around 4:00 p.m..

Cedaredge also has a few good restaurants. **The Divot**, at the Deer Creek Golf Course south of town, (970) 856-7781, features authentic Italian food, such as Caesar salad, minestrone, eggplant Parmesan, or tortellini covered with a red sauce, fresh basil, and tomatoes. Lunch is served 11:00 a.m. to 4:30 p.m., dinner, 5:00 p.m. to 8:30 p.m. **Sylvia's Frog Pond Café**, 415 South Grand Mesa Drive, (970) 856-3566, has breakfast, lunch, and dinner from 6:00 a.m. to 8:00 p.m., closed Wednesdays. Breakfast is less than $5, with a biscuits and gravy special on the weekends for $2.50. Lunch, $5, features sandwiches like the Texas melt—turkey with cheese, peppers and onion on Texas toast—or a great Philly cheese steak. On Friday nights, Sylvia features Mexican food, and on Saturdays, prime rib for $9.95.

LODGING

There is no shortage of hotel rooms along Horizon Drive. The third weekend of June, this area hosts Country Jam, jamming all of the hotel rooms in Grand Junction. The concerts feature big-name country stars like Garth Brooks and Dolly Parton, so plan accordingly. The **Days Inn**, 733 Horizon Drive, (970) 245-7200, has special deals for families, with prices in the $40 to $50 range.

Downtown Grand Junction has more unique lodging, such as the **Historic Hotel Melrose and International Hostel**, 337 Colorado Avenue, (970) 242-9636. Accommodations include either private rooms with their own baths ($22–$40) or a dormitory ($12.50).

Sometimes it gets a little noisy because of its popularity with younger travelers, but if you're on a tight budget or looking for out-of-the-ordinary lodging, you might appreciate this historic hotel, which has period antiques and is very clean. The **Junction Country Inn**, 861 Grand Avenue, (970) 241-2817, is a restored Victorian bed and breakfast with four rooms, two with private baths. Rates range from $35 to $79 per night for two people.

The **Stonehaven Bed and Breakfast**, 798 North Mesa Street, (970) 858-0898, is a restored Victorian mansion in Fruita with five rooms; prices range from $55 to $95 in the summer and drop 25 percent in fall and winter. The master bedroom features a Jacuzzi and king-size bed, and the Cherry Room Suite is two connecting rooms with a shared bath.

There are several bed and breakfasts and lodges on the Grand Mesa. If you've never been to a working llama ranch, here's your chance. You can spend the night at the **Cedar's Edge Llama Ranch**, 2169 Highway 65, (970) 856-6836, a unique bed and breakfast about 6 miles north of Cedaredge, with private rooms ranging from $35 to $75. The owners will gladly tell you about the friendly nature of these intelligent animals. The **Grand Mesa Lodge**, open May 15 to October 30, near milepost 28 on Highway 65, (970) 856-3250 or (800) 551-MESA, has several cabins with kitchens. The lodge is located in the heart of Grand Mesa, with fishing, hiking, and horseback riding nearby. The prices range from $30 to $65.

CAMPING

The **Saddlehorn Campground in Colorado National Monument** gets crowded in the summertime and is first-come, first-served. Amenities include picnic tables, charcoal grills, restrooms, and water. The fee is $8 from April to October. Address: Colorado National Monument, Fruita, CO 81521. Phone: (970) 858-3617. Backcountry camping is also permitted.

Numerous campgrounds on the **Grand Mesa** have water and fishing access or primitive camping. For more information, contact Grand Mesa Forest Headquarters, 2250 Highway 50, Delta, CO 81416. Phone: (970) 874-7691. Nine of the campgrounds charge a fee.

For RV camping in the Colorado River valley, try the **Fruita Junction RV Park**, across from Devil's Canyon Learning Center

(Rates range from $15 to $30). Exit I-70 at milepost 19, and drive south a quarter-mile. The park is next to the Colorado Welcome Center in Fruita. Phone: (970) 858-3155. Three miles north of Cedaredge is the **Aspen Trails Campground**, 1997 Highway 65, (970) 856-6321, with 30 RV sites, open year-round.

Scenic Route: The Unaweep/Tabeguache Scenic and Historic Byway

This remote highway has been a secret for years. Many people consider this to be the "True West" made famous in Hollywood Westerns. No road penetrated this region until the 1940s. The boom days started during World War II, when mine companies began to tap the region's significant stores of uranium and vanadium used in the nuclear bombs developed at Los Alamos National Laboratories. Most of the larger mines continued to operate here for the next 40 years.

Today many people consider this area isolated and empty, but you will like it here if you savor the solitude and secret discovery associated with an off-the-beaten-track destination. Public lands have ample room for hiking, mountain biking, backpacking, and rock climbing, and the Dolores River is popular for river rafting. A dramatic sandstone monolith called the Palisades towers above **Gateway**, where a gravel cutoff road leads to Moab, Utah. Farther down the canyon, remains of the **Hanging Flume**, a 7-mile wooden trough, still cling to the eastern wall of the sandstone canyon. A confident gold miner

UNAWEEP/TABEGUACHE BYWAY

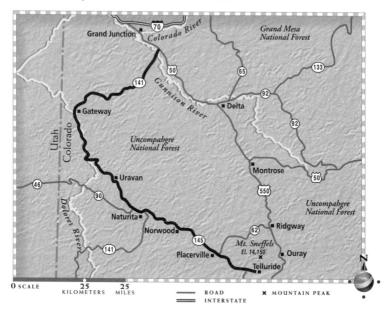

built the structure in the 1890s to carry water to his remote placer mine. But building it cost five times more than he estimated, and he abandoned the mine and the flume after he went bankrupt.

Uravan, a former uranium mining town, once housed more than 3,000 miners and their families, but very little remains of this once-bustling community and mine today. The UMETCO Mine Company closed the mine in the 1980s and dismantled the homes and mine structures. They offered to leave two buildings as a museum to explain both Uravan's role in making nuclear bombs during World War II and the uranium industry as a whole. The museum, operated by the Rimrock Historical Society, will be open in late 1996. For more information, contact the Rimrock Historical Society at P.O. Box 505, Naturita, CO 81422. Phone: (970) 865-2286.

The highway eventually parallels the scenic San Miguel River Canyon all the way to Telluride. But before you reach the cosmopolitan oasis of Telluride, stop and spend some time in Naturita, Norwood, or Placerville to get a taste of a western Colorado ranching community. ◣

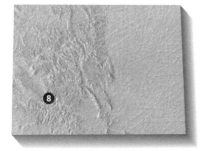

8
THE NORTHERN SAN JUAN MOUNTAINS

The San Juan Mountains, a massive range stretching through south-western Colorado, feature some of the state's most impressive and rugged scenery. They are also richly laden with a variety of minerals that sparked a major mineral rush in the 1870s. For centuries before, these venerable mountains belonged to the Ute tribe. As early as the 1760s, Spaniards knew that gold lay in these mountains, but it wasn't until the 1870s that angry Coloradans began clamoring for the right to enter Ute lands and exploit the precious minerals. The Utes lost their mountain homeland to Colorado Territory in 1874. Immediately thereafter, the area became a hotbed of feverish bonanzas and get-rich-quick schemes.

While many gold-seekers never intended to put down roots, others immediately set to work putting their infant settlements on the map. Wealthy businessmen in the more populous mining camps soon built permanent homes and commercial buildings, in only the finest Victorian tradition. Today these buildings and homes are preserved in the National Historic Districts of Telluride, Ouray, and Silverton.

Many people rightly think of this area as the "Wild West," the place of great Western legends and shoot-'em-ups. In fact, the San Juans have been the set for many famous Hollywood Westerns, such as *True Grit* and *How the West Was Won*. Both the mythical and historical West still lurk here, in frontier mining towns and forgotten ghost towns, but today these mountain communities are also modern in every sense of the word. ∎

NORTHERN SAN JUAN MOUNTAINS

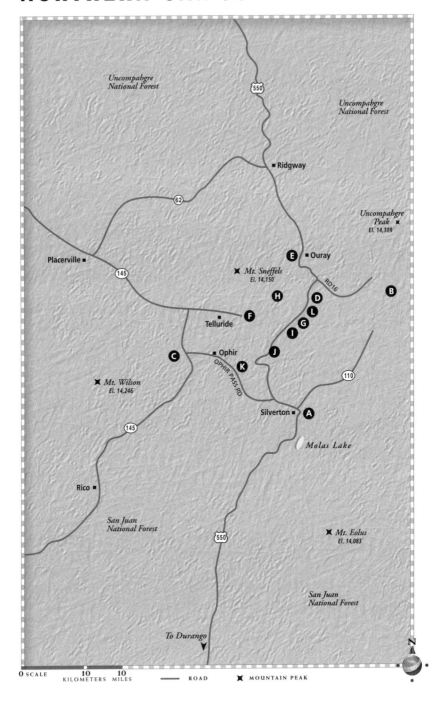

Uncompahgre
National Forest

Uncompahgre
National Forest

550

Ridgway

62

Uncompahgre
Peak ✖
El. 14,309'

Placerville ■

145

E ■ Ouray

✖ Mt. Sneffels
El. 14,150'

RD16

B

H

D

F

L

Telluride ■

G

I

J

C

■ Ophir

K

110

✖ Mt. Wilson
El. 14,246'

OPHIR PASS RD

Silverton ■ A

145

Molas Lake

Rico ■

San Juan
National Forest

550

✖ Mt. Eolus
El. 14,083'

To Durango
▼

San Juan
National Forest

N

O SCALE   10   10
KILOMETERS MILES   —— ROAD   ✖ MOUNTAIN PEAK

Sightseeing Highlights

Ⓐ A Theater Group

Ⓑ Alpine Loop

Ⓒ Ames Power Station

Ⓓ Bear Creek National Recreation Trail

Ⓔ Box Canyon Falls

Ⓕ Bridal Veil Falls

Ⓖ Chattanooga

Ⓕ Galloping Goose

Ⓗ Imogene Pass

Ⓘ Ironton

Ⓙ Million Dollar Highway/Road between Ouray and Silverton

Ⓐ One Hundred Gold Mine Tour

Ⓚ Ophir Pass

Ⓔ Ouray Hot Springs Pool

Ⓛ Riverside Slide

Note: Items with the same letter are located in the same area.

A PERFECT DAY IN THE NORTHERN SAN JUANS

Experience the San Juans with a jeep tour, long hike, or mountain bike ride. Although there is a lot to see from the main highways of the San Juans, much more awaits visitors who take to one of the many back country roads. After a long day of sightseeing and using your muscles, head to the Ouray Hot Springs Pool (or the hot tub of your choice) for a soak. Afterwards, walk the streets of the National Districts in Ouray, Telluride, or Silverton, taking in the ambience of a great bar or restaurant.

HISTORIC SAN JUAN FREIGHTING AND TOLL ROADS

Most early explorers thought that crossing this range was simply impossible, winter or summer. The lure of riches in the mountains proved these early travelers wrong. Men hacked and blasted freighting roads, and later railroads, from the sheer mountains and canyons. These early roads lace this country today, as with the road between Ouray and Silverton, now part of Highway 550, and the dozens of back country roads now accessible to four-wheel drive vehicles, adventurous mountain bikers, and hardy hikers.

The options for exploring these historical routes are many. Some of the roads follow scenic state highways, such as the San Juan Skyway, a national forest and Colorado Scenic Byway, called by some the most beautiful drive in America. The 236-mile route tours the best of southwestern Colorado along major roads beginning on Highway 145 from Cortez to Telluride and Placerville, then east on Highway 62 to Ridgway. From Ridgway, the road turns south on Highway 550 to Ouray, Silverton, and Durango, where it heads west on Highway 160 to return to Cortez. In addition to this major route, there are dozens of back country roads that take intrepid travelers deep into the San Juan's dramatic geology and mining history.

Roads that wind through this region aren't ordinary. They follow steep switchbacks, hairpin turns, and narrow curves along the sides of mountains and canyons, all requiring a driver's careful attention. There are usually numerous pull-offs along the sides of the road, where drivers can stop to enjoy the marvelous views. Speed limits are posted low for good reason. Frequent summer rainstorms and snowstorms at other times of the year can turn a dry road into a slick ribbon in a matter of minutes. Always ask about road conditions before making your trip.

Some unimproved roads, if in good condition, are navigable by a regular passenger car. But when a road gets rough, it can be negotiated only by a four-wheel drive vehicle, preferably with a manual transmission and high clearance. If you aren't used to driving on rough mountain roads, or don't have an adequate vehicle, you can always take a guided jeep tour or rent a vehicle in a nearby town. Ouray, Silverton, and Telluride all have several jeep touring companies that specialize in taking eventful trips into the mountains.

SIGHTSEEING HIGHLIGHTS

✮✮✮ **Million Dollar Highway/Road between Ouray and Silverton**—There are many stories told about the naming of the Million Dollar Highway. When road builders constructed the road after World War I, the costs soared to more than $1 million, a huge sum in those days. Others say the road is named for the worth of its views. Otto Mears, one of this area's most influential men, built the first toll road connecting Ouray and Silverton in the early 1880s. Today this road is the well-maintained and paved U.S. Highway 550. Many Coloradans consider it the state's most beautiful scenic highway. If you are a first-time driver on this road, you will want to take it slow, not only to savor the exceptional views, but because its twists and turns can be tricky and dangerous. Please be considerate of other drivers behind you, and pull off onto one of the many overlooks to let faster vehicles pass. The Colorado Department of Transportation does an excellent job of keeping the road in good condition. Heed their warnings in inclement weather.

Mears blasted almost half of his toll road from solid rock—hundreds of feet above the canyon floor. Today Highway 550 is generally higher on the rock walls than Mears' original road. Just 2 miles south of Ouray, you will come to the **Bear Creek National Recreation Trail**, a moderate hiking trail that takes you past several former mine sites. The trail continues on to American Flats and Engineer Mountain, returning on Horsethief Trail back to Ouray. Consult the Forest Service in Telluride for trip distances and the difficulties of this trail, 2740 Highway 145, (970) 728-4211.

The **Riverside Slide** is 3 miles from the Bear Creek Trail head at milepost 87. A snowshed here protects the highway from frequent avalanches. This part of the highway is subject to more slides than any other highway in the country, and has claimed many lives throughout the years. A monument at the base of Red Mountain Pass is dedicated to those who have died in avalanches along this stretch.

You will continue your drive past several former mines and towns, such as **Ironton** (milepost 82) and **Chattanooga** (milepost 78 on the other side of Red Mountain Pass). Ironton is the first of several settlements stacked like dominos in this cramped gulch. During its heyday, this mining district produced over $1 billion worth of minerals. Chattanooga served as a staging point for freighters and mule skinners traveling between Silverton and the outlying mining camps. This bare patch of ground once had over 75 buildings. After Chattanooga, you will drive more than 10 miles before beginning your descent into Silverton. You will first see the town hundreds of feet below you at about milepost 68. Even though it is only 23 miles between Ouray and Silverton, this drive will take you at least an hour, depending on how many times you stop.

✯✯ **Imogene Pass**—This extremely rough road is not for beginning mountain drivers, and requires a four-wheel drive vehicle. Imogene Pass, the high road between Telluride and Ouray, is usually passable only from late July to mid-September. The road summits at an amazing 13,114 feet, the second highest automobile pass in North America for four-wheel drive vehicles (the highest is near Leadville).

To take this drive from Telluride to Ouray, start on North Oak Street in Telluride. Turn right on the Imogene Pass Road, marked as Forest Road 869. You will climb out of Telluride, and soon see some beautiful views of the town and valley. Continue on Road 869, and you will encounter the remains of the massive Tomboy Mine. This area once had a mill, numerous houses, a boarding house, a store, and even a bowling alley for the men working the mine. The Rothschilds bought this property in 1897 for a mere $2 million. A famous book, *Tomboy Bride*, by Harriet Backus, is partly about this small settlement.

Imogene Pass is a little over 2 miles from the Tomboy. Fort Peabody once sat on the summit of this pass and played a significant role during turn-of-the-century labor disputes in the mines. The fort kept union supporters from sneaking into Telluride to cause more labor unrest. After descending the other side of the pass, you'll come upon the famous Camp Bird Mine Complex, continuously operated since the late 1890s. From here you will take Forest Road 853 and descend into the town of Ouray south of town at Box Canyon Falls. (½–full day)

✩✩ **Ouray**—Rimmed on all sides by the Uncompahgre Mountains, Ouray was first known as Uncompahgre City, established in 1876. Town founders later changed the name to honor Chief Ouray, a great Ute leader who died in 1880. The town quickly became respectable, as seen in the quality of buildings constructed from 1880 to 1900, many of which are still standing.

The Ouray Recreation Association opened the **Ouray Hot Springs Pool** in 1926. Today the facilities include a fitness center and a pool separated into three sections. The outdoor hot springs are especially soothing during the winter. Admission: $5.50 for adults, $4 for children 7–17 and seniors, $2.50 for children 3–6. Winter hours: Weekdays 12:00 p.m. to 9:00 p.m., weekends 10:00 a.m. to 9:00 p.m. Summer hours: Open daily 10:00 a.m. to 10:00 p.m., except Thursdays, 10:00 to 8:00 p.m. Phone: (970) 325-4638.

Box Canyon Falls, a narrow gorge created by a pounding waterfall, can be seen from several vantage points. One path leads to an area beneath the falls, another to a 1900s-era steel bridge that spans a gap above the falls, and a third fairly steep and rocky trail takes you to the top of the falls for a stunning view of the surrounding mountains. Admission: $1.25 for adults, 75 cents for children 5–12, $1 for seniors. The falls are usually open mid-May to mid-October, 8:00 a.m. to dusk. They are located just south of Ouray off Highway 550 near the Box Canyon Motel. From there, follow the signs. Phone: (970) 325-4464.

✩✩ **Silverton**—The story of Silverton, one of the earliest centers of mining activity in the San Juans, is one of a hardy community continually overcoming adversity. Known as the "Treasury Chest of the San Juans," Silverton has at times faced severe depressions, as when silver prices plunged after the great 1893 Silver Panic. Still, the town managed to survive. Mining continues to support many Silverton residents, but the town relies largely on its historic charm to attract visitors.

The **One Hundred Gold Mine Tour**, built by hardrock miners, gives you the rare chance to explore a mine in the heart of a mountain. Miners demonstrate drilling with working equipment, and point out gold and other mineral veins as well as several mining shafts and tunnels within the mountain. The tours, which last about an hour, are given May 15 through October 15, weather permitting. They run on the hour, from 10:00 a.m. to 4:00 p.m. Admission: $8.95 for adults, $4.95 for kids 5–12, free for kids 5 and under, $8 for seniors. Wear warm clothes and shoes, as temperatures inside the mountain are chilly. To get there, head east on Highway 110 from Silverton to Howardsville, today a ghost town. Turn right on County Road 4 and then left on County Road 4-A to the mine. Phone: (800) 872-3009 or (970) 387-5444.

Silverton's **A Theatre Group** is a unique company of volunteer actors. Each summer the group produces a George Bernard Shaw festival, in addition to several other American plays. During December they offer a special holiday production. Wednesday through Sunday performances start at 8:00 p.m. Admission: $7. Address: Located in the historic Miners Union Theatre, 1069 Greene Street. Phone: (970) 387-5337 or (800) 752-4494.

★★ **Telluride**—Telluride is situated in a heavenly valley at the base of grand and imposing mountains. This robust little ski town is crawling with celebrities, who have raised Telluride's status to that of an international resort, with lodging and restaurant prices to match. Telluride's modern, pleasant streets are a far cry from the dusty, crowded streets of yore, when long wagon trains, lines of gruff oxen, and braying burros laden with supplies often clogged the streets. This noisy scene played each morning, as Telluride once was a major shipping and freighting center between the mountain mining camps and the train depot at Ridgway. Incorporated in 1878, Telluride enjoyed relative prosperity until the Depression of the 1930s crippled most of the mines in the area.

No one would have predicted a tough future for Telluride when the Rio Grande and Southern Railroad arrived in the fall of 1891. Telluride was finally connected directly to ports east and west. Freight prices became more affordable overnight, and the heavy machinery brought in by the railroad helped miners dig deeper and more efficiently for the ore. But eventually the railroad also fell on hard times. As automobile roads began to be built throughout the area, the Rio Grande and Southern struggled to compete. A last-ditch effort to save the railroad came with the invention of the **Galloping Goose**, a bizarre hybrid of freight car cum passenger car, actually a Pierce-Arrow automobile fitted to the rails and refashioned to carry 6 to 7 tons of freight as well as numerous passengers. Today you can see a surviving Galloping Goose in Telluride's Town Park.

Bridal Veil Falls, a magnificent landmark east of town, boasts the longest drop in Colorado—365 feet! The private home that sits at the top of the falls was once a hydroelectric power plant for the Smuggler-Union Mine, Telluride's most famous mine. It was one of the first discovered in the district, and proved to be one of the greatest. A great hike from downtown Telluride up to the falls affords a spectacular view. Just head east up Colorado Avenue toward the falls and walk up the rough road to the top, about 2 miles one way. The hike continues on past the falls through beautiful fields of wildflowers.

Telluride is known internationally for its innovative festivals. The **Telluride Bluegrass Festival** started in 1973 and has grown more popular every year. It is usually held in mid-June and is one of the best (and most crowded) ways to experience bluegrass in Colorado. The concerts are held at the Telluride Town Park. July features the famous **Nothing Festival**, while August usually hosts **Jazz and Chamber Music Festivals** as well as a serious gathering known as the **Telluride Mushroom Festival**. During the first week of September is the heralded **Telluride Film Festival,** a star-studded event with award-winning films.

✸ **Alpine Loop**—The Alpine Loop travels through the San Juans over high back country roads from Ouray and Silverton to Lake City. See the Lake City/Creede chapter for a description of this challenging route.

✸ **Ophir Pass**—The trip over Ophir Pass Road takes you over an easy four-wheel drive road, great for drivers just getting used to four-wheel mountain driving. The road starts 5 miles north of Silverton on Highway 550. The Ophir Pass Road (Forest Road 679) is a one-way route, heading west towards Ophir. Views from the summit of the pass are truly spectacular. The lofty peaks to the west, all Fourteeners, are Mt. Wilson, El Diente, and Wilson Peak. To the east are the stained mountains of Red Mountain Pass, with their varying shades of yellow, red, and purple.

Ophir, named for King Solomon's mines in the Bible, got its start as a silver camp in the 1870s. Just outside of Ophir is the **Ames Power Station**, a pioneering success as the world's first plant to use an alternating current to supply power to a nearby mine. Until this successful adaptation of Nicola Tesla's alternating current design, Thomas Edison's direct current was the only type of power used. The alternating current, financed by George Westinghouse, soon surpassed direct current as the most inexpensive and efficient method for powering mines, factories, and towns throughout the world. (½ day)

If you'd like to take a portion of this drive from Telluride, head south on Highway 145 until you reach Forest Road 625, which leads to the Ames Power Plant. After viewing this site, head back to Highway 145 to the town of Ophir, Forest Road 630. (1 hour)

FITNESS AND RECREATION

Skiers are always pleased to ski **Telluride Ski Area**, one of the best in Colorado for advanced skiers. The Telluride Resort Company recently added something called a "chondola," a cross between a chair-lift and gondola, the first such contraption to be built in Colorado. Even though it is often known as an expert area, almost half of Telluride's runs are rated for intermediate skiers. The **Telluride Nordic Center** has more than 19 miles of cross-country ski trails. For more information, call (970) 728-6900.

Cross-country skiing on **Lizard Head Pass** is popular, as is skiing from hut to hut in the **San Juan Hut System**. The entire trail stretches 205 miles from Telluride to Moab, and during the summer it is a paradise for hikers and mountain bikers. For more information on the San Juan Hut System, write to P.O. Box 1663, Telluride, CO 81435. Phone: (970) 728-6935.

Backcountry opportunities for hiking, mountain biking, and backpacking abound in the northern San Juans. Summer brings hiking and backpacking in **Lizard Head Wilderness Area**, southwest of Telluride (accessible from Lizard Head Pass on Highway 145), the **Weminuche Wilderness** (accessible from Highway 550 near the Purgatory Ski Resort or from the Durango & Silverton Narrow Gauge Railroad and Colorado Trail), and the **Mt. Sneffels Wilderness** (north of Telluride). Mountain biking is not allowed in wilderness areas, but the variety of trails that wind through these former mining districts will keep any rider busy. Outdoor equipment stores in Silverton, Ouray, and Telluride all have suggestions on trails to suit your taste.

FOOD

You could probably blow your whole trip budget on one meal in Telluride. I've given you a sampling of reasonably priced restaurants in this notoriously expensive town. **Sofio's**, 110 East Colorado Avenue, (970) 728-4882, serves excellent Mexican food and margaritas; the menu includes just about every Mexican dish you could ever desire. Prices range from $8 to $12, open 5:30 p.m. to 10:00 p.m. **Baked in Telluride**, 127 South Fir, (970) 728-4775, is a standard bakery and coffeehouse, with stuffed croissants, sandwiches, bagels, and bread. This is a good place for a light meal. For a pizza, try **Eddie's**, 300 West Colorado, (970) 728-5335.

In Ouray, the **Bon Ton Restaurant**, in the St. Elmo Hotel, 426 Main, (970) 325-4951, specializes in Italian cuisine and continental specials. They often feature beef and seafood dishes, as well. Dinners range from $11 to $20. Open from 5:30 p.m., with the last seating around 8:30 p.m. The **Coachlight Restaurant,** 118 West 7th Avenue, Ouray, (970) 325-4361, is more of a family-style restaurant, also specializing in steak and seafood. Dinner runs $11 to $20. Open May to October 5:30 p.m. to 9:30 p.m.

For a great sandwich in Silverton, go to **The Pickle Barrel**, 1304 Greene Street, (970) 387-5713. Hot and cold sandwiches of every variety run no more than $6.

LODGING

Rooms in Telluride are much more expensive during the peak of the summer and festival season (mid-June through September) and in the peak of the ski season (December through March). Other times of the year, the prices scale back considerably. A variety of lodging can be found through **Telluride Resort Accommodations**, (800) 538-7754, where rooms can start as low as $60 during the summer.

A unique place to stay in Telluride is the **New Sheridan Hotel**, 231 West Colorado Avenue, (970) 728-4351. When it was built in 1895, it rivaled the Brown Palace, Denver's finest establishment. Today this restored hotel continues to pamper its guests in high style. High-season rates range from $100 to $170, but during the off-season, they drop considerably. Rates include a full breakfast. Also in Telluride is the **Bear Creek Bed and Breakfast**, 221 East Colorado Avenue, (970) 728-6681 or (800) 338-7064. This Victorian hotel contains ten rooms, each with a private bathroom. The high-season rates run from $67 to $190, off-season from $55 to $92.

If Telluride is out of your price range, there are several other places to stay in the northern San Juans that won't take a huge bite out of your pocketbook. During ski season, several nearby towns, including Ridgway, Ouray, and even Cortez, 77 miles from Telluride, offer half-price deals on lodging or ski tickets. Norwood is a small ranching community about 30 miles west of Telluride on Highway 145, where the **Back Narrows Inn**, 1550 Grand Avenue, (970) 327-4417, has two types of rooms, either with or without a telephone, that range from $45 to $55 for two people. Ridgway is 38 miles north of Telluride on Highway 62. The **Adobe Inn**, 251 Liddell Drive, (970) 626-5939, has

NORTHERN SAN JUAN MOUNTAINS

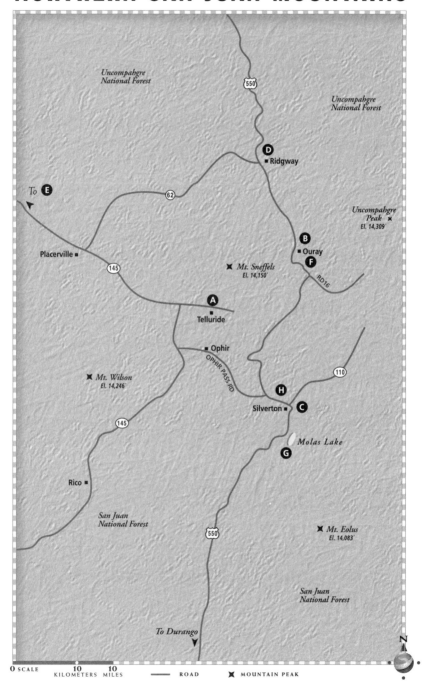

Uncompahgre
National Forest

550

Uncompahgre
National Forest

D
■ Ridgway

To **E**

62

Uncompahgre
Peak ✖
El. 14,309´

Placerville ■

145

B
■ Ouray
F

RD 16

✖ *Mt. Sneffels*
El. 14,150´

A
■
Telluride

■ Ophir

OPHIR PASS RD

110

✖ *Mt. Wilson*
El. 14,246´

H

Silverton ■ **C**

145

Molas Lake

G

Rico ■

San Juan
National Forest

550

✖ *Mt. Eolus*
El. 14,083´

San Juan
National Forest

To Durango

N

0 SCALE   10   10
KILOMETERS MILES   —— ROAD   ✖ MOUNTAIN PEAK

Food

Ⓐ Baked in Telluride

Ⓑ Bon Ton Restaurant

Ⓑ Coachlight Restaurant

Ⓐ Eddie's

Ⓒ The Pickle Barrel

Ⓐ Sofio's

Lodging

Ⓓ Adobe Inn

Ⓔ Back Narrows Inn

Ⓐ Bear Creek Bed and Breakfast

Ⓑ Box Canyon Lodge and Hot Springs

Ⓒ Grand Imperial Hotel

Ⓐ New Sheridan Hotel

Ⓑ St. Elmo

Ⓒ Teller House Hotel

Camping

Ⓕ Amphitheatre Campground

Ⓖ Molas Lake Park

Ⓗ Silverton Lakes Campground

Ⓐ Town Park Campground

Note: Items with the same letter are located in the same area.

three rooms and an excellent Mexican restaurant of the same name. The rooms share a bath, and rates run from $35 to $50.

In Silverton, the **Grand Imperial Hotel**, 1219 Greene Street, (970) 387-5707, is a historic hotel with 40 rooms, each with a private bath. Summer prices start at $59 and go up to $80 for one or two people. During the winter, the rates are halved. The **Teller House Hotel**, 1304 Greene Street, (970) 387-5423, a Victorian hotel built in the late 1890s, is decorated with period furnishings. This hotel is reasonably priced year-round, with rates starting at $31 for a room with a shared bathroom and $47 with a private bathroom, including breakfast at the French Bakery restaurant.

The **St. Elmo**, established in 1898 in Ouray, 426 Main Street, (970) 325-4951, is a wonderful historic hotel, tastefully decorated with antique furnishings. Rooms start at $84 in the high season and $58 in the off-season. The **Box Canyon Lodge and Hot Springs**, 45 Third Avenue, (800) 327-5080 or (970) 325-4981, has its own mineral hot springs tubs situated on a secluded mountainside, affording a spectacular nighttime view of the stars. A variety of rooms are available, from one-bedrooms to suites with or without kitchens and fireplaces. Rates start at $50 and go up to $80.

CAMPING

The **Amphitheatre Campground** in the Uncompahgre National Forest is just outside of Ouray. A reservation is needed for one of the 30 units here, which cost $10 per night. Telluride's **Town Park Campground** is often full, but give it a try if you're traveling on a weekday or during off-season.

Molas Lake Park is 5 miles south of Silverton on Highway 550. There are 60 campsites at Molas Lake, with trout fishing, a store, showers, fishing licenses, and horseback rides. From Highway 110 in Silverton is the **Silverton Lakes Campground**, 2100 Kendall Street, (970) 387-5721, with full RV hookups, picnic tables, and grills. Open May to November.

9

DURANGO AND CORTEZ

A ncient and modern cultures have shaped the unique heritage of the Durango-Cortez region. Between A.D. 1000 and 1300, the population in the region, now known as the Mancos River Valley was double what it is today. The valley's early residents, called the Anasazi peoples, abruptly disappeared from their homes in the year 1300. While there are several plausible explanations for their disappearance, no one knows for sure why they left. Remains left behind, such as cliff houses, baskets, and pottery give us scant clues as to their way of life.

The Utes, who once claimed all of Colorado's mountains as their home, have probably been in this area since at least 1300, but are not related to the Anasazi. This tribe began losing portions of their home-land beginning in 1849 through a series of controversial treaties with the United States. They eventually lost almost all of their original lands. Today they inhabit two small blocks of land in the southwest corner of Colorado, the Ute Mountain Ute Reservation and the Southern Ute Reservation. Of the many Native peoples who once lived in what is today Colorado, the Utes are the only tribe to retain any land holdings in the state.

Southwest of Cortez lies legendary Sleeping Ute Mountain. One Ute legend says the landform is a sleeping god. His headdress flows to the north, his arms are folded on his chest, and his legs and knees stretch toward the south. When clouds collect over Sleeping Ute, the god is said to be changing his blankets for the new season. ◼

DURANGO AND CORTEZ

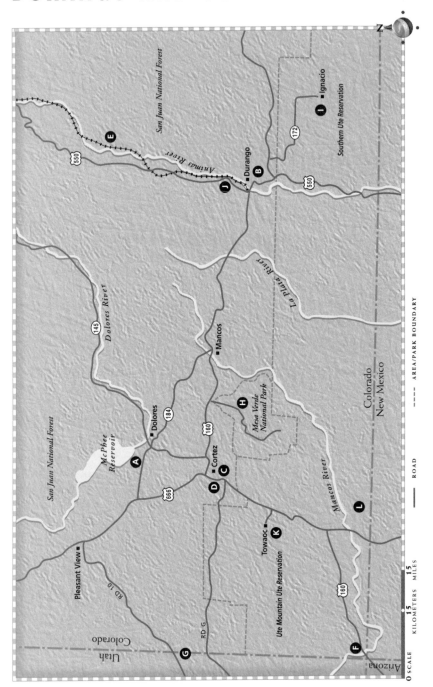

Sightseeing Highlights

(A) Anasazi Heritage Center

(B) Animas School Museum

(C) Cortez Center

(D) Crow Canyon Archaeological Center

(E) Durango-Silverton Narrow Gauge Railroad

(F) Four Corners Monument

(G) Hovenweep National Monument

(H) Mesa Verde National Park

(I) Southern Ute Reservation, Ignacio

(J) Trimble Hot Springs

(K) Ute Mountain Ute Reservation, Towaoc

(L) Ute Mountain Ute Tribal Park

A PERFECT DAY IN DURANGO AND CORTEZ

Spend the entire day exploring the Anasazi cliff dwellings at either
Mesa Verde National Park, Ute Mountain Tribal Park, or Hovenweep
National Monument. Mesa Verde is the most accessible but also the
most crowded. The Ute Mountain Tribal Park and Hovenweep will be
appreciated by adventurous travelers wanting to see some of the more
remote dwellings. In the evening, attend one of the excellent (and usually free) programs at the Cortez Center to learn more about Native
cultures of the Southwest.

THE ANASAZI

The people we call the Anasazi, which means "ancient enemies" in
Navajo, lived in the Mancos and Dolores River Valleys from approximately A.D. 1 to 1300. Over the centuries, they slowly changed their

mesa-top village sites to homes built under rock overhangs, giving them their other name, the "Cliff Dwellers." Although the Anasazi are usually associated with the cliff dwellings, the time they spent in them accounts for only about 10 percent of the entire time they lived in the region.

After they moved to the cliff houses, the Anasazi became more sedentary, developing advanced horticultural and food storage technologies to support a larger population. They planted terraced crops, built canals and dams, grew corns, beans, and squash, and hunted wild turkey and other game. Traveling on established trade routes, they traded these goods with larger pueblos to the south. The descendants of the Anasazi are believed to be the Pueblo and Hopi Indians today living in New Mexico and Arizona.

The Anasazi cliff dwellings were multistoried and made of stone. The complex included towers, large plazas surrounded by "apartments" with windows, and underground structures known as kivas, used for sacred ceremonies. The rock overhangs protected the homes from the wind, and the dwellings' openings all faced south to soak up the sun's rays. The Anasazi collected water from seeps and springs in the canyon walls.

Why did the Anasazi leave their cliff homes and the Mancos River Canyon? Perhaps they had to move because of changing environmental conditions, such as a long drought, or cooler weather which shortened the growing season. They might have been overpowered by the stronger pueblos to the south, or had to abandon their homes because they became too crowded and had used all available natural resources. Whatever the reason, these people never returned, but they left behind intriguing archaeological clues for us to examine. Throughout this region are many locations where you can examine the remnants of this once-thriving civilization.

SIGHTSEEING HIGHLIGHTS

☆☆☆ **Cortez Center**—If you're interested in learning more about the diverse peoples of this area, attend one or several of the cultural events held at the Cortez Center. The Native American Culture Series held during the summer includes programs of dance, concerts, art exhibits, lectures, sandpainting demonstrations, or storytellers elaborating on the history and culture of native peoples. The Octubre Fiesta in the fall focuses on all ethnic groups in the area, and might include cowboy poetry or a classical music concert. During the summer, programs run nightly, except Sundays, beginning at 7:30. Address: 25 North Market. Phone: (970) 565-1151.

✩✩✩ **Durango-Silverton Narrow Gauge Railroad**—This historic railroad line, today Durango's most popular attraction, fittingly pays tribute to the reason for Durango's existence. The Denver & Rio Grande Railroad built a narrow gauge line through the Animas River Valley in 1882 to reach the rich mines in the San Juan Mountains to the north. Platted by the railroad, the town of Durango blossomed overnight, becoming a commercial supply center for the mining camps. Like many Western towns, Durango aggressively promoted itself, struggling to become the biggest and best city in southwestern Colorado. The railroad quickly saw the value of advertising the stunning scenic views of the San Juans on the Durango-Silverton line and ran special excursion trains for visitors.

Today the Durango-Silverton Narrow Gauge Railroad continues to carry thousands of passengers through the Animas River Valley on the original Denver & Rio Grande route. The restored steam engines are fired by coal, and the railroad uses only authentic turn-of-the-century railroad equipment. The train runs 45 miles (90 miles round-trip) between Durango and Silverton daily from May to October, with several different departure times. There are also special winter excursions from late November through April.

The round-trip between Durango and Silverton takes a full day, or you can spend the night in Silverton and return the next day (see the Telluride/Silverton chapter for sightseeing, lodging, and restaurants in Silverton). Many people like to disembark mid-way and go hiking or backpacking in the Weminuche Wilderness of the San Juans, returning on the railroad the same day or several days later.

Advance reservations for the train are advisable. The round-trip fare is $42.70 for adults and $21.45 for children 11 and under. Address: 479 Main, Durango. Phone: (970) 247-2733. (Full day)

✩✩✩ **Mesa Verde National Park**—First photographed in 1874 by pioneer photographer William Henry Jackson, the cliff dwellings preserved in Mesa Verde have long been a source of wonder and amazement for both archaeologists and laypeople. You will understand why when you explore the dwellings for yourself. Take at least one of the tours guided by park rangers who do a great job of explaining the dwellings and Anasazi culture.

Start your visit at the Far View Visitor Center (open only during the spring, summer, and fall, 8:00 a.m. to 5:00 p.m.), 15 miles inside the park. From here you can get tickets to see Cliff Palace and Balcony House. These are two of the more popular dwellings, and free tickets are given out on a first-come, first-served basis.

Hiking is allowed only in designated areas of the park, and hikers must register at Park Headquarters at Chapin Mesa, located 5 miles from Far View Visitor Center. There are two trails from Spruce Tree House: Petroglyph Point Trail (2.8 miles round-trip), which ends at a wall of petroglyphs, and Spruce Canyon Trail (2.1 miles round-trip), which takes you along the lush canyon bottom. Chapin Mesa is home to a fascinating archaeological museum (open 8:00 a.m. to 6:30 p.m. in the summer; 8:00 a.m. to 5:00 p.m. during the winter).

The park is open year-round, but during the winter some of the sites are closed. Still, many visitors prefer this season because they usually have the park to themselves. The beauty of snow gracing the mesa tops and dwellings is an incomparable sight. The Cliff Palace and Balcony House Loop are open from 9:00 a.m. to sunset during the winter for cross-country skiing.

You will find your own "Anasazi saturation rate," but I recommend spending at least one or two full days exploring this wonderful cultural resource. Admission is $5 for a week pass. The entrance to the park is 9 miles east of Cortez on Highway 160, or 36 miles west of Durango. Phone: (970) 529-4461.

★★★ **Ute Mountain Ute Tribal Park**—This secluded park is twice the size of Mesa Verde National Park—and much less crowded. Ute Mountain Ute guides give interpretive tours of the park's Anasazi cliff dwellings and Ute petroglyph sites. This is a terrific opportunity to explore seldom-seen Anasazi ruins and to learn about the Ute Mountain Ute tribe.

You can take a full-day tour, bringing your own lunch and vehicle with a full tank of gas, or a guided backpacking trip for up to four days. All trips leave from the Tribal Park Visitor Center at the junction of Highways 666 and 160, south of Tribal Headquarters at Towaoc. Phone: (970) 565-3751. For more information, write to the Ute Mountain Ute Tribal Park, Towaoc, CO 81334. (1–4 days)

★★ **Anasazi Heritage Center**—This museum is devoted to understanding and preserving Anasazi artifacts. The damming of the Dolores

River to construct McPhee Reservoir would have flooded several significant Anasazi locations. Archaeologists worked for eight years to record the places and their artifacts before construction of the dam started. The artifacts from these significant sites are displayed today at the Heritage Center.

A nice feature of the center is that it offers several hands-on experiences, such as learning to weave on a loom, grind corn with a metate, and handle actual Anasazi artifacts. You can also take short hikes to two remains of 12th-century settlements. Free. Address: 27501 Highway 184. Phone: (970) 882-4811. (2 hours)

✫✫ **Crow Canyon Archaeological Center**—If you're itching to work at an Anasazi dig with a professional archaeologist, here is your chance. This hands-on experience can be hot, dirty, and exhilarating. In addition to digging, there are several other programs offered, such as lectures by scholars or workshops by Native American artists on weaving or ceramics. You can sign up for day trips or weeklong seminars. Address: 23390 County Road K, Cortez, CO 81321. Phone: (800) 422-8975 or (970) 565-8975.

✫✫ **Southern Ute Reservation, Ignacio**—The Southern Utes operate the Sky Ute Lodge in Ignacio, a casino with limited stakes gaming. For a more educational experience, visit the Southern Ute Museum, with an art gallery and exhibits on Ute history. Sky Ute Downs is an equestrian center where rodeos are often held. For more information, write to Box 737, Ignacio, CO 81137. Phone: (970) 563-9583.

✫✫ **Ute Mountain Ute Reservation, Towaoc**—In addition to the Ute Mountain Ute Tribal Park, this reservation operates the Ute Mountain Casino just outside of Towaoc. The Ute Mountain Pottery Plant blends ancient Anasazi and Ute styles with original handpainted designs. The plant, which is open to the public, is located on the east side of Highway 666 just before the turnoff to Towaoc, roughly 12 miles south of Cortez. For more information, contact the pottery plant at (970) 565-8548.

✫ **Animas School Museum**—Ranchers, farmers, and businessmen began settling in the Animas River Valley during the 1870s to supply mining camps to the north with beef, flour, vegetables, lumber, and many other items. Founded in 1876, Animas City was the first prominent community in the valley. The residents optimistically looked forward to a bright future for their small town, but, by 1880, their hopes were dashed.

When the Denver & Rio Grande Railroad planned to build through the valley, the railroad directors tried, and failed, to negotiate a settlement with the founding fathers of Animas City. The railroad instead planned its major hub 2 miles south, creating the town of Durango. Soon Durango eclipsed Animas City as the commercial center for the San Juans. When the smelters from the mining district moved to Durango, it sealed the fate of Animas City.

The Animas School Museum, housed in an historic building, has many more stories about Durango's past. Open Memorial Day through Labor Day, Monday through Saturday 10:00 a.m. to 6:00 p.m. and, after November 1, by appointment. Address: 3065 West 2nd Avenue (at intersection of 31st Street and West 2nd). Phone: (970) 259-2402.

✹ **Hovenweep National Monument**—This remote monument straddles the Colorado/Utah border and is open year-round. Although there is always a ranger on duty here, other services are limited, and you can usually appreciate these impressive stone villages from around A.D. 1200 in solitude. The Square Tower Ruins are easy to get to, but the other five Anasazi villages in the monument can be reached only from hiking trails varying in length. There is no telephone service at Hovenweep, but you can call Mesa Verde National Park, (970) 529-4461, for more information.

There are two ways to get to Hovenweep. Before leaving, inquire about road conditions, as the dirt roads leading to the monument can be impassable when wet. The first route takes you south of Cortez, on Highway 666/160 for 4 miles. At County Road G, head west up McElmo Canyon 25 miles to the Ismay Trading Post (you can obtain gas, firewood, and camping supplies here). Continue another 14 miles from the trading post until you reach the access road into the monument in Utah.

The second, and more popular, route heads north of Cortez on Highway 666 to Pleasant View, about 20 miles. Take County Road CC a little over 6 miles to the junction of County Road 10 and head south. You will take this road directly to the monument access road, approximately 20 more miles.

✹ **Trimble Hot Springs**—First discovered and promoted by the arthritic W. F. Trimble in 1874, this natural hot springs pool has been a favorite of locals for many years. The facility has several different pools, and provides spa treatments such as massage therapy and acupuncture. Admission: $7 for adults, $5 for children 12 and under. Hours: Sunday through Thursday 8:00 a.m. to 10:00 p.m., Friday and Saturday 8:00 a.m. to 11:00 p.m. During the winter, the springs open at 9:00 a.m. Located 6 miles north of Durango on Highway 550 on Trimble Lane. Address: 6475 County Road 203. Phone: (970) 247-0111.

Four Corners Monument—This is the only place in the United States where four states meet (Colorado, Utah, Arizona, and New Mexico). The monument, on the Ute Mountain Ute Reservation, is 38 miles southwest of Cortez off Highway 160.

FITNESS AND RECREATION

Numerous outfitters provide a variety of adventure trips in this region, such as rafting or kayaking on the Dolores and Animas Rivers, horseback rides in the San Juan National Forest, and jeep tours along bumpy mountain roads. Durango has recently become the center of a thriving bicycle culture and sponsors the Iron Horse Bicycle Classic over Memorial Day weekend. Several mountain bike trails are accessible right from town. Contact **Mountain Bike Specialists**, 949 Main Avenue, (970) 247-4066, for information on tours, rentals, and ideas for trails in the area.

The **Purgatory Ski Resort** is 25 miles north of Durango. A shuttle bus runs from Durango to Purgatory during the winter. As one of Colorado's lesser-known ski areas, Purgatory's terrain is varied, with beginning trails at the base village, and the harder runs farthest back on the mountain. Address: 1 Skier Place. Phone: Snow report, (800) 525-0892; lodging, (800) 525-0892.

Some of the best hiking in Colorado is found just outside of the Durango area. Because there are so many options, I suggest contacting a Forest Service district office in the area for more information. There are Forest Service district offices in Durango, 701 Camino Del Rio, (970) 385-1286; Dolores, 100 North 5th, (970) 882-7296; and Mancos, 41595 East Highway 160, (970) 533-7716.

For those who like to fish, trophy-size rainbow trout are found in the Dolores River below McPhee Dam, just outside of Dolores. McPhee Reservoir is considered one of the best fishing spots in the whole San Juan Basin. Vallecito Lake, northeast of Durango is also a popular fishing hole. If you'd like some advice on where to go, contact **Duranglers Flies and Supplies**, 801 Main Avenue, (970) 385-4081.

FOOD

Carver's Bakery Café and Brewery, 1022 Main Avenue, (970) 259-2545, in Durango, is a moderately priced restaurant that specializes in healthier fare. The menu includes vegetarian burgers, sandwiches, pizzas, and stews in bread bowls. Prices are in the $5 to $10 range. This hearty fare can be supplemented by a range of house beers. Open Monday through Saturday 6:00 a.m. to 10:00 p.m., Sunday 6:00 a.m. to 1:00 p.m.

Father Murphy's Pub and Gardens, 636 Main Avenue, (970) 259-0334, serves one of the best burgers in town, plus a variety of salads, hot and cold sandwiches, chicken specialties, and a mean chile relleno. Prices are in the $5 to $12 range. Open daily 11:00 a.m. to 9:00 p.m. One of the local favorites is the **Durango Diner**, 957 Main Avenue, next to Woolworth's, (970) 247-9889. It opens at 5:00 a.m. every day to serve up steaming plates of eggs, hash browns, toast, and other breakfast dishes. Traditional lunch fare, such as chicken-fried steak and mashed potatoes, is served until 2:00 p.m. on weekdays, and 1:00 p.m. on Sunday. Meals cost $3 to $5.

Sweeney's, in north Durango on Highway 550, (970) 247-5236, is housed in a rustic setting that resembles the interior of a mine. The dinners here are elegant, meant for a special night out. Specialties are steaks, seafood, duck, and chicken. Prices average about $16 per person. Open for dinner at 5:30.

In Cortez, the **Main Street Brew Pub**, 21 East Main, (970) 564-9112, serves several handcrafted beers in addition to a reasonably priced and inventive menu of specialty pizzas, salads, pastas, and excellent dinner entrees, such as chicken Florentine, aged steaks, and pork tenderloin, priced from $6 to $15. Their appetizers are also delicious, including baked Brie, escargot, and marinated beef ribs, for $4 to $5. Open 11:30 a.m. Monday through Saturday, and 4:30 p.m. on Sunday.

Nero's Italian Restaurant, 303 West Main, (970) 565-7366, has been a Cortez tradition for years. Specialties of the house include wonderful pestos, grilled chicken in lime sauce, and beef tenderloin, ranging from $11 to $17. Open every night except Sunday at 5:00 p.m. to approximately 9:00 p.m. Another Cortez favorite is **Nashio's**, 1020 South Broadway, (970) 565-1257. The steaks are very reasonable and delicious, from the top sirloin for $11.25 to the chateaubriand feast (enough for three people) for $47. A variety of grilled shrimp and scampi dishes run about $17. Open 5:30 p.m. to 10:00 p.m.

LODGING

If you are planning a trip to this area during the summer, be sure to reserve lodging beforehand. Accommodations in Durango and Cortez are usually booked through the summer, especially on the weekends, and rates here are usually higher. There are several excellent places to stay in smaller towns nearby, such as Dolores or Mancos. You shouldn't have any problems finding accomodations during the spring, fall, or winter.

If you'd like to spend two or more days exploring Mesa Verde, stay within the park, at **Far View Lodge**, open spring, summer, and fall, (970) 529-4421. Rates are from $76 to $89. Standard motels are found en masse in Cortez. The **Sand Canyon Inn**, 301 West Main Street, (970) 565-8562, is affordable and clean. Rates start at $38.

In Dolores, the **Rio Grande Southern Hotel**, 101 South 5th, (970) 882-7527, was originally built as a railroad hotel in 1893. Two of the rooms have private bathrooms, while 11 rooms share three bathrooms. Rates are $35 to $60, which includes a full breakfast served in the dining room.

The **Bauer House**, 102 Bauer Avenue, Mancos, (970) 533-9707 or (800) 733-9707, is open usually from April through November. This 1890s Victorian mansion has three private rooms and a penthouse, all nonsmoking. Rates run $75 to $125 (for the penthouse). Also in Mancos is the **Mesa Verde Motel**, 191 Railroad Avenue, (970) 533-7741. During the summer, rates start at $40.

When the **Strater Hotel** opened its doors in 1888, Durango celebrated its first high-class hotel, which rivaled the finest establishments in Denver. The hotel still offers elegant lodging, decorated in the Victorian style of the late 19th century. Address: 699 Main. Phone: (800) 247-4431 or (970) 247-4431. Summer rates are $105 to $155. Durango also has a variety of lodging in different price ranges. One of the most economical is the **Spanish Trails Motel**, 3141 North Main Avenue, (970) 247-4173, with summer rates starting at $30. The **River House Bed and Breakfast**, 495 Animas View Drive, (970) 247-4775 or (800) 254-4775, has seven rooms, all with private baths. Rates start at $65 during the summer. The full breakfast is gourmet and healthy. It is located north of Durango, just off Highway 550.

DURANGO AND CORTEZ

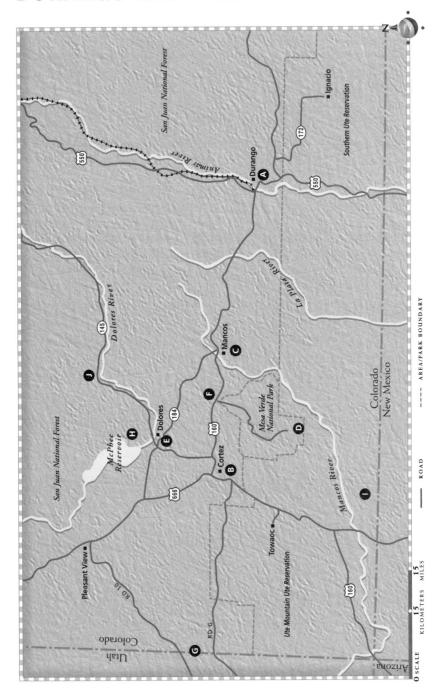

N

San Juan National Forest

Antinas River

Durango ■ Ⓐ

550

550

172

■ Ignacio

Southern Ute Reservation

Colorado
New Mexico

La Plata River

Dolores River

145

Ⓙ

San Juan National Forest

McPhee
Reservoir

Ⓗ

■ Dolores

Ⓔ

184

Ⓕ

160

■ Cortez

Ⓑ

666

Mancos ■
Ⓒ

Mesa Verde
National Park

Ⓓ

Mancos River

Ⓘ

Towaoc ■

Ute Mountain Ute Reservation

160

Pleasant View ■

RD 10

Ⓖ

RD G

Utah
Colorado

Arizona

0 SCALE
15 KILOMETERS   15 MILES

—— ROAD

---- AREA/PARK BOUNDARY

Food

A Carver's Bakery Café and Brewery

A Durango Diner

A Father Murphy's Pub and Gardens

B Main Street Brew Pub

B Nashio's

B Nero's Italian Restaurant

A Sweeney's

Lodging

C Bauer House

D Far View Lodge

C Mesa Verde Motel

E Rio Grande Southern Hotel

A River House Bed and Breakfast

B Sand Canyon Inn

A Spanish Trails Motel

A Strater Hotel

Camping

F A & A Mesa Verde RV Resort Park

A Cottonwood Camper Park

G Hovenweep National Monument

H McPhee Reservoir

D Mesa Verde National Park

I Ute Mountain Ute Tribal Park

J West Fork Campgrounds

Note: Items with the same letter are located in the same area.

CAMPING

Morefield Campground in **Mesa Verde National Park** has almost 500 sites, and is open from spring to fall. Camping at **Hovenweep National Monument** is possible year-round at Square Tower Ruins. The National Park Service charges between $6 and $16 for camping. To camp at either site you'll need a permit from Mesa Verde National Park. For more information, call (970) 529-4465.

Camping is available at the **Ute Mountain Ute Tribal Park**, but it also requires a permit from the tribe. Call (970) 565-3751 for more information. Camping at **McPhee Reservoir,** west of Dolores, (970) 882-2257, with several RV hookups, runs between $8 and $12. The **West Fork Campgrounds** in the San Juan National Forest are a series of campgrounds accessed from Highway 145. From Dolores, drive 13 miles northeast, then go north on Forest Service Road 535. Some have RV pull-throughs and dump stations. The fee is $6 to $8. Call the Forest Service in Durango for more information, 701 Camino del Rio, (970) 247-4874.

Cottonwood Camper Park, on Highway 160 one-third of a mile west of Highway 550, (970) 247-1977, is centrally located near downtown Durango. It is open year-round. Closer to Mesa Verde is the **A & A Mesa Verde RV Resort Park**, across from the entrance to Mesa Verde, (970) 565-3517 or (800) 972-6620. There is a playground, courts for basketball and volleyball, and a heated pool. They also stable horses for trail riding.

NIGHTLIFE

The students at Fort Lewis College in Durango support several watering holes and music spots. The most popular, **Farquahrts,** (970) 247-5442, 725 Main Avenue, also serves great pizza. If you're just looking for a fun place to have a drink, **Henry's,** at the Strater Hotel, 699 Main Avenue, (970) 247-4431, is an Old West throwback, complete with honky-tonk piano, plush red velvet walls, and interestingly (scantily) attired waitresses.

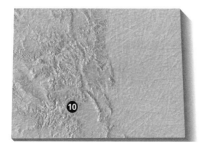

10

THE UPPER RIO GRANDE VALLEY

Summers in the Upper Rio Grande River Valley bring glorious sunny days, wildflowers, and lots of out-of-town visitors. In the winter, this area falls into a restful slumber, stirred only by an occasional cross-country skier or snowshoer.

People often return to the Upper Rio Grand Valley year after year, staying in the same lodge or guest ranch until it begins to feel like a second home. Once you discover the beauty of this area for yourself, you might also want to return. It's just that kind of place. ◪

UPPER RIO GRANDE RIVER VALLEY

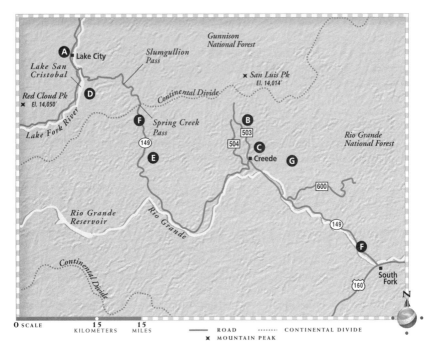

Sightseeing Highlights

- **A** Alfred Packer Massacre Site
- **B** Bachelor Loop Driving Tour
- **C** Creede Museum
- **C** Creede Repertory Theatre
- **C** Creede Underground Mining Museum
- **A** Hinsdale County Historical Museum
- **D** Lake San Cristobal
- **E** North Clear Creek Falls
- **F** Silver Thread Scenic and Historic Byway
- **C** Underground Firehouse
- **G** Wheeler Geologic Wilderness Area

Note: Items with the same letter are located in the same area.

A PERFECT DAY IN THE LAKE CITY/CREEDE AREA

Spend the day exploring the vast untamed wilderness between Lake City and South Fork. Drive the highway between these towns, known as the Silver Thread Scenic and Historic Byway, to appreciate the beautiful views. Stop at various locations along the way, such as North Clear Creek Falls, or take a longer side trip to the Wheeler Geologic Area. Enjoy a relaxing evening in either Lake City or Creede, both of which have several good restaurants, and attend one of the plays at the Creede Repertory Theater.

SIGHTSEEING HIGHLIGHTS

✭✭✭ **Creede Repertory Theatre**—Housed in a prominent building on Creede's Main Street, this theater has earned its reputation as one of the best in the Southwest. It started as a struggling company in 1966 and has developed into a well-known playhouse, featuring actors from all over the country who perform a different play each night, in true repertory style. One recent season featured *A Streetcar Named Desire*, *You Can't Take It With You*, and *Steel Magnolias*. Regular tickets run $12 to $14. Phone: (719) 658-2540. (Evening or matinee shows, 2 hours)

✭✭✭ **Silver Thread Scenic and Historic Byway**—This 75-mile route links the communities of Lake City, Creede, and South Fork. The Rio Grande, which begins high in the Weminuche Wilderness, lazily meanders through the landscape. Paralleling the drive from South Fork to Creede are the former Denver & Rio Grande railroad tracks that carted many loads of ore extracted from Creede silver mines. Residents are currently trying to remove the rails and turn the railroad grade into a multi-use recreational trail.

In this valley, cattle ranching has proven profitable and certainly much more reliable than mining. While miners are known to be a transitory lot, homesteaders and ranchers set up permanent ranches here in the last years of the nineteenth century. Several large family-owned spreads remain in the area, some of which have been converted into guest ranches.

One of the most beautiful places to stop along this route is **North Clear Creek Falls**, a little more than 20 miles from Creede. North Clear Creek is a quiet meadow stream until it comes to a steep basalt cliff, where it plummets more than 100 feet and travels through a narrow canyon before uniting with the mighty Rio Grande. The falls overlook is a nice place to stop for a picnic. From Highway 149, drive east on Forest Road 510 about a mile to the scenic overlook.

Six miles outside of Lake City is a creeping earthflow that started sliding down the landscape about 700 years ago. Called the "Slumgullion Earthflow" because it resembles a thick stew of that name favored by miners, this weak volcanic tuff and breccia (ash) became oversaturated with water and succumbed to the force of gravity. You can tell where the slide begins by looking for trees leaning precariously on top of what looks like a yellowish mud.

Along this spectacular drive you will cross the Continental Divide twice, at Spring Creek Pass and Slumgullion Pass. The road takes you through a delicate subalpine forest with an abundance of wildlife. In the space of two days, I happened upon a herd of bighorn sheep, two soaring bald eagles, more elk and antelope than I could count, and even a couple of moose rummaging in the willow bottoms. (2 hours–½ day)

☆☆ **Bachelor Loop Driving Tour**—This 17-mile tour travels through Mineral County's rich mining history, starting at the south end of Creede. Although it travels over steep and narrow roads, it can be navigated, albeit carefully, by passenger cars. A highlight of the tour is seeing what remains of the Amethyst and Last Chance Mines, two of the greatest producers in the district. As the story goes, a prospector discovered the Amethyst while cursing his stubborn burros that refused to move from a nearby hill. In desperation, he began to pick at the mountainside, and found a rich vein that he quickly laid claim to.

While it is fun to explore this former mining country, please remember to be careful near mine sites. Never climb on the unstable structures and watch for shafts sunk in the cliffs. You can get an informative guidebook to the Bachelor Loop for $1 from Creede's Chamber of Commerce, which describes interpretive stops marked with wooden timbers along the way. (2 hours)

☆☆ **Lake San Cristobal**—The 3-mile long Slumgullion Slide dammed the Lake Fork of the Gunnison River, forming this natural lake. Located 3½ miles from Lake City, Lake San Cristobal is known for its fishing, scenic views, and picnic spots. (2 hours)

☆☆ **Wheeler Geologic Wilderness Area**—Once a national monument, this 640-acre wilderness area encompasses a maze of volcanic tuff eroded into fantastic formations. The volcanic debris settled here after a violent volcanic episode 30 million years ago. To get to the area from Creede, drive 7.3 miles southeast on Highway 149 to Pool Table Road (County Road 600) and head northeast. After about 10 miles, the road becomes extremely rough, and can only be driven by four-wheel drive vehicles for the next 14 miles into the area. For more information, contact the Rio Grande National Forest at (719) 658-2556. (Full day)

✯ **Alfred Packer Massacre Site**—A party of six eager prospectors foolishly entered the San Juan Mountains during the harsh winter of 1873. They hoped to reach the Los Pinos Indian Agency to the south, and then get a jump start on the gold fields recently opened in Breckenridge. The following April, only one man of the party, Alfred Packer, made it to Los Pinos. He looked surprisingly fit and supple for someone who had just survived such an ordeal. He was observed with a large amount of money, causing many to suspect him of murdering his fellow travelers. When questioned, Packer revealed that the men resorted to cannibalism as several members of the party began to die from starvation and illness. When just Packer and another man named Bell remained, Packer claimed Bell went mad and attacked him, forcing him to kill Bell in self-defense. A reporter from *Harper's Weekly* stumbled upon five bodies northeast of Lake San Cristobal in August 1874. They were quickly identified as the original five men who had accompanied Packer. Coloradans demanded a trial and anticipated execution of the cannibal. But before a trial could begin, Packer escaped from a Saguache jail. After being re-apprehended in 1883, his infamous trial took place in Lake City. Dubbed the "Maneater," Packer spent the next 18 years in the state penitentiary for his crime.

In 1989, the bodies of that unlucky prospecting party were exhumed to re-examine the case against Alfred Packer, Colorado's infamous cannibal. Investigators did find marks on the bones, proving that they had been hacked at to remove the flesh, but were uncertain as to whether Packer alone was the cannibal, or if the men ate one another to keep from starving.

Lake City likes to toast poor Alfie by sponsoring an annual rib dinner Memorial Day weekend. You can visit the grave of the five men on Cannibal Plateau by heading south on Highway 149 for a little over 2 miles. The site is well-marked on the road as the "Alfred Packer Massacre Site." (1 hour)

✭ **Creede**—With the discovery of an enormous silver vein in Willow Creek Canyon in 1889, the rush to Creede began. The tent town quickly gained a wild reputation where revelers never slept—day or night. The railroad line entered town two years later to ship ore, freight, and passengers, and Creede's population soared to 10,000 people. The **Creede Museum** has early mining tools, photos, and other pioneer artifacts housed in the 1891 Denver & Rio Grande depot on Main Street. Admission is free. Hours: Memorial Day through Labor Day, Monday through Saturday 10:00 a.m. to 4:00 p.m. (½ hour)

After the last mine pulled out of Mineral County in the mid-1980s, Creede lost 32 percent of its population and its economic mainstay—hard rock mining. Residents of the town built the **Creede Underground Mining Museum** as a tribute to hard rock mining in Mineral County. The museum, dug into the side of a mountain, is a replica of a working mine. Exhibits depict mining in Creede and Mineral County from the 1890s to the 1980s. Silver still lies waiting in many mines here, but it just isn't profitable to extract it.

Creede's **Underground Firehouse**, next to the mining museum, is still used today. The fire department volunteers, all miners, preferred to blast underneath a mountain than build a new structure for their firehouse. This firehouse is known far and wide as one of the most unusual in the country. Admission to the museum is $3, or $4 with a guided tour given during the summer. Hours: Starting Memorial Day weekend, both the museum and firehouse are open daily 10:00 a.m. to 4:00 p.m. In the winter, the museum is open 10:00 a.m. to 3:00 p.m., and closed on the weekends. Phone: (719) 658-0811. (1 hour)

✭ **Lake City**—In an era known for rough-and-tumble mining towns, Lake City was a breed apart. A road builder discovered a rich vein of gold while surveying this area for a road near Lake San Cristobal in 1874. His discovery spawned Lake City, one of the first incorporated towns on the Western Slope. While miners hastily threw together ramshackle log cabins and tents when they first came here, the more permanent homes and commercial buildings of Lake City boasted Greek, Gothic, Italianate Revival, and Queen Anne Victorian building styles.

In keeping with its sophisticated architecture, the late nineteenth-century residents of Lake City enjoyed many refinements of a respectable town, with residents regularly attending socials, church gatherings, and concerts. Many original buildings from the late 1870s and 1880s still stand in this National Historic District, one of the largest in Colorado. During the summer and fall, the Hinsdale County Historical Society sponsors house tours.

The **Hinsdale County Historical Museum** is located in a mercantile building that dates from 1877. Changing exhibits on the Utes, early mining history, and the geology of the Upper Rio Grande River Valley are featured. Admission: $2 for adults, 50 cents for children. Hours: Open daily Memorial Day to Labor Day. Address: 130 Silver Street, Lake City. Phone: (970) 944-9515. (1 hour)

FITNESS AND RECREATION

Fishing is the preferred summer activity on the **Rio Grande**, known for its 16- to 18-inch rainbow trout. The best stretch on the river starts from the bridge on Highway 149 in South Fork and goes downstream towards Del Norte at the Rio Grande Canal diversion structure. This area has been designated one of Colorado's Gold Medal Waters. Although much of this stretch is privately owned, there are several public access spots. For more information on fishing, contact the **Division of Wildlife** Area Office in Monte Vista at 1035 Park Avenue, (719) 852-2731.

An active walking club in the Creede area sponsors several group hikes from June to October. Joining one of their events is a great way to see and learn about the area with some experienced walkers. They offer walks for every ability, usually 10 kilometers in length. Contact the **Upper Rio Grande Mountain Walkers** at P.O. Box 272, Creede, CO 81130, (800) 327-2102 or (719) 658-2736.

During the cold months, pull on a pair of cross-country skis or snowshoes and experience the glorious winter landscape. There are trails for every ability in this region, and several beginner trails are groomed periodically. The **Bachelor Loop/East West Willow Trail** starting from Creede has levels for every type of skier. The first 3 miles are suitable for beginners; the trail then gets progressively more difficult.

FOOD

The restaurant at **Crystal Lodge**, 2 miles south of Lake City, is a year-round gourmet's delight. Breakfast, lunch, and dinner all feature unusual and delicious entrees. Some of the dinner specials served include a spicy jumbo shrimp with a special Cajun seasoning, New York steak, macadamia nut–crusted halibut served with green chile

UPPER RIO GRANDE RIVER VALLEY

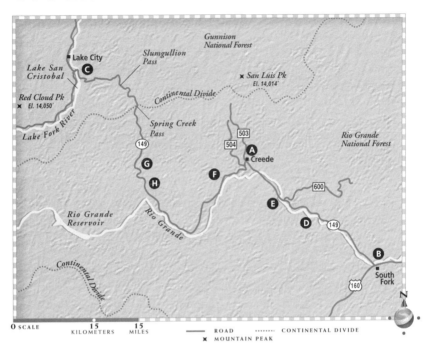

Food

- **A** The Blessings Inn
- **B** Brown's Country Store
- **B** La Casita
- **A** Creede Hotel
- **C** Crystal Lodge
- **A** Mucker's Bucket Saloon

Lodging

- **D** Cottonwood Cove
- **A** Creede Hotel
- **C** Crystal Lodge
- **C** Moncrief Mountain Ranch and Lodge
- **A** Old Firehouse Bed and Breakfast

Camping

- **E** Broadacres Guest Ranch
- **D** Cottonwood Cove
- **C** Lake City Campground
- **F** Marshall Park
- **G** North Clear Creek
- **H** Silver Thread

Note: Items with the same letter are located in the same area.

cilantro sauce, or a roasted stuffed chicken breast. Vegetarian specials might be a Mediterranean torte or penne pasta with a basil cream sauce. Breakfast runs $4 to $7; lunch, $5 to $7; and dinner, $9 to $16.

The **Creede Hotel**, (719) 658-2608, serves fresh and well-prepared meals and homemade baked goods and pastries. Breakfast starts with big cinnamon rolls or other pastries, and includes traditional egg dishes. Lunch features homemade soups, salads, and burgers, from $3 to $7. The dinner menu is more elegant, with entrees such as tamari honey chicken, salmon, prime rib, and several vegetarian pasta dishes, from $10 to $15.

Most of the restaurants in Creede and Lake City are closed during the winter. Luckily, the **Mucker's Bucket Saloon**, (719) 658-9997, on Highway 149 in Creede, stays open (7:00 a.m. to 9:00 p.m.). The saloon serves delicious and inexpensive meals, such as fried chicken, burgers, and french fries. **The Blessings Inn** bills their morning meal as a "stick to your ribs breakfast." They make fluffy pancakes and waffles, and standard egg breakfasts for under $3. On Main Street in Creede, (719) 658-0215.

At **La Casita**, 76 West Highway 149, South Fork, (719) 873-5556, every dish is made from scratch by the owner. The specialties include tacos, enchiladas, and chile rellenos, all accompanied with rice and beans for about $8. A la carte options start at $2. For a quick submarine sandwich, go to **Brown's Country Store**, 29411 U.S. Highway 160 in South Fork, (719) 873-5582. Subs are about $4.

LODGING

The most common form of lodging in the Creede/Lake City area is the summer guest cabin, usually a tiny cottage with one or two bedrooms and a small kitchenette. Most are open only in the summer, but a few are available year-round.

Cottonwood Cove, at the historic Wagon Wheel Gap about 10 miles southeast of Creede, (719) 658-2242, continues to uphold a long-standing tradition of guest ranches in this region. The accommodations include small cabins with one, two, or three bedrooms, and an RV park. Rates for the cabins range from $50 to $89, and RV sites are $17.50 per night, with the seventh night free. They also have horseback rides in the summer, $12 per person for one hour, or $20 per person for two hours.

Each of the rooms at the **Old Firehouse Bed and Breakfast**, (719) 658-0212, in Creede, is filled with interesting antiques and collectibles. The owner did a remarkable job converting this former firehouse into a bed and breakfast. Rates are $70 during the summer, and $60 during the winter (it's one of the few places that stays open).

The **Creede Hotel**, (719) 658-2608, on Main Street, has four comfortable rooms with private bathrooms, ranging $69 to $79. The hotel also has an annex, with a kitchen, that can sleep up to 11 people. Usually open from mid-March to mid-October.

For a luxurious treat near Lake City, stay at the **Moncrief Mountain Ranch and Lodge**, (970) 944-2796. Ten rooms in this log-cabin bed and breakfast range from $60 to $125. The whole ranch can be reserved for reunions, retreats, or weddings. It is located 8 miles south of Lake City on County Road 30.

The **Crystal Lodge**, 2 miles south of Lake City, has rooms starting from $55 in the summer, $45 in the winter. Also available are suites starting at $85, and cottages starting at $95.

CAMPING

For rustic camping, there are several good campgrounds in the **Rio Grande National Forest**, such as **Marshall Park, North Clear Creek**, and **Silver Thread**. There is a nominal fee for each site. Contact the Rio Grande National Forest on Third and Creede Avenues in Creede, (719) 658-2556, for more information.

Cottonwood Cove at Wagon Wheel Gap (see description under "Lodging," above) has pull-through RV sites, as does the **Broadacres Guest Ranch**, 4 miles southwest of Creede, (719) 658-2291. The **Lake City Campground**, (970) 944-2920, at 8th and Bluff Streets, is located right in Lake City, close to the downtown district, shops, and restaurants.

Scenic Route: The Alpine Loop

This route covers 65 miles of dirt and gravel back country roads from Lake City over Engineer Pass to Ouray, or over Cinnamon Pass to Silverton. While you can negotiate lower sections of the route in a passenger car, you'll definitely need a four-wheel drive with high clearance to travel over the high mountain passes. You can also mountain bike or walk part of the route to experience the high-altitude country.

If you don't have a four-wheel drive vehicle, rent one in Lake City or take a four-wheel drive jeep tour and let someone else do the driving. To inquire about renting a vehicle or taking a guided jeep trip, contact either **Rocky Mountain Jeep Rental**, (970) 044-2262, or **Hummer Adventures**, (970) 944-2780.

Freighters and miners used these rough roads to haul ore and equipment to and from mines in the San Juan Mountains. When you visit this area today, you can appreciate the remoteness of these former mines and forgotten settlements. Enterprising men like Otto Mears, the great "Pathfinder of the West,"

THE ALPINE LOOP

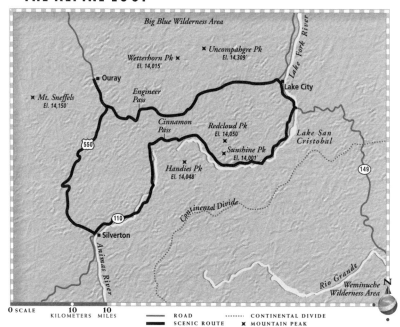

labored to bring stagecoaches and freight wagons to the fledgling camps.

The highest point on the road is at Engineer Pass, on the way to Ouray from Lake City, summiting at 12,800 feet. You can see numerous 14,000-foot peaks from this pass, with Mt. Sneffels (14,150 feet) to the west, and the craggy Mt. Uncompahgre (14,309 feet) to the northeast. Try to imagine a stagecoach crossing this same road in the late 1870s.

The backcountry access from the Alpine Loop is tremendous. The Big Blue and Weminuche Wildernesses, as well as two other wilderness study areas are readily accessible and laced with hiking trails and backcountry camping spots. The Alpine Loop also connects, at both Ouray and Silverton, to the San Juan Skyway Scenic and Historic Byway, which travels through some of the finest scenery in Colorado (see the Durango/Cortez chapter). ◼

11
UPPER ARKANSAS
RIVER VALLEY

The Arkansas River begins its 1,400-mile journey to the Mississippi in the high reaches of the Sawatch Range, a broad swath of mountains that start near Leadville and end just southwest of Salida. This range is home to 15 mountains above 14,000 feet, including Colorado's highest: Mt. Elbert, at 14,433 feet. The Collegiate Peaks Wilderness is in the southern section of the range and includes Fourteeners named after the Ivy League universities: Yale, Harvard, Princeton, and Columbia. The Sangre de Cristo Mountains frame the eastern border of the Arkansas Valley. Spanish explorers named the Sangre de Cristos, meaning "Blood of Christ." During sensational sunsets, this range is bathed in crimson hues, and the reason for its name is quite clear.

The Sawatch Mountains shelter this broad valley from harsh winters, which is why it is known locally as the Banana Belt. Most outdoor activities are possible here year-round. You can still hike or mountain bike on many trails at lower elevations during the winter months. The bodies of water rarely ice over, even during January and February, and year-round fishing in creeks, streams, lakes, and beaver ponds is usually possible. Locals claim the best fishing is in the fall, when the rivers are running at their lowest. ◧

UPPER ARKANSAS RIVER VALLEY

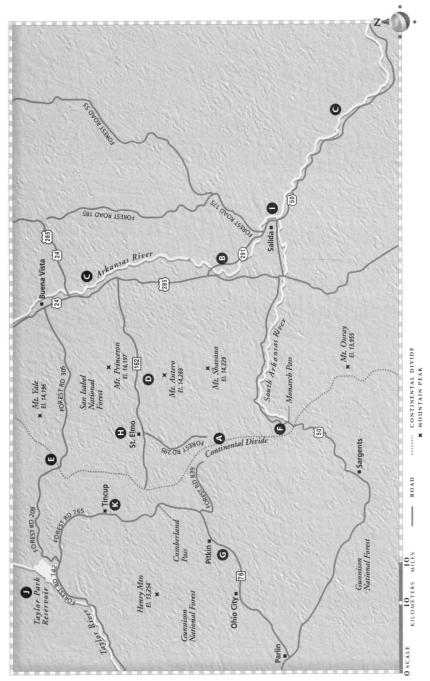

Z

FOREST ROAD 53

FOREST ROAD 185

FOREST ROAD 175

C

I

B

285

24

285

■ Buena Vista

C

24

Arkansas River

291

■ Salida

FOREST RD 305

× Mt. Yale
EL 14,196'

San Isabel
National
Forest

Mt. Princeton ×
EL 14,197'

162

D

× Mt. Antero
EL 14,269'

Mt. Shavano ×
EL 14,229

South Arkansas River

Monarch Pass

× Mt. Ouray
EL 13,955'

H

St. Elmo

A

FOREST RD 295

Continental Divide

F

50

■ Sargents

E

FOREST RD 209

FOREST RD 765

■ Tincup

K

FOREST RD 839

Cumberland
Pass

Pitkin ■

G

76

Taylor Park
Reservoir

FOREST RD 742

J

Henry Mtn
EL 13,254'
×

Gunnison
National Forest

Ohio City ■

Gunnison
National Forest

Taylor River

Parlin ■

0 SCALE

10   10

KILOMETERS MILES

·········· CONTINENTAL DIVIDE
× MOUNTAIN PEAK

──── ROAD

Sightseeing Highlights

Ⓐ Alpine Tunnel at Alpine Pass

Ⓑ Arkansas Headwaters Recreation Area

Ⓒ Arkansas River

Ⓓ Chalk Creek Canyon

Ⓔ Cottonwood Pass

Ⓕ Monarch Ski Area

Ⓖ Pitkin

Ⓗ St. Elmo

Ⓘ Salida

Ⓘ Salida Aquatic Hot Springs Pool

Ⓘ Salida Steam Plant

Ⓙ Taylor Park

Ⓚ Tincup

Note: Items with the same letter are located in the same area.

A PERFECT DAY IN THE UPPER ARKANSAS RIVER VALLEY

Sign up for a river rafting trip for a half-day, and spend the other half exploring St. Elmo, a remarkably well-preserved ghost town near Salida. Camp at one of the numerous campgrounds in the San Isabel National Forest, or spend the night in a lodge or bed and breakfast in Salida, where you can browse through the downtown National Historic District.

GHOST TOWNS

Several mute ghost towns stand today in this range of mountains, as reminders of the booming gold rush that once took place here. Places like Tincup, St. Elmo, and Pitkin once harbored aspirations to be the county seat—if not the state capital—but the decline of the mines and their isolation eventually buried those dreams under the thick winter snows.

A wonderful way to explore these ghost towns is to take a scenic drive on the back country roads. Most roads can be negotiated by a two-wheel drive vehicle, but I've noted where four-wheel drive is necessary. Take your time to explore the beautiful and serene alpine environment, the tremendous vistas, and the interesting historical attractions along the way.

SIGHTSEEING HIGHLIGHTS

★★★ **Arkansas River**—From its start at the crest of the Continental Divide, the Arkansas River is one of the major drainages that flow eastward across Colorado's plains to carry water eventually destined for the Gulf of Mexico, through the southeastern United States. Cascading through beautiful granite canyons and open valleys, the Upper Arkansas is also a source of numerous water sports, such as river rafting, kayaking, and fishing.

As many outfitters in this area will tell you, this river offers more excitement per mile than any other river in the West. A raft trip could be the highlight of your stay in the Upper Arkansas River Valley. The season usually runs from May to September, but peaks in June when the rivers are at their highest. A variety of trips are possible, from exciting adrenaline rushes on the boiling white-water rapids to gentle floats down the milder sections. Brown's Canyon, 8 miles south of Buena Vista, is known as the ultimate in white-water rafting because of the number of rapids encountered along the route. At least 20 companies in the area run trips. Among the more reputable are American Adventure Expeditions, 12791 U.S. Highway 24 and 285, Buena Vista, (719) 395-2409; and Bill Dvorak Kayak and Rafting Expeditions, 17921 Highway 285, Nathrop, (800) 824-3795 or (719) 539-6851. (½ day, full day, and multi-day trips available)

Headquartered in Salida, the **Arkansas Headwaters Recreation Area** begins in Leadville and ends in Pueblo, encompassing 150 miles of state parks, campgrounds, picnic areas, boat ramps, and fishing access along the Arkansas River. The United States Bureau of Land Management and the Colorado Department of Parks and Outdoor Recreation teamed up to create this unique recreation area and to protect the riparian environment. For more information, contact the Arkansas Headwaters Recreation Area, P.O. Box 126, Salida, CO 81201, (719) 539-7289.

★★★ **Chalk Creek Canyon**—This backcountry drive takes you through some of Colorado's richest mining and railroad history. About 15 miles north of Salida on Highway 285, you will come to County Road 162, just south of the town of Nathrop. Head west on this road. After about 5 miles, you will come to the Mt. Princeton Hot Springs Resort, where you can take a dip in the hot springs for $6.

Twelve miles west is **St. Elmo**, one of Colorado's best known and well-preserved ghost towns. In the 1880s, this town served as the transportation and supply hub for mining camps in the district, yet today it is isolated from the busy highways and towns of the Arkansas Valley. Miners from all over the area flocked to St. Elmo on the weekends to kick up their heels in the town's saloons. St. Elmo slowly withered as the demand for silver decreased, and by 1950, only two people lived here.

The Denver, South Park and Pacific Railroad built a narrow gauge line to service the mines in this area in 1880. The owners optimistically planned for their railroad to stretch all the way to the Pacific, but first the Continental Divide had to be conquered. The line came through St. Elmo and continued south past the Mary Murphy Mine, the best producer in the district. Instead of attempting to build the tracks over the Divide, railroad engineers decided instead to bore a tunnel beneath it. They designed the 1,772-foot Alpine Tunnel, the first ever burrowed under the Continental Divide.

The Alpine Tunnel closed in 1910 because the harsh winter conditions caused too many fatal accidents. You can see the eastern portal of the **Alpine Tunnel at Alpine Pass**. Head south of St. Elmo about 4½ miles on Forest Road 295 until you reach the former railroad station of Hancock. Head west here, and take the right fork of the road up to the tunnel. This road is very rough. You can drive it if you have a four-wheel drive with high clearance, or you can hike up the road about 3 miles to see the tunnel. A short trail from the east portal will take you over the Divide to the western portal, seen from the scenic drive over Cumberland Pass.

This drive should take you about 2¼ hours, excluding the time you will spend exploring sites and stopping to enjoy the scenery along the way.

★★ **Cottonwood Pass/Taylor Park/Pitkin**—This well-maintained paved road takes you over the Continental Divide, summiting at Cottonwood Pass at 12,126 feet. Several trailheads for Fourteeners and the Colorado Trail are accessed from the Cottonwood Pass Road. From the stoplight in Buena Vista, head west 20 miles on Forest Road 306 to

Cottonwood Pass. The road is paved until just before you reach the top, but the gravel portions can be driven by a two-wheel drive passenger car.

At the summit of Cottonwood Pass, a moderate hike starts at an elevation of 12,100 feet and gains about 1,000 feet. Walking at this elevation will be much harder than down in the valley, so don't overdo it. This short walk will take you south along the Continental Divide to higher views of the surrounding region. Taylor Park is on the western slope of the Divide, while to the north is the majestic Sawatch Range.

After hiking or enjoying the views from the pass, continue to descend into Taylor Park and toward Taylor Park Reservoir. From the reservoir, head south on Forest Road 742 until you reach Forest Road 765, which takes you into **Tincup**. The town probably was named after a miner who carried out his earnings in a tin cup. During the mining boom of this area in the late nineteenth century, Tincup's major thoroughfare to the outside world was through St. Elmo over the treacherous Tincup Pass. Be sure to visit the cemetery just outside of town and take time to read the inscriptions on the headstones, poignant reminders of the bygone mining era. (½ day)

For a longer trip from Tincup, continue south on Forest Road 765 over Cumberland Pass (12,000 feet) to the small historic community of **Pitkin** on Quartz Creek. You can camp in one of the many campgrounds along the way or spend the night at a hostel or bed and breakfast in Pitkin. Just outside of town, Forest Road 839 will take you to the western portal of the historic narrow gauge Alpine Tunnel, described in the Chalk Creek Canyon section in "Sightseeing Highlights," above.

The Pitkin Museum keeps odd hours, so if you'd like to see it, contact the Pitkin Historic and Community Association at P.O. Box 141, Pitkin, CO 81241, or call (970) 641-2685. To get back to Salida from Pitkin, take County Road 76 through Ohio City to Parlin, on Highway 50. You will be about 50 miles west of Salida on Highway 50. (1 long day or 2 days)

★★ **Monarch Ski Area**—This ski area has been tremendously popular because it is reasonably priced and known for its volume of snow: almost 36 feet are dumped here annually. The ski area offers both alpine and Nordic skiing, and caters to expert and intermediate skiers, but there are also several beginner trails and a ski school. The Monarch Ski Area grooms 3 kilometers of Nordic trails on Old Monarch Pass over the top of the Continental Divide. The trail begins just west of the ski area. Located 22 miles west of Salida on Highway 50. Phone: (719) 539-3573.

✦ **Salida**—This large National Register Historic District has several interesting art galleries, antique stores, restaurants, and bookshops. The springs supplying the **Salida Aquatic Hot Springs Pool** are actually piped in from 8 miles away, near Poncha Springs. The Works Progress Administration built the hot springs building and pool facilities during the 1930s. An Olympic-size pool offers lap swimming, aerobics, and water games; there's also a soaking pool and a child's pool. Admission: $5 for adults, $3 for kids 6–17 and seniors. Hours: Memorial Day to Labor Day, open daily 1:00 p.m. to 9:00 p.m.; during the winter, Tuesday through Thursday 4:00 p.m. to 9:00 p.m., Friday through Sunday 1:00 p.m. to 9:00 p.m. Address: 410 West Highway 50 (Rainbow Street). Phone: (719) 539-6738. (1–2 hours)

The **Salida Steam Plant** first brought electricity to the streets of Salida in 1887. This historic landmark is now an innovative community space for theater, dance, lectures, or whatever else comes to town. An outdoor sculpture garden sits next to the building. During your stay in Salida, look for community notices or posters announcing current events. For more information, contact the Steam Plant Committee, P.O. Box 758, Salida, CO 81201. Address: 312 West Sackett Street. Phone: (719) 539-7848.

Beginning in mid-July, Salida brings musicians from the Aspen Music Festival to town for six Saturday evening performances, known as the Salida-Aspen Music Festival. The performances start at 8:00 p.m. at the John Held Auditorium, 10th and D Streets. Phone: (719) 539-6441.

If you visit Salida in mid-June, you will encounter a crazy festival known as the FIBArk Boat Race Weekend. The weekend event is built around a 26-mile kayak race from Salida to Cotopaxi. People come to watch the race and take part in the festival activities, such as a bed race, parade, live music, and art booths. This event is billed as the most prestigious downriver kayak race in North America. For more information, contact FIBArk (it stands for "First In Boating on the Arkansas") at P.O. Box 762, Salida, CO 81201, (719) 539-7254.

FITNESS AND RECREATION

Eighty percent of Chaffee County is public land. The **San Isabel National Forest, Collegiate Peaks Wilderness, Sangre de Cristo**

Wilderness, Buffalo Peaks Wilderness northeast of Buena Vista, and sections of the **Colorado Trail** all offer an unlimited variety of trails for hiking and backpacking. Maps and information about these areas can be purchased from several wilderness equipment stores in Salida, Buena Vista, or Poncha Springs. The San Isabel National Forest office, 325 West Rainbow Boulevard in Salida, (719) 539-3591, also has detailed maps of the National Forest, including trails and campgrounds.

Summer afternoons in the mountains usually bring thunder and lightning storms. Always be aware of changing weather conditions when outdoors for an extended period of time. Pack a raincoat and several layers of clothing to keep you comfortable if there is a severe change in the weather. Even if you are only going for a day hike, carry extra water and food in case of an emergency. When camping, stay off the trail and at least 200 feet from any water sources to avoid damaging these fragile areas.

Hikers who are in good physical condition and accustomed to the altitude will be challenged by the many Fourteeners in this region, such as **Mt. Yale** and **Mt. Princeton**, both strenuous day-hikes. There are also countless number of mountain bike trails in the **Salida/Buena Vista** area, thanks to the many former railroad beds and rocky roads to the mountain mining districts. The **Monarch Crest Trail** from the crest of Monarch Pass to Marshall Pass has been called the best mountain bike ride in the state. The **Banana Belt Fat Tracks Mountain Biking Club** can recommend several good rides and provide more detailed information. Address: c/o Otero Cyclery, 108 F Street, Salida, CO 81201. Phone: (719) 539-6704.

FOOD

The **First Street Café**, 137 East First Street in Salida, (719) 539-6499 or 539-4759, has an excellent and varied menu, including many vegetarian dishes. Huevos rancheros, breakfast enchiladas, and other standard breakfasts run up to $5.95; Mexican specials, quiche, or sandwiches for lunch range from $5 to $9; and New York strip steak, stuffed chicken, or trout dinners run $10 to $18. Hours: Monday through Saturday 8:00 a.m. to 10:00 p.m., closed Sunday. **Il Vicino**, 136 E. 2nd Street in Salida, (719) 539-5219, fires pizzas in a wood oven and brews its own beer. They also serve calzones and paninos (sort of like pizza sandwiches). Both lunch and dinner run from $5 to $7. Open daily from 11:30 a.m.

The unique recipes at **Casa del Sol**, 303 North Highway 24, in Buena Vista, (719) 395-8810, are inspired by regional recipes from Mexico and New Mexico. Popular dishes include the *pechega suiza*, a folded flour tortilla sautéed in butter with chicken and green chiles, and enchiladas, with a carefully prepared red sauce that uses homegrown chiles from New Mexico. During the summer the restaurant is open every day, with lunch served 11:30 a.m. to 3:00 p.m. and dinner 4:30 p.m. to 9:30 p.m. Winter hours are erratic, so call ahead. Lunch is from $5 to $8; dinner, $8.50 to $12.

The **Mt. Princeton Restaurant** is located at the Mt. Princeton Hot Springs Resort, 15870 County Road 162, 5 miles from Nathrop, (719) 395-2361 and open for breakfast, lunch, and dinner. For dinner, the chef prepares several different pasta dishes, in addition to several excellent cuts of meat, chicken-fried steak, or vegetarian lasagna. The dining room is open from 7:00 a.m. to 9:00 p.m. in the summer. Breakfast runs $2 to $7; lunch, $5 to $7; dinner, $9 to $15.

LODGING

There is no shortage of standard motels in Salida or Buena Vista. However, plenty of out-of-the-ordinary lodging options can also be found. **The River Run Inn**, 8495 County Road 160, (800) 385-6925 or (719) 539-3818, is a Victorian mansion on 5 acres outside of Salida. The house has a huge front porch, 12-foot ceilings, and four-poster beds in each room. There are seven private rooms ($55–$70) and a coed dorm ($25) for large groups or families. The historic **Meister House**, 414 East Main Street, Buena Vista, (800) 882-1821 or (719) 395-9220, has five Southwestern-style rooms. Rates, including breakfast, are $60 to $75. The owners of the Meister House also rent a cabin with a two-night minimum stay, and a home on the Arkansas River which sleeps up to eight people.

The **Redwood Lodge**, 7310 Highway 50 West, (800) 234-1077 or (719) 539-2528, is a refreshing change from the standard motels that line the highway coming into Salida. This lodge has 27 different units, which range from rooms with queen-size beds to suites with a private Jacuzzi. The rates are $44 to $140.

If you stay at the **Jackson Hotel**, 220 South Main Street, Poncha Springs, (719) 539-4861, you become another name on their illustrious guest register, alongside Susan B. Anthony, Ulysses S. Grant, Kit Carson, Jesse James, and Billy the Kid. The hotel has been a resting

UPPER ARKANSAS RIVER VALLEY

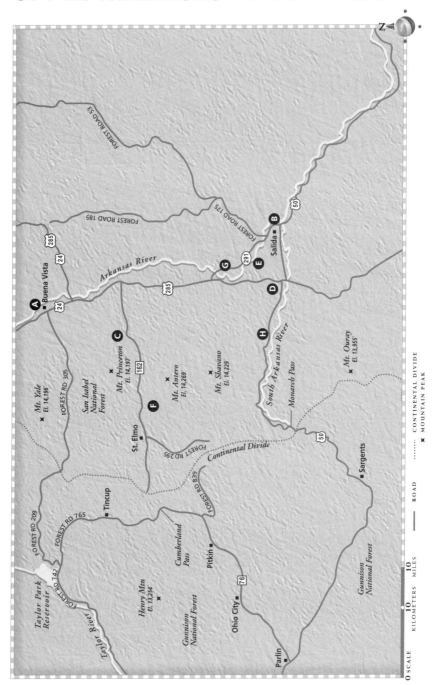

Food

Ⓐ Casa del Sol

Ⓑ First Street Café

Ⓑ Il Vicino

Ⓒ Mt. Princeton Restaurant

Lodging

Ⓐ The Adobe Inn

Ⓓ Jackson Hotel

Ⓐ Meister House

Ⓑ Redwood Lodge

Ⓔ The River Run Inn

Ⓕ Streamside Bed and Breakfast

Camping

Ⓖ Arkansas Headwaters Recreation Area

Ⓗ Heart of the Rockies Campground

Note: Items with the same letter are located in the same area.

place for travelers since 1878, and some rooms still have the hand-carved furniture bought by the original owner. Year-round rates are $25 to $55.

The **Adobe Inn**, 303 North Highway 24, next to the Casa del Sol Restaurant in Buena Vista, (719) 395-6340, has three rooms, each of which features distinct and tasteful furnishings. The rooms range from $59 to $79 in the winter and $69 to $89 in the summer, including a complete breakfast.

The **Streamside Bed and Breakfast**, 18820 County Road 162, 8 miles west of Nathrop, (719) 395-2553, has as its backdrop the magnificent Mt. Princeton, Mt. Antero, and Chalk Cliffs. The owners like to suggest trails for hiking, skiing, wildlife viewing, and other non-motorized recreation. Their rooms cost approximately $70 in the summer and $65 in the winter.

CAMPING

Campgrounds located along this section of the **Arkansas Headwaters Recreation Area**, (719) 539-7289, include Five Points, east of Salida; and Hecla Junction and Ruby Mountain, both north of Salida. To enter all Arkansas Headwater recreation sites you have to have a Colorado State Parks Pass, which costs $1 per person. Camping costs $2 per site, per night.

Some campgrounds in the San Isabel National Forest must be reserved and cost from $5 to $9. You can make reservations by calling (800) 280-CAMP (2267) for an additional $7.50. There are also backcountry camping sites in the national forest boundaries. For more information on camping, contact the San Isabel National Forest, 325 West Rainbow Boulevard, Salida, (719) 539-3591.

The **Heart of the Rockies Campground**, 16105 Highway 50 West, 11 miles east of Monarch Pass and 5 miles west of Poncha Springs, (800) 496-2245 or (719) 539-4051, has 45 RV sites with picnic tables, grills, and campfire rings. An arcade room, swimming pool, evening movies, and scenic horseback rides will also keep the kids busy.

NIGHTLIFE

The **Victoria Hotel and Tavern**, 143 North F Street, (719) 539-4891. About the only thing going on in Salida after 9:00 p.m. is found at "The Vic," open daily from noon to 2:00 a.m. On Friday and Saturday, you'll find live music here, usually rock 'n' roll or rhythm and blues.

12
SAN LUIS VALLEY

In 1598, Spain laid claim to all lands drained by the Rio Grande, including the San Luis Valley. As in the Southwest, this land belonged to Native Americans who had lived in the region for thousands of years. The Spanish subjugated the Pueblo peoples of New Mexico, but several other tribes, such as the Utes and Apaches, remained free from Spanish control and continued to roam the broad San Luis Valley. The horses brought by the Spanish came to be owned by several nomadic tribes, dramatically changing their way of life. As Indian people adopted the horse to their culture, they became more mobile and wealthy.

Extended families from northern New Mexico began settling permanently in the San Luis Valley during the first part of the nineteenth century. They lived along waterways, growing crops and tending flocks of sheep. Their homes, called *plazas*, were self-enclosed structures that helped them defend themselves during Indian raids. The isolation of this area from both Mexico and the United States protected the traditions of these early Hispanic settlers from outside influences, even after the area became part of the United States in 1848. Today many of the residents of the San Luis Valley still remain somewhat isolated, preferring to follow their longstanding traditions.

Anglo homesteaders began moving to the valley in the 1860s, plowing their fields and practicing agriculture differently than their Hispanic neighbors. Today these two cultures live side by side in the valley, each utilizing its abundant and diverse resources. ◣

SAN LUIS VALLEY

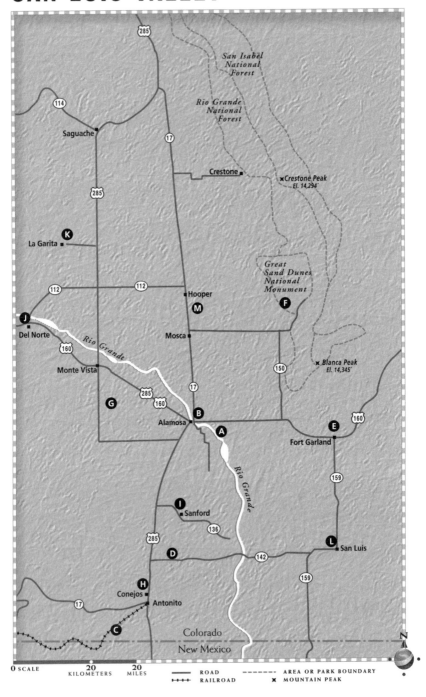

San Isabel National Forest

Rio Grande National Forest

285

114

Saguache

17

Crestone

✕ Crestone Peak
El. 14,294'

285

K
La Garita

112

112

Hooper

Great Sand Dunes National Monument

M

F

J
Del Norte

Rio Grande

160

Mosca

Monte Vista

150

✕ Blanca Peak
El. 14,345'

285

160

G

17

B

Alamosa

A

E
Fort Garland

160

Rio Grande

159

I
Sanford

136

285

D

142

L
San Luis

159

H
Conejos

17

Antonito

C

Colorado

New Mexico

N

Sightseeing Highlights

Ⓐ Alamosa National Wildlife Refuge

Ⓑ Luther Bean Museum

Ⓒ Cumbres & Toltec Narrow Gauge Railroad

Ⓓ Jack Dempsey Museum

Ⓔ Fort Garland Museum

Ⓕ Great Sand Dunes National Monument

Ⓖ Monte-Vista National Wildlife Refuge

Ⓗ Our Lady of Guadalupe Church

Ⓘ Pike's Stockade

Ⓙ Rio Grande County Museum and Cultural Center

Ⓚ San Juan Art Center

Ⓛ San Luis Museum and Cultural Center

Ⓜ San Luis Valley Alligator Farm

Ⓝ Splashland

Ⓞ The Stations of the Cross Shrine

Note: Items with the same letter are located in the same area.

A PERFECT DAY IN THE SAN LUIS VALLEY

Spend about three hours exploring the Great Sand Dunes National Monument. Afterwards, drive to the Fort Garland Museum, a reconstructed frontier military post from the early 1860s. Continue south through Fort Garland to San Luis and visit the Stations of the Cross Shrine. The shrine is a series of 15 sculptures situated along a path up a high bluff that overlooks the San Luis Valley and surrounding mountains.

ART OF THE SAN LUIS VALLEY

Much of the art produced in the valley today reflects the area's rich Hispanic heritage. The traditional artwork is a blend of early Spanish and Native American influences. The weaving style of the San Luis Valley and northern New Mexico, known as the Rio Grande style, can be found in several galleries, along with murals, *santos*, *milagros*, and other representations of Hispanic religious art. Eppie Archuleta, known throughout the world for her fine weaving, runs a weaving school in the valley. She is Colorado's only recipient of a National Heritage Fellowship, the highest honor given to folk artisans.

A recent influx of artists to this area has resulted in more modern influences in photography, pottery, paintings, watercolors, and sculpture. If you are interested in the work of a certain local artist, you can usually make an appointment to visit his or her studio. Inquire at art galleries in Alamosa, San Luis, and La Garita.

SIGHTSEEING HIGHLIGHTS

★★★ **Cumbres & Toltec Narrow Gauge Railroad**—Take a trip back in time on this steam powered narrow gauge railroad line between Antonito, Colorado, and Chama, New Mexico. Today the railroad carries only passengers, but the Denver and Rio Grande originally built this narrow gauge extension to haul minerals extracted from the San Juan Mountains. The line also picked up chiles from northern New Mexico villages, giving it the nickname "The Chile Line." The trip runs 64 miles through the San Juans, over trestles, curves, and bridges that afford incredible scenic vistas.

Prices for different trips on the line range from $16 to $26 for children, and $32 to $50 for adults. Seniors over 60 receive a 10 percent discount if they notify the agent when they make a reservation. Hours: Memorial Day weekend through mid-October, with various morning departure times. Phone: (719) 376-5483. (Full day)

★★★ **Great Sand Dunes National Monument**—For centuries, high winds crossing the San Luis Valley deposited millions of grains of sands to create these 700-foot-high sand dunes at the base of the Sangre de Cristo Mountains. The Dunes actually cover an area of 39 square miles. Exploring this stark environment can evoke an African desert experience—without the camels. Hiking to the summit takes about two hours uphill, and an hour downhill. For a fun and fast way down, try "skitching" on a plastic sled or windbreaker.

To get to the Great Sand Dunes from Alamosa, head east on Highway 160 to Highway 150. Turn north and drive about 18 miles.

Address: 1150 Highway 150, Mosca, 38 miles northeast of Alamosa.
Phone: (719) 378-2312. (3 hours–full day)

★★★ **The Stations of the Cross Shrine**—Built by the Sangre de
Cristo Parish, this shrine sits atop a bluff on the northern side of the
town of San Luis. Religion is the glue for many communities of the
San Luis Valley, as seen in the huge volunteer effort that went into
constructing this sanctuary for prayer and solace. Fifteen dramatic
bronze sculptures depicting the last hours of Christ's life, sculpted by
local artist Huberto Maestas, are positioned at intervals along a half-
mile trail to the top of the bluff. At the top, the scenic vistas of the
Sangre de Cristos, San Juans, and the valley itself, are very powerful.
Try to go just before the sun goes down—you may be rewarded with a
legendary San Luis Valley sunset. For more information on the shrine,
call (719) 672-3355. (1 hour)

★★ **Alamosa-Monte Vista National Wildlife Refuge**—In spring,
more than 20,000 greater sandhill cranes and a handful of their
cousins, the endangered whooping cranes, migrate through the San
Luis Valley on their way north. Approximately 20 whooping cranes
raised at these refuges return annually, usually between February and
the beginning of April. The Monte Vista Refuge is south of Monte
Vista on Highway 15. The Alamosa Refuge can be reached from
Highway 160 east of Alamosa, and south of County Road S-116.
Phone: (719) 589-4021. (½ day)

★★ **Fort Garland Museum**—Established in 1858, this frontier military outpost protected San Luis Valley homesteaders from attacks by
Ute and Apache warriors retaliating against settlement in the area.
From 1866 to 1867, the frontiersman Kit Carson commanded the post,
in charge of largely Hispanic troops. For a short time, "Buffalo
Soldiers," African-Americans who enlisted in the frontier army, were
also stationed here.

Recent archaeological excavations by the Colorado Historical
Society have unearthed many artifacts that illuminate the daily activities of soldiers and their families at the fort. Life at a frontier outpost
was seldom exciting, more often a humdrum repetition of marching
and orders. Several displays here explain the fort's history. Admission:
$2.50 for adults, $2 for seniors, $1.50 children 6–16. Children under 6
and Colorado Historical Society members are admitted free. Hours:

Open daily 9:00 a.m. to 5:00 p.m.; Address: U.S. Highway 159. Phone: (719) 379-3512. (1–2 hours)

★★ **San Juan Art Center**—Housed in the historic La Capilla de San Juan Bautista (the Church of Saint John the Baptist), this women's art cooperative is dedicated to Hispanic folk art. Hours: Memorial Day to Labor Day, Monday through Friday 10:00 a.m. to 5:00 p.m., Saturday and Sunday 1:00 p.m. to 5:00 p.m. Location: In La Garita, 6 miles from Highway 285 between Saguache and Monte Vista. The church can be seen from a rise northwest of town. Mailing address: P.O. Box 627, Center, CO 81125. Phone: (719) 754-3191, winter, or (719) 589-4769. (1 hour)

★★ **Luther Bean Museum**—On the campus of Adams State College in Alamosa, this museum has a unique collection of Native American and Hispanic Folk Art, including a bronze sculpture by noted Apache artist Alan Houser, Rio Grande–style weavings, and extensive anthropological collections. The museum features the work of regional artists. Admission is free. Hours: Open weekdays 1:00 p.m. to 4:30 p.m.; special tours can also be arranged. Phone: (719) 589-7121. (1 hour)

★★ **San Luis Museum and Cultural Center**—The exhibits in this center reflect the rich history of San Luis, Colorado's oldest incorporated town (1851), and of the whole San Luis Valley. Recent exhibits have focused on the area's multicultural heritage. Hours: Memorial Day to Labor Day, Monday through Friday 8:00 a.m. to 4:30 p.m., Saturday and Sunday 10:00 a.m. to 4:00 p.m. Address: 402 Church Street. Phone: (719) 672-3611. (1 hour)

★★ **Splashland**—Located north of Alamosa, Splashland is a geothermal swimming pool supplied by an artesian well kept a constant 94 degrees Fahrenheit. There are smaller pools for soaking and a larger pool with diving boards. Admission: $3. Hours: Memorial Day through Labor Day, weekdays (closed Wednesday) 10:00 a.m. to 6:30 p.m.; weekends, noon to 6:00 p.m. Location: The pool is 1 mile north of Alamosa on Highway 17. Look for the colorful 1950s marquee of a woman in a bathing suit. Phone: (719) 589-6307. (2 hours)

★ **Jack Dempsey Museum**—Jack Dempsey, the famous boxer and world heavyweight champion, hailed from Manassa, Colorado. Known as the "Manassa Mauler," he earned his title boxing in rough mountain camps such as Creede. Dempsey's former home, a 20-by-30-foot cabin, is now a museum in Manassa and a tribute to the town's favorite son. Highlights include boxing paraphernalia and rare film footage of Dempsey fighting. Hours: Memorial Day to October, Monday through Saturday 9:00 a.m. to 5:00 p.m. Address: 401 Main Street, Manassa. Phone: (719) 843-5207. (½ hour)

✯ **Pike's Stockade**—In 1806, Thomas Jefferson sent Zebulon Pike to explore lands west of the Mississippi River acquired through the Louisiana Purchase. Pike traveled through the San Luis Valley during a harsh winter and crossed the Sangre de Cristos in January 1807. His party of 12 men camped along the Conejos River, where they built a stockade and hoisted an American flag in the northern reaches of Spanish territory. In late February, one hundred Spanish soldiers traveled north from Santa Fe to the stockade to arrest Pike for trespassing. The soldiers took Pike prisoner and forced him to journey to Chihuahua, Mexico, where he was held for roughly a year.

A property of the Colorado Historical Society, Pike's Stockade has the distinction of being the first U.S. fort built on Colorado soil. To get to this site from Alamosa, travel south on Highway 285 to La Jara. Turn east on Highway 136 and drive about 4 miles to Sanford. Take County Road 20 6 miles northeast of Sanford and follow the signs. Hours: Memorial Day to Labor Day 9:00 a.m. to 5:00 p.m. For more information about the stockade, inquire at the Fort Garland Museum, (719) 379-3512. (½ hour, plus 45 minutes' drive from Alamosa)

✯ **Rio Grande County Museum and Cultural Center**—Displays include artifacts from the disastrous John Fremont expedition in the San Juan Mountains and a Native American rock art exhibit with carefully reproduced copies of art found in Rio Grande County. There are also many changing exhibits, lectures, and events. Hours: May to September, Monday through Saturday 10:00 a.m. to 5:00 p.m.; October to April, Monday through Friday 11:00 a.m. to 4:00 p.m. Address: 580 Oak Street, Del Norte. Phone: (719) 657-2847. (½ hour)

✯ **San Luis Valley Alligator Farm**—This farm is supported by geothermal hot springs. The Rocky Mountain White Tilapia, prized for its moist meat, is a fish delicacy that was developed here. The alligators consume the byproducts of the fish plant, but they are now the farm's most popular attraction. You can buy fresh and smoked fish delicacies here, as well as alligator meat. Admission: $2 for adults, $1.50 for children 6–12. Hours: June through August 7:00 a.m. to 7:00 p.m., September through May 10:00 a.m. to 3:00 p.m. Address: On Road 9N, from Highway 17, between Hooper and Mosca. Phone: (719) 378-2612. (1 hour)

Our Lady of Guadalupe Catholic Church—Before Catholic parishes and churches came to the valley, residents met informally on Sundays to recite the rosary, or gathered when the rare traveling priest came to the area to perform marriages, baptisms, and other holy rites. Our Lady of Guadalupe, in Conejos, formed in 1856, is the earliest congregation in the San Luis Valley and in Colorado. The parish's original adobe church, blessed by the Bishop of Santa Fe in 1860, has been replaced by a more modern structure.

FITNESS AND RECREATION

The stacked loop at Zapata Falls is a good mountain bike trail for beginners. The trail features four different loops winding through a piñon-juniper forest. From the trail you can see the San Luis Valley and the Great Sand Dunes and visit the nearby Zapata Falls. To get to the trailhead, head east from Alamosa on Highway 160. Turn left on Highway 150, the Great Sand Dunes Road, and drive 12 miles north to a gravel road. A sign here will direct you to Zapata Falls, 4 miles away. To rent a bike or get suggestions on rides in the area, contact **Kristi Mountain Sports**, in Villa Mall on Highway 160, Alamosa. Phone: (719) 589-9759.

Adams State College rents a variety of outdoor equipment, and you don't have to be a student or local resident to take advantage of the program. Available equipment includes bikes, backpacks, kayaks, rafts, life jackets, tents, sleeping bags, and more. Call ahead for reservations. The college also schedules trips to Creede, Taos, Santa Fe, and sites within the San Luis Valley. For more information, call (719) 589-7813.

FOOD

Emma's Hacienda, in San Luis, (719) 672-9902, is known far and wide for its tasty, authentic Mexican dishes. Emma's special consists of two cheese enchiladas, one smothered in green chile, the other in red chile, with beans, rice, a taco, and sopaipillas for $6.50. The bowl of green chile with two sopaipillas is also a favorite. The **R&R Grocery** on the main street of San Luis is the oldest grocery in Colorado.

True Grits Steak House, at the junction of Highways 160 and 17 in Alamosa, (719) 589-9954, is the best place in town for a steak. It also serves lobster, crab legs, and shrimp. Lunch prices start at $3.95; dinner starts at $4.99 for the food bar and goes up to $24.95 for the steak and lobster combination. Also in Alamosa is **Lara's Soft Spoken**, 801 State Avenue, (719) 589-6769. Lara's serves a little bit of everything, including pasta, sandwiches, soups, Mexican food, steaks, and seafood. Open Monday through Friday 11:00 a.m. to 9:00 p.m., and Saturday 4:30 p.m. to 9:00 p.m. (8:00 p.m. in the winter); closed Sunday. Entrees are $3.50 to $11.50. For something lighter, **Muggs**, 810 Main Street, Alamosa, (719) 589-8855, is a traditional bookstore and coffee shop, serving gyros and deli sandwiches for $4 to $5.

LODGING

Alamosa offers the most choices for standard motel lodging. The **Days Inn**, (719) 589-9037, a quarter-mile east of the junction of Highways 17 and 160, is the most economical. Prices start around $40. For more unique lodging in Alamosa, there is the comfortable **Cottonwood Inn Bed and Breakfast**, 123 San Juan Avenue, (800) 955-2623 or (719) 589-3882. A room with a shared bath starts at $52, including breakfast, for two people. Private baths are in the $75 range. The inn features artwork by regional artists. The gourmet breakfasts include homemade breads and jellies.

El Convento Bed and Breakfast, 512 Church Place, San Luis, (719) 672-4223, is housed in an adobe building that dates to 1905. Built by Father Jose Samuel, it used to be a religious school. Four guest rooms, each with a private bath, are decorated with handcrafted furniture and colorful Southwestern fabrics. The year-round rate is $60, which includes breakfast. Centro Artesano, a gallery featuring the work of local artists, is on the first floor of the bed and breakfast. The 1906 Victorian **Casa de Oro Bed and Breakfast**, also in San Luis, (719) 672-3608, has three rooms that sleep up to three people each. Rates are $40 to $50, including a continental breakfast on weekdays and full breakfast on weekends.

The **Wild Iris Inn**, (719) 754-2533, is located on the 155-acre La Garita Creek Ranch. The lodging here is comfortable and affordable,

SAN LUIS VALLEY

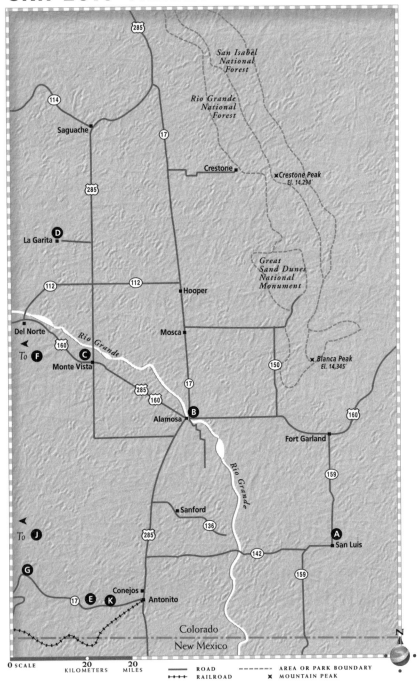

San Isabel National Forest

Rio Grande National Forest

285

114

Saguache

17

Crestone

✕ Crestone Peak
El. 14,294'

D
La Garita

285

112

112

Hooper

Great Sand Dunes National Monument

Del Norte

Rio Grande

160

Mosca

C

160

Monte Vista

150

✕ Blanca Peak
El. 14,345'

To F

285

160

17

B

Alamosa

Fort Garland

160

159

Sanford

136

To J

285

142

159

San Luis

A

G

17

E

K

Conejos

Antonito

Rio Grande

Colorado

New Mexico

N

| 0 SCALE | | 20 | 20 |
| KILOMETERS | | MILES | |

———— ROAD   — — — — — AREA OR PARK BOUNDARY
╟━━━━┤ RAILROAD   ✕ MOUNTAIN PEAK

Food

- **Ⓐ** Emma's Hacienda
- **Ⓑ** Lara's Soft Spoken
- **Ⓑ** Muggs
- **Ⓐ** R&R Grocery
- **Ⓑ** True Grits Steak House

Lodging

- **Ⓐ** Casa de Oro Bed and Breakfast
- **Ⓑ** Cottonwood Inn Bed and Breakfast
- **Ⓑ** Days Inn
- **Ⓐ** El Convento Bed and Breakfast
- **Ⓒ** Movie Manor
- **Ⓓ** Wild Iris Inn

Camping

- **Ⓔ** Aspen Glade
- **Ⓕ** Big Meadows
- **Ⓖ** Elk Creek
- **Ⓗ** Great Sand Dunes National Monument
- **Ⓘ** Great Sand Dunes Oasis
- **Ⓙ** Lake Fork
- **Ⓚ** Mogote
- **Ⓛ** Twin Rivers RV Park and Cabins

Note: Items with the same letter are located in the same area.

and the ranch offers a variety of outdoor amenities, including a tennis court and swimming pool. Rates start at $42, and there is a family cabin for $102. To get to the inn, drive to La Garita from Highway 285 south of Saguache or Highway 112 northeast of Del Norte. The inn is 3½ miles from La Garita; follow the signs.

Perhaps the most original place to stay in the San Luis Valley, and for that matter, all of Colorado, is **Movie Manor**, at 2830 West Highway 160 in Monte Vista, (800) 528-1234 or (719) 852-5921. The motel rooms are wrapped around a drive-in movie screen. During the summer, movies are shown nightly, and guests can watch from their rooms, with the sound piped in from outside. Rates start at $40.

CAMPING

Piñon Flats Campground in the **Great Sand Dunes National Monument**, 11500 Colorado State Highway 150, (719) 378-2312, is open year-round. It fills up quickly from April to October on a first-come, first-served basis. Backcountry camping is allowed with a permit in designated sites, but fires are prohibited. Many campgrounds in the **Rio Grande National Forest**, 1803 Highway 160, Monte Vista, (719) 852-5941, have fishing access, space for travel trailers, and numerous camp units. Some, at **Big Meadows, Lake Fork, Elk Creek, Aspen Glade**, and **Mogote**, can be reserved through the National Campground Reservation System, (800) 280-2267. Nightly fees for camping range from $5 to $10.

Numerous RV sites are clustered around Antonito and the Conejos River Canyon. One of the more secluded is the **Twin Rivers RV Park and Cabins,** 5 miles west of Antonito at the mouth of the Conejos River Canyon, (719) 376-5710 or (800) 376-5710. Fishing access is nearby, as are mountain bike trails and four-wheel drive routes. Closer to the Sand Dunes is the **Great Sand Dunes Oasis**, (719) 378-2222, which also has a grocery store and café.

13
TRINIDAD/LA JUNTA

In the early 1820s, the great Santa Fe Trail linked the United States with Mexico in commerce, forever changing relations between the two countries. After Mexico gained independence from Spain in 1821, enterprising American traders from Missouri capitalized on the open trade decreed by Mexico. Long trading caravans set off from Missouri filled with cloth, kitchen utensils, knives, and firearms, and slowly labored more than 1,200 miles to reach the New Mexico settlements. They returned with silver coins, horses, burros, blankets, hides, and wool. The burgeoning trade was an economic boon to both the trading centers of Missouri and the northern settlements of New Mexico.

In Colorado, the mountain route of the Santa Fe Trail followed the Arkansas River, the boundary between the United States and Mexico until 1848. Bent's Fort was the major rest stop and trading center along this portion of the trail. The trail then went southwesterly into Mexican territory, crossing Raton Pass, and continued south for the final leg of the trip to Santa Fe.

Today the Santa Fe Trail is a National Historic Trail managed by the National Park Service, running through parts of Missouri, Kansas, Oklahoma, Colorado, and New Mexico. There are many private and public historic sites where the story of this fabled commercial trail are told. In Colorado, sites such as Bent's Fort, actual trail ruts, and other remnants bring alive the memories of the trail for today's travelers. ◼

TRINIDAD TO LA JUNTA

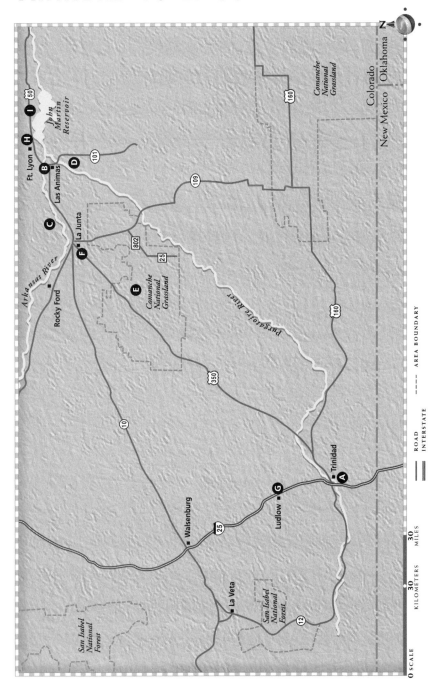

Sightseeing Highlights

Ⓐ A.R. Mitchell Museum of Western Art

Ⓐ Baca House

Ⓑ Bent County Courthouse

Ⓒ Bent's Fort

Ⓐ Bloom House

Ⓓ Boggsville

Ⓔ Comanche National Grasslands

Ⓐ Corazon de Trinidad National Historic District

Ⓔ Iron Springs Historic Area

Ⓑ Kit Carson Museum

Ⓐ Kit Carson Statue

Ⓕ Koshare Indian Museum

Ⓐ Louden-Henritze Archaeology Museum

Ⓖ Ludlow Monument

Ⓗ New Fort Lyon

Ⓕ Otero Museum

Ⓔ Picket Wire Canyonlands

Ⓐ Santa Fe Trail Museum

Ⓔ Sierra Vista Overlook

Ⓔ Timpas Picnic Area

Ⓘ Trail Ruts, John Martin Reservoir

Ⓐ Trinidad Children's Museum

Ⓐ Trinidad History Museum

Ⓔ Vogel Canyon

Note: Items with the same letter are located in the same area.

A PERFECT DAY IN TRINIDAD/LA JUNTA

Don't miss the experience of visiting Bent's Fort. You'll park your car about a half-mile from the fort and approach it on foot, just as travelers in the 1830s and 1840s did. After your visit to the fort, explore the pristine canyons and prairies of the Comanche National Grasslands from several points along Highway 350. Then drive to Trinidad and visit the Trinidad History Museum, which provides an excellent opportunity to learn more about the history and cultures of this area.

SIGHTSEEING HIGHLIGHTS

✯✯✯ **Bent's Old Fort, National Historic Site**—Around 1834, Bent, St. Vrain and Company established this fur trading post in United States territory on the north side of the Arkansas River (today just east of La Junta, Colorado). The Southern Cheyennes promised William Bent, who operated the fort, that they would trade buffalo robes with him if he established the post in their hunting grounds along the river. Bent capitalized on this successful partnership with the Cheyennes, as well as other Plains Indian tribes, making him much more successful than other traders.

Every caravan on the trail stopped at Bent's Fort to rest, catch up on the latest news, and conduct trade. The fort was the most important cultural center of exchange among Indians, Mexicans, and Americans between Missouri and New Mexico. Bent's Fort flourished until 1849, when William Bent abandoned it. A cholera epidemic brought by travelers on the trail may have been the reason Bent left for a new site up the river.

The National Park Service reconstructed the frontier trading post in the 1970s. Living history activities feature Santa Fe Trail customs, characters, and trivia. From La Junta on Highway 50, take Highway 194 8 miles to the site. Admission: $1 to $3. Hours: Memorial Day through Labor Day 8:00 a.m. to 6:00 p.m., the rest of the year 8:00 a.m. to 4:30 p.m. Address: 35110 Highway 194 East, La Junta, CO 81050-9523. Phone: (719) 384-2596.

✯✯ **Boggsville**—This early pioneer settlement used to be the agricultural and commercial seat of Bent County. In 1862, Thomas O. Boggs, following the example of Hispanic settlers who preceded him, built an adobe house for his family near the junction of the Purgatoire and Arkansas Rivers. William Bent had a ranch nearby, and other men who figured prominently in the history of this area also joined Boggs here, such as Kit Carson and John Prowers. The site was a major stop for Santa Fe Trail travelers in the 1860s.

The Boggsville Revitalization Committee has restored several of the original buildings of this settlement. Interpretive signs and a self-guided walking tour give detailed information about the site. To visit Boggsville, drive to Las Animas (east of La Junta), and turn south of Highway 101. Drive about 2 miles, and you will see the site to the east. For more information, call (719) 384-8113. (1 hour)

✯✯ **Comanche National Grasslands**—This high plains prairie is home to grasses that seldom grow more than two feet in height, but have deep root systems to consume large amounts of moisture and nutrients deep within the soil. Yucca and cholla, or candelabra cactus, thrive where the grasses have been disturbed because of overgrazing or other events.

Since 1954, the United States Forest Service has managed the Comanche National Grasslands as a legacy to the devastating Dust Bowl years of the 1930s. The multi-use management of today focuses on grazing, recreation, and preservation of cultural remains of the grasslands. More than 275 species of birds migrate through here, including quail, pheasant, dove, prairie falcon, bald eagle, golden eagle, hawks, and the endangered lesser prairie chicken. While bison no longer blanket this prairie, several other species roam the area, including the rarely seen mountain lion, pronghorn antelope, fox, coyote, and bobcat.

Although primarily a grassland, the land is also crisscrossed with creek beds and river canyons studded with piñon and juniper trees. These canyons reveal some of the most lush and scenic portions of the Comanche National Grasslands. **Vogel Canyon** has loop trails to view rock art, a stagecoach stop, and old structures from a former homestead. The canyon is about 13 miles south of La Junta on Highway 109. Just beyond the intersection of County Road 802 and Highway 109 is the access road to Vogel Canyon.

Another remarkable place in the grasslands is the **Picket Wire Canyonlands**. There are several hiking trails, historical remnants, and a trail of dinosaur footprints from 150 million years ago. To get to the Picket Wire, head south on Highway 109 to County Road 802. Turn right and drive southwest 8 miles until you reach County Road 25. Head south on this road to the canyon access, a little over 5 miles.

From Highway 350, there are several scenic pull-offs with interpretive signs describing the Santa Fe Trail, weather patterns in this area, and the effect of the Dust Bowl on the grasslands. You will see these at the **Iron Springs Historic Area**, the **Sierra Vista Overlook**, and the **Timpas Picnic Area**. If you don't have time to explore the grasslands for a full day, these interpretive pull-offs will help you better appreciate this area. For more information, contact the grasslands headquarters in La Junta, 1321 East 3rd Street, (719) 384-2181. (2 hours–full day)

✯✯ **Corazon de Trinidad (Heart of Trinidad) National Historic District**—The long wagon trains and freighting caravans on the

Mountain Branch of the Santa Fe Trail rolled through downtown Trinidad, literally right down Main Street. Incorporated in 1866, Trinidad quickly became the commercial center for sheep and cattle ranchers with large holdings in the area. The downtown area remains relatively unchanged, with many historic structures that have been preserved. The Trinidad Historical Society has published an interesting walking guide to the history of downtown Trinidad that you should seek out when you get to this city.

The **Trinidad History Museum**, a museum complex in downtown Trinidad, includes several properties, the **Baca House, Bloom House**, and **Santa Fe Trail Museum**, all of which have vital links to Trinidad's past. In the 1860s, Don Felipe Baca encouraged several families from New Mexico to settle in the fertile river valleys surrounding Trinidad. Baca soon became a prominent sheep rancher, and in 1873, moved into a two-story adobe house in the center of Trinidad. The Baca House is filled with elegant New Mexican furnishings, including colorful woven blankets, handcarved furniture, and religious folk art, depicting the lifestyle of this prominent Hispanic family. Next door to the Baca House is the Bloom House, the home of Frank Bloom, a prominent Anglo cattle rancher. In contrast to the Baca House, the Bloom House exhibits period furnishings from the 1880s Victorian era, with ornate furniture, patterned wallpaper and carpets, and delicate china. Tour guides give informative and interesting tours of both houses.

Behind the Baca and Bloom Houses is the Santa Fe Trail Museum. Devoted to the history of the Mountain Branch of the Trail, the museum exhibits several early trail and pioneer artifacts; the tour is self-guided. The Colorado Historical Society manages all three properties. Admission: $2.50 for adults, $2 for seniors or students, and $1.50 for kids 6–16. Hours: May through September 10:00 a.m. to 4:00 p.m., the rest of the year by appointment. Address: 300 East Main Street. Phone: (719) 846-7217. (2 hours)

The **A.R. Mitchell Museum of Western Art** displays some of the oil paintings of Arthur Roy Mitchell, born on a homestead west of Trinidad in 1889. Mitchell illustrated early Western scenes of cowboy life straight out of his own experiences living on a cattle ranch in Las Animas County. His love for this region can be seen in many of his paintings and in his efforts to preserve Trinidad's history for later generations. In addition to a rare collection of Hispanic and Native American art, the museum also includes the Aultman Photography Collection, vintage photographs that encompass more than a century of Trinidad history. Free. Hours: Monday through Saturday 10:00 a.m. to 4:00 p.m. Address: 150 East Main. Phone: (719) 846-4224. (1 hour)

Other museums in Trinidad include the **Louden-Henritze Archaeology Museum**, (719) 846-5508, open May through September 10:00 a.m. to 4:00 p.m., on the campus of Trinidad State Junior College; and the **Trinidad Children's Museum**, 314 North Commercial Street, open June through August 12:00 p.m. to 4:00 p.m. Both museums are free to the public.

✸ **Kit Carson Statue**—Kit Carson Park sits at the corner of Kansas Avenue and San Pedro Street in Trinidad. The most prominent feature of this beautiful park is a striking bronze of Kit Carson, considered by many one of the finest equestrian statues ever made. (½ hour)

✸ **La Junta and Las Animas**—Both La Junta and Las Animas are railroad towns, incorporated in the early 1870s with the arrival of the Kansas Pacific Railroad. La Junta's **Koshare Indian Museum** features a large collection of Native American art. For many summers, the Koshare Indian Dancers, actually a local Boy Scout troop, has performed Indian dances in the Koshare Kiva. Admission: $2 for adults, $1 for children and seniors. Hours: June through August, Monday through Saturday 9:00 a.m. to 5:00 p.m., Sunday 12:30 p.m. to 5:00 p.m.; September through May, daily 12:00 p.m. to 5:00 p.m. Address: 115 West 18th Street, on Otero Junior College grounds. Phone: (719) 384-4411. The **Otero Museum**, in La Junta at Second and Anderson Streets, houses artifacts from early pioneer history, complete with old buildings and an 1867 Overland Stagecoach. Free. Hours: June through September 1:00 p.m. to 5:00 p.m. For information, call (719) 384-7406 or 384-7121. (½ hour)

In Las Animas, the **Bent County Courthouse** is the oldest continuously used courthouse in Colorado. Dating back to 1883, this handsome building has recently been restored to its original beauty. The **Kit Carson Museum** features exhibits on railroads, agriculture, Fort Lyon, the Santa Fe Trail, as well as other aspects of local history. Several older structures from the area have been preserved here, such as the 1876 county jail and a stagecoach station and blacksmith shop dating to the early 1860s. Free. Hours: Memorial Day to Labor Day 1:00 p.m. to 5:00 p.m. Address: 425 Carson. Phone: (719) 456-2005. (1 hour)

✴ **Ludlow Monument**—Ludlow, a small coal town on the Colorado and Southern Railway, was the scene of a violent miners' strike in April 1914. The miners and their families had been evicted from their homes in town and were living in a tent colony. When the state militia attempted to disperse them, a fire swept through the tents, killing two women and 11 children. The site is 10 miles north of Trinidad, exit 27 on I-25, to the west of the highway. The tragic event has been memorialized with a United Mine Workers of America monument. (1 hour)

✴ **New Fort Lyon**—This fort, built in 1867, replaced the older Fort Lyon, which had been erected too close to the banks of the Arkansas River. The original officers' quarters, made from limestone, are preserved. In May 1868, Kit Carson died here in the post surgeon quarters, now the Kit Carson Chapel. Today the fort is a veteran's hospital. (½ hour)

✴ **Raton Pass**—Dreaded and cursed by freighters, this pass was the major obstacle on the Mountain Branch of the Santa Fe Trail. It took over a week for heavily loaded wagons to make this leg of the trip, totaling less than 25 miles. In 1866, Richens "Uncle Dick" Wootton improved the road, and opened a tollbooth on the pass. Although he charged 25 cents per wagon, he shortened the time needed for the trip and eased many problems. Today, thanks to an interstate highway and a 65-mph speed limit, travel time over the pass has been reduced to 15 minutes.

The views of the Spanish Peaks and the Sangre de Cristos seen to the northwest from Raton Pass on a clear day are simply breathtaking. The pass is the border between Colorado and New Mexico. To visit Raton Pass, drive south from Trinidad on I-25 about 13 miles. You'll have to exit at the weigh-in station before the border and take the overpass to the other side of the road. (½ hour)

✴ **Trail Ruts, John Martin Reservoir**—Unfortunately, this dam destroyed historic sections of the Santa Fe Trail. One section of ruts was preserved, however. To see the ruts, drive to the small town of Hasty on Highway 50. Turn south and follow signs to the reservoir. A dirt road will intersect this road before you reach the lake. Head west on the dirt road. You will quickly reach the access road and see a small granite Daughters of the American Revolution monument pointing out the ruts. Phone: (719) 336-3476. (½ hour)

FITNESS AND RECREATION

Southeastern Colorado is the site of many reservoirs, which provide a variety of outdoor recreation. Fishing, wildlife-watching, and boating are all popular. **John Martin Reservoir**, east of La Junta, doesn't allow motorboats but is good for canoeing. **Trinidad Lake State Park** offers picnicking, boating, swimming, fishing, and hiking.

The **Comanche National Grasslands** has numerous hiking trails. To pick up a map of the grasslands and get more information on outdoor activities, contact the Comanche National Grasslands in La Junta, 1321 East 3rd Street, (719) 384-2181.

The **Cuchara Ski Area** is Colorado's southernmost ski area, recently reopened. While it is somewhat off the beaten track, the mellow atmosphere here is great for families or beginning skiers. For information, contact the Cuchara Valley Resort, 946 Panadero Avenue, Cuchara, CO 81055; snow report, (719) 742-3163; lodging, (800) 227-4436.

FOOD

From August through September, fresh produce stands line Highway 50 from Rocky Ford to Swink. This river valley proudly produces the famous Rocky Ford cantaloupe, full of flavor and very sweet. Farmers also sell fresh asparagus, cucumbers, sweet corn, tomatoes, beans, and many other vegetables at the stands.

Excellent traditional Mexican food can be found in La Junta. The **El Camino Inn**, 816 West 3rd Street, (719) 384-2871, has served food in the La Junta area for more than 30 years. The #16 special combination includes a beef taco, cheese enchilada, and potato burrito, served with rice and vermicelli for $8. Other meals cost about $6. Open from 10:30 a.m. to 1:30 p.m. for lunch and 3:30 p.m. to 10:30 p.m. for dinner, closed Sunday and Monday. **Felisa's**, 27948 Frontage Road, (719) 384-4814, serves lighter Mexican fare than the El Camino.

A nice surprise in La Junta is the **Café Grandmere**, 408 West 3rd Street, (719) 384-2711. The fixed price menu, $20, includes five courses, creatively prepared from locally grown products. The meal might include a salad of baby greens, a seasonal soup, a sorbet, and entrees such as Delmonico grilled steak or chicken Marsala, all finished by outstanding desserts.

Chef Liu's Chinese Restaurant and Lounge, in Trinidad, 1423 Santa Fe Trail Drive, (719) 846-3333, serves Chinese dishes that compete with restaurants in larger cities. Specials include vegetarian dishes

TRINIDAD TO LA JUNTA

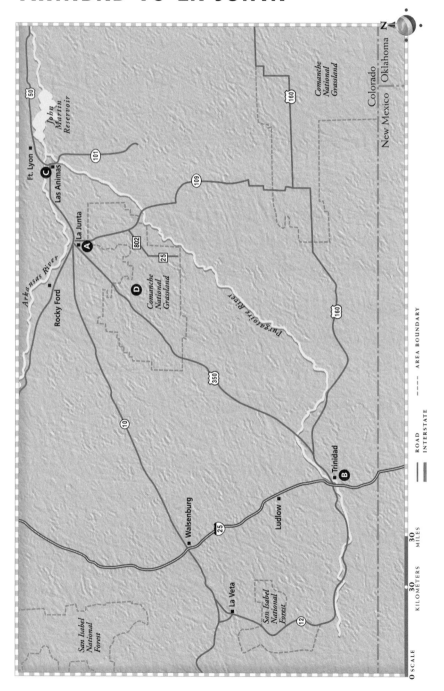

Food

- Ⓐ Café Grandmere
- Ⓑ Chef Liu's Chinese Restaurant and Lounge
- Ⓐ El Camino Inn
- Ⓐ Felisa's
- Ⓑ Monteleone Deli
- Ⓑ Nano & Nana's Pasta House

Lodging

- Ⓒ Best Western Bent's Fort Inn
- Ⓑ Best Western Country Club Inn
- Ⓑ Chicosa Canyon Bed and Breakfast
- Ⓑ Inn on the Santa Fe Trail
- Ⓐ Mid-Town Motel
- Ⓐ My Wife's Inn

Camping

- Ⓓ Comanche National Grasslands
- Ⓐ La Junta KOA
- Ⓑ Trinidad State Park

Note: Items with the same letter are located in the same area.

and family dinners for under $10. Hours: 11:00 a.m. to 9:30 p.m., closed Mondays. For the best in traditional Italian food, try **Nano & Nana's Pasta House**, 415 University, (719) 846-2696. Prices range from $5 to $11. Open for dinner from 4:30 p.m. to 8:00 p.m. The **Monteleone Deli** next door is great for a quick sandwich ($3–$5).

LODGING

La Junta's **Mid-Town Motel**, 215 East 3rd, (719) 384-7741, is well located away from the highway and railroad tracks. Year-round rates are $25 for a single and $32 for a double. **My Wife's Inn**, 801 Colorado, (719) 384-7911, is clean, nicely decorated, and comfortable. Two $45-rooms in the main house offer private baths. A cottage that sleeps up to four people is $65 for two, plus an additional $15 for each adult. A full and healthy breakfast is included.

In Las Animas, the **Best Western Bent's Fort Inn**, 10950 Highway 50, (719) 456-0011, boasts a pool, restaurant, and bar. Rates range from $40 to $56; rooms have queen- or king-size beds.

For standard lodging in Trinidad, try the **Best Western Country Club Inn**, 900 West Adams, from exit 13A off I-25, (719) 846-2215. The **Chicosa Canyon Bed and Breakfast**, (719) 846-6199, is great for a relaxing getaway. There are three rooms in the main house and a lodge that sleeps four. Several hiking trails are accessible from the ranch, which sits on 68 acres of canyon country northwest of Trinidad. Rates vary but range from $55 to $125, including breakfast. The **Inn on the Santa Fe Trail**, 402 West Main Street, (719) 846-4636, is in downtown Trinidad. There are seven rooms in this circa 1900 Victorian, and the rates ($35 to $85) include a three-course breakfast.

CAMPING

Trinidad State Park, 32610 Highway 12, (719) 846-6951, has more than 60 camping spots for RVs, trailers, or tents. You can reserve the sites, for an additional $7.50 fee, by calling (800) 678-CAMP (2267). The camping fee at the park is $7 per night, in addition to a $3 daily park pass. The **La Junta KOA**, on Highway 50, 1½ miles west of the junction with Highway 109, (719) 384-9580, features a playground, pool, and two recreation rooms.

For information on camping in the **Comanche National Grasslands**, contact the Forest Service headquarters at (719) 384-2181.

Scenic Route: Highway of Legends

There is an intriguing story about the name of the Purgatoire River, running alongside the southern part of the Highway of Legends. The full name, *El Rio de Las Animas Perdidas en Purgatorio* means "The River of the Souls Lost in Purgatory." In 1594, a Spanish exploration party from Mexico came through this area in search of the fabled Seven Cities of Cibola. Frustrated with their futile search, the members of the expedition quarreled and the leader was killed in a heated argument. The party then split; the first faction returned to Mexico and the second continued to search for the golden cities. The second faction was never seen again, and it was said the men perished on the banks of this river. Without the benefit of last rites, their souls roamed endlessly in Purgatory. French trappers in this area shortened the name to *La Purgatoire*, and later Anglo settlers mangled the name to the Picketwire. Today, the river is called variously the Purgatoire, the Purgatory, or the Picketwire.

The legend of the Purgatoire River is only one of many surrounding the Highway of Legends. This route can be driven from Trinidad in a day. Along the way are several interesting

HIGHWAY OF LEGENDS

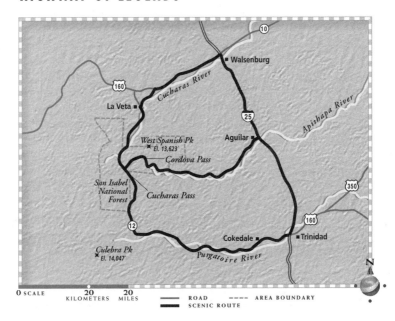

sights, and if you choose to stop at one or several of these spots, it will take a full day to complete the 100-mile loop.

Hispanic plazas are intermingled with historic coal towns throughout the Purgatoire River Valley. In the early 1860s, several families from New Mexico migrated permanently to this river valley, taking up farming and sheepherding. When coal mines opened here in the 1900s, many Hispanic natives started to work in the mines. Seven miles west of Trinidad is the former company town of **Cokedale**, today on the National Register of Historic Places. Established in 1907 by the Carbon Coal and Coke Company, this town housed workers and families until 1947, when the mine closed. Many of the mine workers purchased their homes from the company and incorporated their town in 1948. You can still see ruins of the old coke ovens on the south side of the highway. The ovens removed all moisture, sulphur, and phosphorus from the coal, burning it down to carbon and ash that was used in the process of smelting iron. The former Cokedale Company Store is now a museum, and a guided walking tour of the town is available .

As you drive north on Highway 12, you will have first-rate views of the majestic **Spanish Peaks**, which dominate the Cuchara River Valley. These peaks are seen from several high points throughout southeastern Colorado, and for centuries have been landmarks for travelers going to the southern mountains. The Spanish Peaks are actually two massive volcanoes, with more than 400 volcanic dikes radiating from their bases. Many of the remains of the volcanic dikes can still be seen in this area today, as at **Devil's Stairsteps** and **Profile Rock**, both seen south of La Veta at mileposts 59 and 61, respectively.

As you drive into La Veta, you will see a large adobe structure, the **Fort Francisco Museum**. John Francisco, the first settler in this area, built this plaza here in 1862. It became an important trading center for Anglo and Hispanic families living in the Cuchara Valley. The museum is open from Memorial Day to Labor Day 9:00 a.m. to 5:00 p.m. From La Veta, you will continue following the Cucharas River on Highway 160 to Walsenburg. The 37-mile trip back to Trinidad on I-25 is quick but can't rival the Highway of Legends (Highway 12). ◼

14

COLORADO SPRINGS

General William Jackson Palmer, the ambitious president of the Denver & Rio Grande Railroad, founded Colorado Springs during the 1870s as a genteel and refined community at the foot of Pikes Peak. Palmer's settlement attracted English aristocrats and well-heeled Americans, prompting the nickname "Little London." But his wasn't the first community in the area. Colorado City had been founded during the Pikes Peak Gold Rush of 1859 and served briefly as the first territorial capital of Colorado. Its bawdy and dusty streets didn't meet Palmer's sophisticated tastes, however, and he chose to develop his exclusive community a few miles south. Despite his precautions, the two settlements eventually merged into one sprawling city. Today Old Colorado City is a pleasant treelined street filled with galleries and restaurants, while the older sections of Palmer's Colorado Springs retain an aristocratic flavor with stately homes, wide avenues, and quiet streets.

Colorado Springs is the hub for five major military installations in the surrounding area: Fort Carson Army Base, the United States Air Force Academy, Peterson Air Force Base, Falcon Air Station, and the North American Air Defense facility (NORAD) housed within Cheyenne Mountain. In fact, one out of every five workers in Colorado Springs is employed by the military. ◼

COLORADO SPRINGS AREA

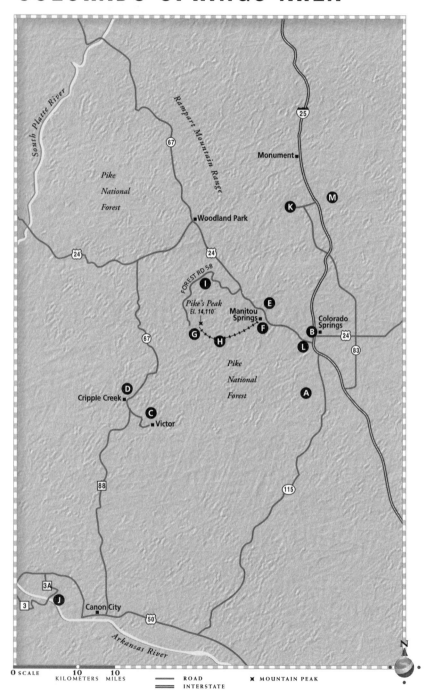

South Platte River

Rampart Mountain Range

25

Monument

67

Pike

National

Forest

Woodland Park

24

24

FOREST RD 58

I

Pike's Peak
El. 14,110´

E

Manitou
Springs

F

Colorado
Springs

B

24

K

M

G

H

L

83

67

A

Pike

National

Forest

D

Cripple Creek

C

Victor

88

115

3A

J

3

Canon City

50

Arkansas River

N

0 SCALE   10   10
KILOMETERS MILES   ROAD   ✖ MOUNTAIN PEAK
                         INTERSTATE

Sightseeing Highlights

(A) Cheyenne Mountain Zoo & Will Rogers Shrine of the Sun

(B) Colorado Springs Fine Art Center

(B) Colorado Springs Pioneer Museum

(C) Cripple Creek and Victor Narrow Gauge Railroad

(D) Cripple Creek Museum

(E) Garden of the Gods

(F) Manitou Springs

(F) Miramont Castle

(G) Pikes Peak

(F) Pikes Peak Auto Hill Climb Museum

(H) Pike's Peak Cog Railway

(I) Pikes Peak Highway

(J) Royal Gorge Bridge

(K) United States Air Force Academy

(B) United States Olympic Complex

(L) Van Briggle Pottery

(M) Western Museum of Mining and Industry

Note: Items with the same letter are located in the same area.

A PERFECT DAY IN COLORADO SPRINGS

Spend the morning exploring the Garden of the Gods, a park named by a Pikes Peak prospector who found that its vermilion-colored sandstone walls and shapes formed an unearthly site "fit for the gods." Afterwards, drive to Manitou Springs for lunch, and then take the Pikes Peak Cog Railway to the summit of 14,110-foot Pikes Peak.

More adventurous travelers may opt for this alternative: get up at dawn to hike the 13-mile Barr Trail to the summit of Pikes Peak, and then take the cog railroad back down the mountain. You won't soon forget this exhilarating hike. Afterwards, you'll really deserve that beer at one of Colorado Springs' microbreweries.

SIGHTSEEING HIGHLIGHTS

★★★ **Garden of the Gods**—The phenomenal sandstone formations protected by this unique city park tell an amazing geological story of mountain building and earthquakes. The Lyons Formation, a red sandstone, and the Dakota Hogback, a buff-colored sandstone that caps the ridges of many formations in the area, were both gradually uplifted beginning 300 million years ago. These formations have since weathered into fantastic shapes, such as Toothsome Rocks, Balanced Rock, and the Kissing Camels.

Most memorable is the park's famous panoramic vista: crimson walls played against the blue-purple mass of Pikes Peak. Adding to the breathtaking scenery are nimble rock climbers gracefully poised on the sandstone walls. The area is known internationally for its technical climbs.

Several hiking trails wind through the formations and a diverse variety of life zones, from plains grasslands to juniper and piñon pine forests. The **Garden of the Gods Visitor Center** features informative exhibits on the natural and cultural history of the area and a multimedia presentation in its auditorium. A guided tram tour of the park, with descriptions of the formations and historic sites, starts from the visitor center. Admission to the park is free. The multimedia show is $1.50 for adults, $1 for children; the guided tour, offered Memorial Day through October, is $3.75 for adults and $2.50 for children. Hours: The visitor center is open during the summer from 7:00 a.m. to 9:00 p.m., and during the winter from 8:30 a.m. to 5:30 p.m. Address: 1805 North 30th Street. Phone: (719) 634-6666. (2–3 hours)

★★★ **Pikes Peak**—When explorer Zebulon Pike first gazed upon this majestic mountain in the autumn of 1806, he had no idea that one day his namesake would be America's most famous peak. When gold seekers converged on Colorado during the Pikes Peak Gold Rush of 1859, the mining activity they sought was actually in the hills west of present-day Denver, more than 100 miles to the north. However, Pikes Peak had achieved such notoriety in the eastern states that many uninformed people assumed the mines clustered around its formidable base.

You can hike, drive, or ride a cog railroad car to the summit of this imposing mountain. The 13-mile (one way) Barr Trail departs from Ruxton Avenue near the Pikes Peak Cog Railway station. While Pikes Peak is one of the easiest of the Fourteeners to scale, this is a long trail, and you might consider making this a two-day trip, staying overnight at Barr Camp. Located about 7 miles up the hill, this campsite has two rustic cabins at 10,200 feet. Or you could take the cog railway (see below) one way and hike one way if you'd like to make the trip in a day. To make reservations at Barr Camp, call (719) 635-0670.

You can drive the **Pikes Peak Highway** to the summit in the comfort of your own car. However, you should know that this route will be very hard on your car, as it climbs almost 7,000 feet in 19 miles and twists and turns through more than 150 hairpin curves. Stunning views include the lofty peaks of the Continental Divide, the city of Colorado Springs, and even Denver. Admission: $5 for adults, $2 for children 6–11. Open from December to March, Wednesday through Sunday 9:00 a.m. to 3:00 p.m.; April through May and September through November, daily 9:00 a.m. to 3:00 p.m.; and Memorial Day through Labor Day, daily 7:00 a.m. to 7:00 p.m. Even though the road stays open year-round, severe weather will affect the schedule. The road entrance is in the village of Cascade, west of Manitou Springs on Highway 24. For more information, call (719) 684-9383 or (800) DO-VISIT.

One of the best ways to see the summit without having to expend much energy is to take a trip on the **Pike's Peak Cog Railway**. The train has been carting visitors to the top of Pikes Peak since 1891 and is the world's highest cog railway. The 9-mile trip starts at the depot in Manitou Springs, and the round-trip takes just over three hours. The train runs from May to October, and advance reservations are necessary. Admission: $21 for adults, $9.50 for children 5–11. Address: 515 Ruxton Avenue. Phone: (719) 685-5401. (3 hours by cog railway, 2 hours by highway, and 1–2 full days by the Barr Trail)

★★ **Colorado Springs Fine Arts Center**—A select group of Colorado Springs residents pooled their talents and resources in the mid 1930s to create this center as a haven for art and culture. The Fine Arts Center continues to thrive as a cherished Colorado Springs institution, with intriguing exhibitions, lectures, and performances. Located at the edge of the Colorado College campus at Cascade and Dale, this world-class collection includes works from Native American and Hispanic artists as well as nineteenth- and twentieth-century Western American artists. Admission, free on Saturdays until noon, is otherwise $3 for adults, $1.50 for seniors and students 13–21, and $1 for children 6–12. Hours: Tuesday through Friday 9:00 a.m. to 5:00 p.m., Saturday 10:00 a.m. to 5:00 p.m., Sunday 1:00 p.m. to 5:00 p.m. Address: 30 West Dale. Phone: (719) 634-5581. (1 hour)

★★ **Colorado Springs Pioneer's Museum**—Situated in the stately El Paso County courthouse, this museum has several interesting exhibits on the history of the Pikes Peak region, with Indian artifacts, an historical toy exhibit, and—perhaps the most entertaining—a quilt once owned by a Colorado Springs woman bearing autographs of famous people during the 1930s, with small illustrations stitched next to their names. Exploring this handsome building—and riding the old-fashioned elevator—is a treat. Free admission. Hours: April to September, Tuesday through Saturday 10:00 a.m. to 5:00 p.m., Sunday 1:00 p.m. to 5:00 p.m. Address: 215 South Tejon Street. Phone: (719) 578-6650. (½ hour)

★★ **Cripple Creek and Victor**—The southern slopes of Pikes Peak saw a doozy of a gold rush in the 1890s, with mines of the district out-producing all others in Colorado. This late gold rush also occurred during years of financial setbacks suffered by many silver titans, who went broke because of the repeal of the Sherman Silver Act and were forced to watch the gold barons of Cripple Creek laugh all the way to the bank. Known as the "richest square mile on earth," Cripple Creek attracted every hustler, promoter, lady of the night, and miner eager to prosper in the booming settlement. The town also flourished with bankers, industrialists, and businessmen who transformed the small tent city into the most influential marketing center in the mining district southwest of Colorado Springs.

The town of Cripple Creek today has limited stakes gambling. Casinos line the historic Main Street and hawkers briskly advertise poker, blackjack, and slot machines waiting for visitors inside. In addition to gambling, Cripple Creek also has many family-oriented activities, such as taking a trip along the **Cripple Creek and Victor Narrow Gauge Railroad**. The 4-mile tour highlights historic buildings, mine structures, and former gold mines dotting the landscape. Admission: $6.75 for adults, $3.50 for children 3–12, and $3 for seniors. Tours leave every 45 minutes from the Midland Station depot, beginning at 10:00 a.m. and ending at 5:00 p.m. The season runs from mid-May through mid-October. Location: The depot sits at the top of Bennet Avenue. Phone: (719) 689-2640.

Next door to the depot is the **Cripple Creek Museum**, housed in the former Colorado Midland Railroad Depot that dates to 1896. Focusing heavily on mining and geologic history, the museum also has an excellent historic photograph collection and Victorian furniture display. Admission: $2.25 for adults, 50 cents for children under 12. Hours: June through September, open daily 10:00 a.m. to 5:00 p.m.; October to May, open Saturday and Sunday 12:00 p.m. to 4:00 p.m. Phone: (719) 689-2634.

The distance between Colorado Springs and Cripple Creek is about 45 miles, and driving time is usually an hour. Take Highway 24 west from Manitou Springs, continuing west until you come to the town of Divide. In Divide, take Highway 67 south. (Full day)

★★ **Manitou Springs**—William Blackmore, an Englishman with a fondness for Native American legends, named the bubbling hot springs at this site after Manitou, the Great Indian spirit in Henry Wadsworth Longfellow's romantic poem *Hiawatha*. While the Utes never referred to their Great Spirit as Manitou, they did frequent these hot springs to heal their aches and pains, as did the Cheyennes and Arapahos.

In the latter part of the nineteenth century, the Colorado Springs region gained a reputation for curing any type of illness, no matter how severe. Tuberculosis patients flocked to the region, seeking bed rest and exercise in the crisp mountain air. Health seekers dipped into the springs at Manitou and even drank its soda water to cure everything from cancer to flatulence. A French priest who came to Manitou Springs before the turn of the century to cure his consumption built the four-story **Miramont Castle** to remind him of his European home. The exterior of the castle features nine different types of architectural styles, abounding in peaks, balconies, turrets, and dormers, while the interior includes elegant staircases, a gold ceiling in the drawing room, and a 200-ton native sandstone fireplace. Before becoming a Victorian museum operated by the Manitou Springs Historical Society, the structure was a sanitarium and an apartment house. Admission: $3 for adults, $1 for children 6–11, and $2.50 for seniors. Hours: Open daily 12:00 p.m. to 3:00 p.m. Address: 9 Capitol Hill Avenue. Phone: (719) 685-1011. (1 hour)

After improving the stage road to the summit of Pikes Peak in 1915, promoter Spencer Penrose decided he needed a gimmick to advertise it. The Pikes Peak Auto Hill Climb began on the Fourth of July in 1916 and has occurred annually since that time, attracting nationally ranked race-car drivers such as Bobby Unser and Mario Andretti. The history of this challenging race is told in the **Pikes Peak Auto Hill Climb Museum**, which exhibits historic race cars and other memorabilia. Admission: $4 for adults, $3 for seniors and military, and free for children under 12. Hours: May through September, daily 9:00 a.m. to 5:00 p.m. Address: 135 Manitou Avenue. Phone: (719) 685-5996. (½ hour)

★★ **United States Air Force Academy**—Established in the late 1950s on rolling foothills at the base of the Rampart Range, a visit to the United States Air Force Academy includes the striking Cadet Chapel, a B-52 bomber display, and the Academy Visitor Center with displays on Air Force cadet life. If you're there at noon, you will see the ceremonious cadets marching to lunch. A self-guided driving tour of the grounds points out key sights. Admission is free. Hours: Open daily 9:00 a.m. to 5:00 p.m. Location: North of Colorado Springs at exit 156A. Phone: (719) 472-2025. (1½ hours)

★★ **Western Museum of Mining and Industry**—Chronicling the importance of mining to Colorado and other Western states, this non-profit educational museum collects, restores, and displays mining arti-facts. The historic mining equipment has been restored to working order, so you can actually see and hear how it runs (loudly!). Also on the museum grounds are a restored ten-stamp ore mill, blacksmith shop, and working hoist house, all extremely important operations in the mining industry. Admission: $5 for adults, $2 for children 5–12, $4 for students and seniors. Hours: Monday through Saturday 9:00 a.m. to 4:00 p.m., Sunday 12:00 p.m. to 5:00 p.m., and by special appoint-ment December through February. Location: From exit 156A (the north entrance of the Air Force Academy), take the Northgate/Gleneagle Drive exit from I-25 and follow the signs. Phone: (719) 488-0880. (1 hour)

✸ **Cheyenne Mountain Zoo & Will Rogers Shrine of the Sun**—
Spencer Penrose arrived in Colorado Springs in 1892 practically penniless, but he soon made a fortune in the Cripple Creek Mining
District. He became one of Colorado Springs' most enthusiastic boost-
ers, masterminding promotional successes and leaving behind a legacy
known as the El Pomar Foundation.

Because he had a fondness for European zoos, Penrose built his own
zoo on the slopes of Cheyenne Mountain. Penrose billed the Cheyenne
Mountain Zoo as the "Highest Zoo in the World," and acquired many
exotic animals, including Tessie, the "Largest Elephant in the World."
The zoo continually modernizes its animal habitats, including the Jane
Goodall Primate World and a natural Mexican wolf environment.

Later in life, Spencer Penrose began to design his family burial
plot high above the zoo on the slopes of Cheyenne Mountain. With his
usual promotional flair, Penrose wanted to publicize the beautiful vistas
from his cemetery by building an expensive tourist attraction. The
result was a monumental stone tower more than 300 feet high, boast-
ing the "Most Complete Amplification System in the World" that
played chimes heard from a distance of 20 miles. The building of the
tower coincided with the death of Will Rogers, whom Penrose adored.
In tribute, he named his monument the Will Rogers Shrine of the Sun.
The shrine can be visited with admission to the zoo. Admission: $6.50 for
adults, $5.50 for seniors, $3.50 for children 3–11. Hours: Memorial Day
to Labor Day 9:00 a.m. to 5:00 p.m., otherwise 9:00 a.m. to 4:00 p.m.
Location: The zoo is located above the Broadmoor Hotel. From I-25,
take exit 138 west until you reach the Broadmoor. Turn right and follow the signs. Phone: (719) 633-9925. (3 hours)

✸ **United States Olympic Complex**—Colorado Springs is the proud
home of the United States Olympic Committee, centered on a grassy
36-acre compound. The modern athletic facilities here are used by
America's aspiring athletes who train for summer sports such as gym-
nastics, aquatics, and boxing. There are free 1½-hour tours of the facility, which include a film and walking tour. Hours: Monday through
Saturday 9:00 a.m. to 4:00 p.m., Sunday 12:00 p.m. to 4:00 p.m.
Address: One Olympic Plaza, on the northwest corner of Boulder and
Union. Phone: (719) 578-4618.

✸ **Van Briggle Pottery**—When Artus Van Briggle came to Colorado
Springs in 1899 to cure his tuberculosis, he knew he wanted to live the

rest of his life in the town. He and his wife Anne, both exceptional artists, created a unique Art Nouveau–style pottery, with flower motifs and centuries-old matte glazes, and opened their own pottery factory. Van Briggle Pottery is still run by family members, and many original Van Briggle designs, in addition to modern styles, are still produced at the factory. A free public tour of the pottery factory, in the historic round house of the Colorado Midland Railroad, is available year-round, except on Sunday. Address: 600 South 21st Street. Phone: (719) 633-7729.

✵ **Royal Gorge Bridge**—An hour's drive from Colorado Springs on Highway 115 brings you to the Royal Gorge, a deep canyon created by the rushing Arkansas River. A quarter-mile suspension bridge spans the gap of the chasm, 1,053 feet above the Arkansas River, and is the highest suspension bridge in the world. People who could be declared legally insane have been known to bungee jump off this high bridge. You can see tiny specks in the river below, actually white-water rafts bobbing on the Arkansas. Admission: Summer prices are $10.50 for adults, $8 for children 4–11; winter prices are $8.50 for adults, $6 for children. Hours: During the summer 7:30 a.m. to 8:00 p.m.; winter, 9:30 a.m. to 5:00 p.m. Location: Eight miles west of Canyon City on Highway 115. Phone: (719) 275-7507. (1 hour)

FITNESS AND RECREATION

For a relaxing walk on a quiet path, go to **Bear Creek Canyon Regional Park.** Numerous trails here vary in length, but total approximately 5 miles. The park is open from dawn to dusk. Address and directions: 245 Bear Creek Road. From I-25, take the Cimarron Street exit (#141), and head west. Turn left at 26th Street, which eventually turns into Bear Creek Road. Phone: (719) 520-6387.

The **Monument Creek Trail**, an urban bike path, starts at Monument Valley Park behind Colorado College and travels along the creek a few miles just below downtown Colorado Springs. The **North Cheyenne Canyon Trail** is a nice hike close to town. To get to the trailhead, which is behind the Broadmoor, take exit 140 (Nevada Avenue) southbound from I-25. Turn west (right) on Cheyenne Boulevard until you get to the canyon entrance, where the trail begins on the left side of the road.

There are also several excellent bicycle rides near town, such as through the **Garden of the Gods**, the **United States Air Force**

Academy, or **Palmer Park**. All vary in length and difficulty. Stop in at the **Mountain Chalet**, 226 North Tejon, (719) 633-0732, to ask their helpful staff about trails or any type of outdoor activity in the area.

FOOD

Conway's Red Top Restaurant has been a Colorado Springs tradition for over 50 years, serving the tastiest hamburgers and chocolate shakes in town for under $5. Address: 1520 S. Nevada, phone: (719) 633-2444. **Poor Richard's Restaurant**, 324 ½ North Tejon, (719) 632-7721, is one of those rare treasures you find only in college towns, with a coffee shop, theater, and bookstore all under the same roof. The food is on the healthy side, with plenty of vegetarian options and excellent pizza. Prices range from $1.95 for a slice of pizza, $5.95 for many of the entrees, and $14.95 for a large pizza. Open daily from 11:00 a.m. to 10:00 p.m.

A great place for a sandwich, soup, or salad in Old Colorado City is **La Baguette**, 2417 West Colorado Avenue, (719) 577-4818, a French bakery with heavenly aromas. The sandwiches are reasonably priced, from $3.50 to $5.75, and are, of course, served on freshly baked bread. Their desserts are well worth the extra calories. Open Monday through Saturday 7:00 a.m. to 6:00 p.m., Sunday 7:00 a.m. to 5:00 p.m.

The Hungry Farmer, 575 Garden of the Gods Road, (719) 598-7622, is well known for its generous portions and steak, seafood, and chicken. Open for lunch 11:30 pm. to 2:00 p.m. and dinner 5:00 p.m. to 10:00 p.m., with prices ranging from $11 to $20 for dinner.

The Broadmoor Hotel, 1 Lake Circle, (719) 634-7711 or (800) 634-7711, has several dining rooms, each with a unique style and taste. The **Charles Court** is a formal, elegant dining room in an English manor house, serving breakfast, luncheon, and dinner. Dinner entrees start at $31 and feature wild game and adventurous specials such as a rattlesnake quesadilla. Breakfast is served 7:00 a.m. to 10:00 a.m., lunch 11:30 a.m. to 2:00 p.m., and dinner 6:30 p.m. to 9:30 p.m. **The Tavern** is more casual, especially for a lunch of rotisserie-cooked chicken or duck, averaging $20. Open from 11:30 a.m. to 11:00 p.m.

After dinner, stop in at **Josh & John's Naturally Homemade Ice Creams**, 101 North Tejon, (719) 632-0299, for a well-deserved treat. Their wonderfully rich ice cream can be prepared with mix-ins, such as crushed Oreos, M&Ms, or nuts. Go on, you deserve it.

LODGING

Quirky motor hotels line Colorado Avenue and Manitou Avenue all the way to Manitou Springs. One of the finest is the **El Colorado Lodge**, 23 Manitou Avenue, (719) 685-5485 or (800) 782-2246. Built in the 1920s, this classic motor court has individual adobe units with comfortable Southwestern furnishings, starting at $40. Each room has a Spanish-style fireplace, and the motel will give you firewood to make a cozy fire in your room.

If you can afford elegant and expensive accommodations ($155 and up), stay at **The Broadmoor Hotel**, 1 Lake Circle, (719) 634-7711 or (800) 634-7711. The main seven-story structure, built in 1918, is embellished with a rich Italian marble and pink exterior. A golf club, ice arena, spa, fitness center, tennis courts, and extensive gardens round out this exclusive resort.

The **Best Western Palmer House**, 3010 N. Chestnut Street, (719) 636-5201, is conveniently located off of the interstate at exit 145, north of downtown Colorado Springs. There is a dining room adjacent to the hotel. Rates start at $69. The **Hearthstone Inn**, 506 North Cascade Avenue, (719) 473-4413 or (800) 521-1885, a restored Victorian mansion, sits on a quiet street near Colorado College. The towering old trees that line the street provide a canopy of shade. The private rooms here are perfect for a romantic weekend. Rates, including a full breakfast, start at $75.

Budget travelers will have a hard time beating the rates at the **Mel Haven Lodge**, 3715 West Colorado Avenue, (719) 633-9435. These clean and comfortable rooms start at $35, some with a view of Pikes Peak or the Garden of the Gods.

Conveniently located in downtown Colorado Springs is the **Antler's Doubletree Hotel**, 4 South Cascade Avenue, (719) 473-5600 or (800) 528-0444. This new hotel is a renovated version of the historic Antler's, one of the earliest hotels in town. Recent additions include a health club, pool, and microbrewery called Judge Baldwin's. The views of Pikes Peak to the west are the best in town. Rates range from $105 to $145.

CAMPING

The **Golden Eagle Ranch RV Park** (719) 576-0450 or (800) 666-3841, has more than 400 RV sites and is located on the grounds of the **May Natural History Museum**, which exhibits a collection of the

COLORADO SPRINGS

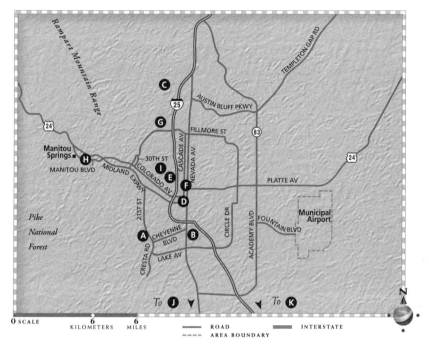

Food

- **A** Charles Court
- **B** Conway's Red Top Restaurant
- **C** The Hungry Farmer
- **D** Josh & John's Naturally Homemade Ice Creams
- **E** La Baguette
- **F** Poor Richard's Restaurant
- **A** The Tavern

- **F** Hearthstone Inn
- **I** Mel Haven Lodge

Camping

- **J** Golden Eagle Ranch RV Park/ May Natural History Museum
- **K** KOA Colorado Springs South

Lodging

- **D** Antler's Doubletree Hotel
- **G** Best Western Palmer House
- **A** The Broadmoor Hotel
- **H** El Colorado Lodge

Note: Items with the same letter are located in the same area.

world's strangest and largest invertebrates. The park is southwest of Colorado Springs on Highway 115. From I-25, take exit 135 and head west to Highway 115, which is South Nevada Avenue. Drive south 5 miles until you see the giant beetle, which is the entrance to the History Museum and RV park.

KOA Colorado Springs South, (719) 382-7575, exit 132 off I-25, is south of Colorado Springs on Fountain Creek (Widefield/Security exit). Facilities include an indoor swimming pool, hot tub, and video game room with numerous campground activities. Open year-round.

NIGHTLIFE

Several brewpubs and microbreweries, all specializing in handcrafted quality beers, have added a new dimension to the nightlife in Colorado Springs. **Beckett's Brewhouse & Restaurant**, 128 South Tejon Street, (719) 633-3230, features four beers on tap, a good dinner menu, and live music on Thursday, Friday, and Saturday nights. Hearty pubfare attracts a younger crowd to the **Phantom Canyon Brewery**, across from the Antler's Hotel at 2 East Pikes Peak Avenue, (719) 635-2800.

Country line-dancing fans flock to **Cowboy's**, 3910 Palmer Park Boulevard, (719) 596-1212, practically every night of the week.

If you're looking for culture, try the **Colorado Springs Symphony Orchestra**, (719) 520-SHOW.

The Golden Bee, (719) 634-7711 or (800) 634-7711, in the Broadmoor Hotel, is a must for a rousing night out on the town. Even the most timid patrons find themselves heartily singing along with the piano player in this nineteenth-century pub—actually imported lock, stock, and barrel from England.

15

APPENDIX

METRIC CONVERSION CHART

1 U.S. gallon = approximately 4 liters
1 liter = about 1 quart
1 Canadian gallon = approximately 4.5 liters

1 pound = approximately $1/2$ kilogram
1 kilogram = about 2 pounds

1 foot = approximately $1/3$ meter
1 meter = about 1 yard
1 yard = a little less than a meter
1 mile = approximately 1.6 kilometers
1 kilometer = about $2/3$ mile

90°F = about 30°C
20°C = approximately 70°F

Planning Map: Colorado

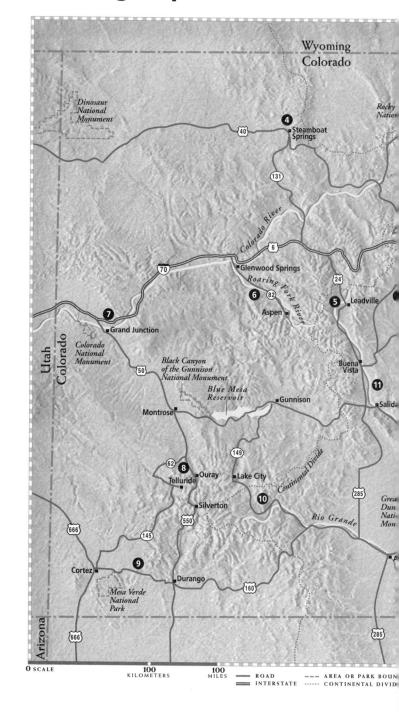

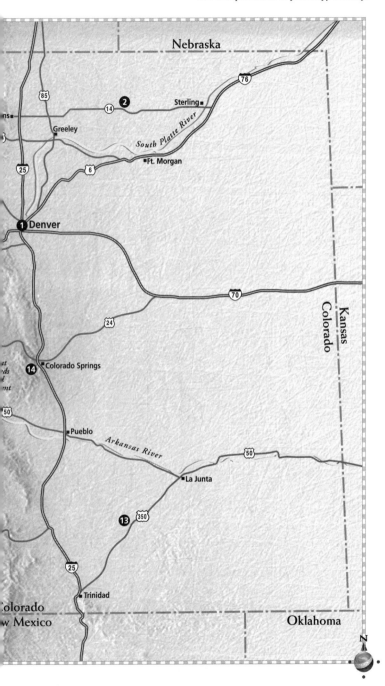

Nebraska

76

85

14 2 Sterling ■

ns ■

Greeley

South Platte River

25 6 ■ Ft. Morgan

1 Denver

70

24

Kansas
Colorado

at
ds
l
nt

14 ■ Colorado Springs

50

■ Pueblo

Arkansas River

50

■ La Junta

13 350

25

■ Trinidad

olorado
w Mexico

Oklahoma

N

Planning Map: Colorado

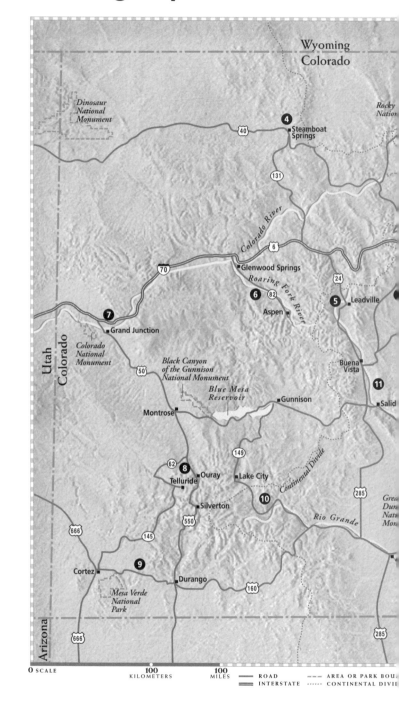

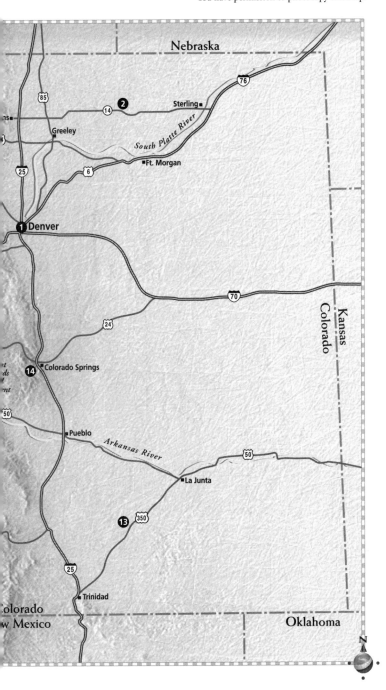

INDEX

African-Americans, 6, 39, 193
airports, 9, 26
Alamosa, 23, 192–196; arts, 16, 192; food, 197; lodging, 197
Alamosa-Monte Vista National Wildlife Refuge, 193
Alfred Packer Massacre Site, 169
Alpine Loop, 145, 175–176
Amtrak, 27
amusement parks, 5, 39
Anasazi Heritage Center, 156–157
Anasazi Indians, 6, 8, 14, 151; cliff dwellings, 153–154, 155–157, 158
Anderson Ranch Arts Center, 6, 116–117
Animas River, 155, 159
Animas School Museum, 157
Antonito, 192; camping, 200
archaeology, 13–14
Arkansas Headwaters Recreation Area, 103, 180; camping, 188
Arkansas River, 14, 17, 19, 20, 30, 95, 103, 177, 201, 204, 208, 224; sightseeing highlights, 180
arts, 6, 15–16, 37, 40–41; in Colorado Springs, 220; the Roaring Fork Valley, 109, 116–117; San Luis Valley, 191–192, 194; Trinidad, 206–207
Aspen, 15, 23, 98, 108, 112, 120, 121; arts, 109; food, 17; music festival, 6, 16, 109, 112, 183
Aspen Center for Environmental Studies, 114, 115, 116

Bachelor Loop Driving Tour, 168
backpacking, 24; Northern San Juans, 146, 176; Unaweep Tabeguache, 135; Upper Arkansas River Valley, 183–184; Ute Mountain Ute Tribal Park, 156
bed and breakfasts, 31
Bent's Old Fort National Historic Site, 8, 14, 201, 203, 204; recommended reading, 30
bicycling, 21, 24, 31; in Colorado Springs, 224; Denver, 41; Durango, 159; Glenwood Canyon, 114; Grand Junction, 128; Rocky Mountain National Park, 75; recommended reading, 30; see also mountain bicycling
birdwatching, 57, 205
Black American West Museum, 6, 39
Boggsville, 8, 204
Boulder, 3, 47–49, 67; arts, 16; hiking, 7
Briggsdale, 65
Buena Vista, 180, 181; food, 185; lodging, 185, 188
Buffalo Bill Memorial Museum and Grave, 39–40

Bureau of Land Management, 31
Byers-Evans House, 36, 37

campgrounds, 24, 27–28, 31; recommended reading, 31; see also recreational vehicles
car rentals, 26–27
Carbondale, 109, 112
casinos, 157, 220
Cedaredge, 125, 126, 132
Chalk Creek Canyon, 181
Cherry Creek, 3, 40
Cheyenne Mountain Zoo, 5, 223
Civic Center Cultural Complex, 3, 6, 36, 37
climate, 24–26; 184
Climax Molybdenum Mine, 100
Cokedale, 214
Colorado Association of Campgrounds, Cabins, and Lodges, 31
Colorado Bicycle Program, 31
Colorado Cross Country Ski Association, 31
Colorado Department of Transportation, 27, 31, 141
Colorado Division of Wildlife, 31
Colorado Dude & Guest Ranch Association, 31
Colorado Historical Society, 8, 21, 29, 36, 37, 101, 193, 195, 206
Colorado Mountain Club, 31
Colorado National Monument, 4, 123,

126; camping, 133–34
Colorado River, 17, 20, 70, 74, 114, 123, 127; river rafting, 114
Colorado Ski Country USA, 31
Colorado Springs, 3, 5, 20, 220, 222, 223, 224; camping, 226, 228; fitness and recreation, 224–225; flora and fauna, 18–19; food, 225; lodging, 226; nightlife, 228; sightseeing highlights, 215–24
Colorado Springs Fine Arts Center, 220
Colorado Springs Pioneer's Museum, 220
Colorado State Capitol, 36
Colorado Trail, 98, 146, 181, 184
Comanche National Grasslands, 203, 205; camping, 212
Conejos River, 195; camping, 200
Continental Divide, 20, 25, 70, 72, 74, 81, 83, 100–101, 168, 175, 180, 181, 182, 219
Coors Field, 39
Corazon de Trinidad National Historic District, 8, 205–207
Cortez, 3, 5, 6, 8, 140, 151, 159; food, 160–161; lodging, 147, 161
Cortez Center, 6, 153, 154
Cottonwood Pass, 181–82
Creede, 167, 169, 171, 195; flora and fauna,

19; food, 173; lodging, 173–174; sightseeing highlights, 170
Creede Repertory Theater, 3, 167
Cripple Creek, 5, 15, 220–221, 223
Crow Canyon Archaeological Center, 157
Crow Valley Recreation Area, 55, 57, 66; camping, 63, cuisine, 16–17, 29
Cumbres & Toltec Scenic Railroad, 8, 192

Denver, 15, 20, 23, 27, 67, 219; arts and cultures, 6, 15; best of, 3, 5, 8, 38–39; fitness and recreation, 41; flora and fauna, 18–19; food, 41–45; lodging, 45–46; nightlife, 46–47; side trips from, 47–52; sights, 33–41
Denver Art Museum, 36, 37
Denver Botanic Gardens, 38
Denver Center for Performing Arts, 6, 16, 47
Denver History Museum, 36, 37
Denver Museum of Natural History, 5, 29, 37, 57
Denver Public Library, 36
Denver Zoo, 5, 38
Devil's Canyon Science & Learning Center, 128
Dexter Cabin, 100–101
dining, see cuisine
Dinosaur National

Monument, 123, 128
dinosaurs, 37, 123, 127, 128, 205
Dolores, 161
Dolores River, 135, 153, 156–157, 159
dude ranches, 31, 77
Durango, 3, 5, 6, 8, 23, 140, 151, 155; food, 160; lodging, 161; museum, 158; nightlife, 164
Durango & Silverton Narrow Gauge Railroad, 5, 8, 155; hikes from, 146, 155

Eaton, 63
Elitch Gardens Amusement Park, 5, 39
Estes Park, 16, 23, 29, 67, 73–74

Farr (Granby) Pump Plant, 74–75
festivals, 6, 16, 24, 38; in Aspen, 16; in Denver, 16; in Estes Park, 74; in Roaring Fork Valley, 109; in Salida, 183; in Telluride, 144–145
Fish Creek Falls, 87
fishing, 21; Arkansas River, 103, 177, 180; Durango, 159–160; Grand Mesa, 125; northeastern Colorado, 59; Rio Grande Valley, 171; Roaring Fork Valley, 117; Rocky Mountain National Park, 75; southeastern Colorado, 209
Flat Tops Wilderness Area, 4, 81, 84–85; camping, 94
flora and fauna, 18–19; Aspen, 114;

Comanche Grasslands, 205; Georgetown, 50; Pawnee Grasslands, 55–56, 59; recommended reading, 29–30; Rocky Mountain National Park, 70, 72; San Luis Valley, 193; southeastern Colorado, 209; Steamboat Springs, 84; Upper Rio Grande Valley, 168

Fort Collins, 53, 62, 63, 67

Fort Francisco Museum, 214

Fort Garland Museum, 8, 191, 193–194

Fort Morgan, 23, 53, 58, 62, 63, 75

Four Corners Monument, 159

four-wheeling, in Northern San Juans, 137, 140, 141, 142, 145, 159; Upper Arkansas River Valley, 180; Upper Rio Grande Valley, 168, 181

Fourteeners (mountains above fourteen thousand feet), 19, 20, 145, 177, 181; Collegiate Peaks, 177, 184; Longs Peak, 75; Mt. Elbert, 98, 106, 177; Mt. Massive, 98, 106; Pikes Peak, 219

fruit stands, 123, 127, 209

Fruita, 123, 127, 128

Garden of the Gods, 3, 218

Gateway, 135

Georgetown, 8, 15, 50–52

ghost towns, 8; Northern San Juans, 142; recommended reading, 30; Upper Arkansas River Valley, 179, 181–182

Glenwood Canyon, 114

Glenwood Hot Springs, 112

Glenwood Springs, 16, 27, 112, 117, 120, 121; arts, 6, 16, 109, 117

Glenwood Springs Center for the Arts, 117

Grand Junction, 4, 13, 17, 20, 125, 126, 128; camping, 133–134; fitness and recreation, 128–129; food, 129–132; flora and fauna, 18; lodging, 132–133; sightseeing highlights, 123–128

Grand Lake, 20, 67, 70, 75

Grand Mesa, 4, 17, 20, 123, 125; camping, 133; fishing, 125, 133

Great Sand Dunes National Monument, 3, 4, 5, 191, 192–193, 196; camping, 200

Green River, 128

Grover, 55, 63, 66

guest ranches, 31, 77

Gunnison River, 123, 127

Hahn's Peak/Steamboat Lake, 85

Hanging Flume, 135

Healy House, 97, 101

Heritage Museum, Leadville, 102–103

Highway of Legends, 8, 213–214

hiking, 21, 24, 26; Boulder, 49;

Colorado Mountain Club, 31; Comanche National Grasslands, 205, 209; Dinosaur National Monument, 128; Durango, 159; Garden of the Gods, 218; Glenwood Canyon, 114–115; Grand Junction, 129; Leadville, 98, 103; Maroon Bells-Snowmass Wilderness, 115; Mesa Verde, 156; Mt. Zirkel Wilderness, 84; Northern San Juans, 140, 146, 155, 176; Pawnee National Grasslands, 57; Pikes Peak, 219; recommended reading, 30; Roaring Fork Valley, 117; Rocky Mountain National Park, 70, 71; San Luis Valley, 192; Steamboat Springs, 87; Telluride, 144–145; Tenth Mountain Division Hut System, 98; Unaweep Tabeguache, 135; Upper Arkansas River Valley, 177, 184; Upper Rio Grande Valley, 171, 181, 182

Hispanics, 6, 14, 40, 58, 204, 206, 213–214; arts and museums, 16, 37, 40, 191–192, 194, 206, 220; in San Luis Valley, 189, 195

horseback riding, in Northern San Juans, 159; in Roaring Fork Valley, 117; in Rocky Mountain National

Park, 75
hot springs, 21;
Glenwood Springs,
112; Mt. Princeton,
181; Ouray, 140, 143;
Salida, 183; San Luis
Valley Alligator
Farm, 195–197;
Splashland, 194;
Steamboat Springs,
83, 87; Trimble,
158–159
Hovenweep National
Monument, 153,
158; camping, 164

Imogene Pass, 142
Independence Pass,
107–108
Indians, 15, 191;
Anasazi, 6, 14, 151,
153, 155–157, 158;
arts and museums,
36–37, 59, 126, 153,
154, 157, 194, 206,
207, 220; early
human habitation,
13; legends, 151,
221; Plains Indian
tribes, 14, 56, 57,
204; Southern
Cheyennes, 204, 221;
Utes, 6, 14, 15, 16,
81, 84, 112, 123, 137,
143, 151, 157, 189,
193, 221

Jack Dempsey Museum,
194–195
John Martin Reservoir,
208, 209

Kawuneeche Visitor
Center, 70, 71–72
Kit Carson Statute, 207

La Garita, 192; lodging,
197
La Junta, 8, 23, 204,
209; food, 209, 212;
lodging, 212; sight-

seeing highlights,
207
Lake City, 167, 168,
169; flora and fauna,
19; food, 171–173;
lodging, 174; scenic
drives, 145, 175–176;
sightseeing high-
lights, 170–171
Lake San Cristobal,
168, 169
Las Animas, 204; lodg-
ing, 212; sightseeing
highlights, 207
Leadville, 8, 108, 177,
180; camping, 106;
fitness and recre-
ation, 98, 103; flora
and fauna, 19; food,
103–105; lodging,
28, 105–106; recom-
mended reading, 31;
sightseeing high-
lights, 98–103
Longs Peak, 29, 57, 72,
73, 74; hiking, 75
Loveland, 67
Ludlow Monument, 8,
208
Luther Bean Museum,
194

Mancos, 161
Mancos River, 151, 153,
154
Manitou Springs, 219,
221–222
Marble, 112, 113
Maroon Bells-
Snowmass
Wilderness, 115
Matchless Mine, 8, 99,
102
Mesa Verde, 3, 5, 153,
155–156; camping,
28, 164; flora and
fauna, 18; lodging,
161
Meeker, 83
microbreweries, 17–18;
Denver, 46;

Colorado Springs,
218, 228; Fort
Collins, 63; Grand
Junction, 132;
Steamboat Springs,
92;
Million Dollar
Highway, 141–142
Mills, Enos, 30, 72–73
Molly Brown House, 40
Monte Vista National
Wildlife Refuge, 4
Mosquito Mountains,
20, 95
Mt. Princeton Hot
Springs Resort, 181
Mt. Zirkel Wilderness
Area, 4; hikes in, 85
mountain bicycling,
Durango, 159;
Grand Junction,
128–129; Leadville,
98, 103; Northern
San Juans, 140, 146;
Roaring Fork Valley,
117; San Luis Valley,
196; Steamboat
Springs, 86, 88;
UnaweepTabeguach,
135; Upper Arkansas
River Valley, 177,
184
mountain ranges, 20
Museo de las Americas,
6, 40
Museum of Western
Art, 36, 40–41,
Museum of Western
Colorado, 125, 127

National Mining Hall
of Fame & Museum,
8, 98–99
National Park Service,
32
New Fort Lyon, 208
New Raymer, 66
Northern San Juan
Mountains, 3, 6, 20,
126, 137, 155, 169,
192, 193, 195; camp-

ing, 150; fitness and recreation, 146; flora and fauna, 19; food, 146–147; lodging, 147, 150; outdoor activities, 7; scenic drives, 8, 175; sightseeing highlights, 141–145

Ophir Pass, 145
Our Lady of Guadalupe Catholic Church, 196
Ouray, 137; food, 147; lodging, 147, 150; scenic drives, 140, 141, 142, 145, 175; sightseeing highlights, 141–145
Ouray, Ute chief, 143
Ouray Hot Springs Pool, 140, 143
outdoor activities, 20; see also backpacking, biking, birdwatching, fishing, fourwheeling, hiking, horseback riding; river rafting, rock climbing, scenic driving, skiing, winter sports

Palisade, 123, 127, 128
Pawnee Buttes, 55, 56, 57, 59, 66
Pawnee National Grasslands, 3, 23; camping, 63–64; fitness and recreation, 59; food, 59–62; lodging, 62–63; sights, 53–59, 65–66
Pawnee Pioneer Trails Scenic and Historic Byway, 65
Pikes Peak, 3, 5, 13, 30, 215, 218, 219, 222
Pikes Stockade, 8, 195
Platte River, see South

Platte River
Poncha Springs, lodging, 185
Pueblo, 180
Purgatoire River, 204, 213–14

railroads, 5, 8, 27, 50, 66, 114, 144, 158, 167, 181, 192, 207, 215, 218, 219, 221
Raton Pass, 201, 208
recreational vehicles (RV's), 24, 27; recommended reading, 31
Redstone, 112, 113–114, 120, 121; arts, 109
Ridgway, 140; lodging, 147
Rio Grande County Museum and Cultural Center, 195
Rio Grande, 20, 167, 168, 189; fishing, 171
river rafting, 5, 21; Animas River, 159; Arkansas River, 103, 180; Colorado River, 114; Crystal River, 117; Dolores River, 135, 159; Green River, 128; Yampa River, 88
road conditions hotline, see Colorado Department of Transportation
Roaring Fork Valley, 6; camping, 121–122; fitness and recreation, 117, 120; food, 120–121; lodging, 121; nightlife, 122; sightseeing highlights, 109–117
rock climbing, in Manitou Springs, 218; Rocky Mountain National

Park, 76; Unaweep Tabeguache, 135
Rocky Mountain National Park, 3, 4, 20, 23; camping, 28, 81; flora and fauna, 19, 70–71, 72; fitness and recreation, 7, 70, 75–76; food, 76–77; lodging, 77, 80; park headquarters, 73; recommended reading, 30; sights, 71–75; wildlife, see flora and fauna; visitor centers, 70, 73
Route of the Silver Kings, 8, 97
Royal Gorge Bridge, 5, 224

Salida, 177, 179, 180; arts, 15–16; flora and fauna, 18–19; food, 184; lodging, 185; nightlife, 188; sightseeing highlights, 183
Salida Aquatic Hot Springs Pool, 183
San Juan Art Center, 194
San Juan Mountains, see Northern San Juan Mountains
San Juan Skyway, 140, 176
San Miguel River, 136
San Luis, 3, 8, 14, 191, 192, 194; food, 196–197; lodging, 197, 200
San Luis Museum and Cultural Center, 194
San Luis Valley, 3, 4, 5, 8, 23; arts, 6, 16, 191–192; camping, 200; fitness and recreation, 196; flora and fauna, 18; food, 196–197; lodging,

197, 200; mountain ranges, 20; sightseeing highlights, 192–196

San Luis Valley Alligator Farm, 195–196

Sangre de Cristo Mountains, 20, 177, 192, 193, 195, 208

Santa Fe Trail, 14, 23, 201, 204, 205, 206, 207, 208

Sawatch Mountains, 20, 95, 177, 182; hiking in, 98

scenic drives, 21, 24; Alpine Loop, 175–176; Highway of Legends, 213–214; Independence Pass, 108; Pawnee Pioneer Trails, 66–67; Pikes Peak, 219; Unaweep Tabeguache, 135–136

shopping, 40

Silver Plume, 50–52

Silver Thread Scenic and Historic Byway, 3, 167

Silverton, 137, 155; food, 147; lodging, 150; scenic drives, 140, 141, 142, 145, 175–176; sightseeing highlights, 143–44

ski areas, 21, 23; Aspen Mountain, 101, 115, 116; Cuchara, 209; Monarch Ski Area, 7, 182–183; Powderhorn, 129; Purgatory, 146, 159; Ski Cooper, 7, 101–102, 106; Ski Sunlight, 115; Steamboat Springs Ski Area, 7, 81, 85–86, 89–90; Telluride, 7, 146

skiing, 21, 24; Colorado Cross Country Ski Association, 31; Colorado Ski Country USA, 31; Grand Mesa, 129; Leadville, 97; Mesa Verde, 156; Roaring Fork Valley, 115–116; Steamboat Springs, 85–86, 87; Telluride, 146; Upper Arkansas River Valley, 182; Upper Rio Grande Valley, 165, 171

Sligo Cemetery, 66

South Fork, 167, 171; food, 173

South Platte River, 20, 30, 58, 59

Spanish Peaks, 208, 214

Splashland, 5, 194

state capitol, 36

Stations of the Cross Shrine, 3, 191, 193

Steamboat Springs, 4, 23; camping, 94; flora and fauna, 18, 81; fitness and recreation, 7, 84–90; food, 17, 90–91; lodging, 91–94; sightseeing highlights, 84–89

Steamboat Springs Swimming Pool, 88

Sterling, 53, 58–59, 62, 63

Storm King Mountain Memorials, 117

Strawberry Hot Springs, 84, 88; camping, 94

Tabor Opera House, 8, 99–100

Tattered Cover Bookstore, 40

Telluride, 3, 6, 23, 136, 137, 140; festivals, 16, 145; food, 17, 146; lodging, 147; scenic drives, 140, 142; sightseeing highlights, 144–145

Tenth Mountain Division Hut System, 98

Trail Ridge Road, 3, 4, 67, 71–72

Tread of the Pioneers Museum, 88–89

Trimble Hot Springs, 158

Trinidad, 8, 201–214; food, 209, 212; lodging, 212

Twin Lakes, 98, 106, 108

United States Air Force Academy, 5, 215, 222

United States Forest Service, 32

United States Mint, 5, 41

United States Olympic Complex, 223

Upper Arkansas River Valley, 5; camping, 188; fitness and recreation, 183–184; food, 184–185; ghost towns, 8, 179–180; lodging, 185–188; nightlife, 188; outdoor activities, 7; sightseeing highlights, 177–183

Upper Rio Grande Valley, 3, 23; camping, 174; fitness and recreation, 171; food, 171–173; lodging, 173–174; sightseeing, 165–171

Uravan, 136

Ute Indians, 6, 14, 15, 16, 81, 84, 112, 123, 137; Chief Ouray,

143; reservations in Colorado, 151, 157, 159, 189
Ute Mountain Tribal Park, 153, 156; camping, 164
Van Briggle Pottery, 223
vineyards, 123, 128

weather, *see* climate
Western Museum of Mining and Industry, 222
Wheeler Geologic Area, 3, 167, 168–69
wildlife, *see* flora and fauna
winter sports, 21; in Steamboat Springs, 85–87

Yampa River, 81, 88; trail, 90
Yampah Spa and Vapor Caves, 116

zoos, 5, 38

Maps Index

Alpine Loop, 175
Boulder, sights, 48
Colorado River Valley, sights, camping, 124
Colorado Springs, food/lodging/camping, 227
Colorado Springs Area, sights, 216
Denver, food/lodging, 42; sights, 34
Durango and Cortez, food/lodging/camping, 162; sights, 152
Georgetown, Silver Plume, sights, 51
Grand Junction, food/lodging, 130
Highway of Legends, 213
Independence Pass, 107
Leadville, sights/food/ lodging, 104
Leadville Area, sights/camping, 96
Northern San Juan Mountains, food/lodging/camping, 148; sights, 138
Pawnee Grasslands, food/lodging/camping, 60; sights, 54
Pawnee Pioneer Trails, 65
Planning Map, 10–11
Roaring Fork Valley, food/lodging/camping, 118; sights, 110
Rocky Mountain National Park,

food/lodging/camping, 78; sights, 68
San Luis Valley, food/lodging/camping, 198; sights, 190
Steamboat Springs, sights/food/lodging, 92
Steamboat Springs Area, sights/food/lodging/camping, 82
Suggested Itineraries, 2–8; The Best of Colorado Tour, 3; Nature Lover's Tour, 4; Family Fun Tour, 5; Arts and Cultures Tour, 6; Outdoor Sports Tour, 7; History Tour, 8
Trinidad/La Junta, food/lodging/camping, 210; sights, 202
Unaweep Tabeguache, 135
Upper Arkansas River Valley, food/lodging/ camping, 186; sights, 178
Upper Rio Grande River Valley, food/lodging/camping, 172; sights, 166

Other Books from John Muir Publications

Rick Steves' Books

Asia Through the Back Door, 400 pp., $17.95

Europe 101: History and Art for the Traveler, 352 pp., $17.95

Mona Winks: Self-Guided Tours of Europe's Top Museums, 432 pp., $18.95

Rick Steves' Baltics & Russia, 144 pp., $9.95

Rick Steves' Europe, 528 pp., $17.95

Rick Steves' France, Belgium & the Netherlands, 256 pp., $13.95

Rick Steves' Germany, Austria & Switzerland, 256 pp., $13.95

Rick Steves' Great Britain, 240 pp., $13.95

Rick Steves' Italy, 224 pp., $13.95

Rick Steves' Scandinavia, 192 pp., $13.95

Rick Steves' Spain & Portugal, 208 pp., $13.95

Rick Steves' Europe Through the Back Door, 480 pp., $18.95

Rick Steves' French Phrase Book, 176 pp., $5.95

Rick Steves' German Phrase Book, 176 pp., $5.95

Rick Steves' Italian Phrase Book, 176 pp., $5.95

Rick Steves' Spanish & Portuguese Phrase Book, 304 pp., $6.95

Rick Steves' French/German/Italian Phrase Book, 320 pp., $7.95

A Natural Destination Series

Belize: A Natural Destination, 344 pp., $16.95

Costa Rica: A Natural Destination, 380 pp., $18.95

Guatemala: A Natural Destination, 360 pp., $16.95

City·Smart™ Guidebook Series

All are 240–256 pages and $14.95 paperback.

City·Smart Guidebook: Cleveland (avail. 2/97)

City·Smart Guidebook: Denver

City·Smart Guidebook: Minneapolis/St. Paul

City·Smart Guidebook: Nashville (avail. 1/97)

City·Smart Guidebook: Portland

City·Smart Guidebook: Tampa/St. Petersburg (avail. 12/96)

For Birding Enthusiasts

The Birder's Guide to Bed and Breakfasts: U.S. and Canada, 416 pp., $17.95

The Visitor's Guide to the Birds of the Central National Parks: U.S. and Canada, 400 pp., $15.95

The Visitor's Guide to the Birds of the Eastern National Parks: U.S. and Canada, 400 pp., $15.95

The Visitor's Guide to the Birds of the Rocky Mountain National Parks: U.S. and Canada, 432 pp., $15.95

Unique Travel Series

All are 112 pages and $10.95 paperback, except Georgia and Oregon.

Unique Arizona

Unique California

Unique Colorado

Unique Florida

Unique Georgia ($11.95)

Unique New England

Unique New Mexico

Unique Oregon ($9.95)
Unique Texas
Unique Washington

Travel✦Smart™ Trip Planners

All are 240–256 pages and $14.95 paperback.

American Southwest Travel✦Smart Trip Planner
Colorado Travel✦Smart Trip Planner
Eastern Canada Travel✦Smart Trip Planner
Florida Gulf Travel✦Smart Trip Planner (avail. 12/96)
Hawaii Travel✦Smart Trip Planner
Kentucky/Tennessee Travel✦Smart Trip Planner
Minnesota/Wisconsin Travel✦Smart™ Trip Planner
New England Travel✦Smart Trip Planner
Northern California Travel✦Smart Trip Planner (avail. 8/96)
Pacific Northwest Travel✦Smart Trip Planner (avail. 8/96)

Other Terrific Travel Titles

The 100 Best Small Art Towns in America, 256 pp., $15.95
The Big Book of Adventure Travel, 384 pp., $17.95
Indian America: A Traveler's Companion, 480 pp., $18.95
The People's Guide to Mexico, 608 pp., $19.95
Ranch Vacations: The Complete Guide to Guest and Resort, Fly-Fishing, and Cross-Country Skiing Ranches, 528 pp., $19.95
Understanding Europeans, 272 pp., $14.95
Undiscovered Islands of the Caribbean, 336 pp., $16.95

Watch It Made in the U.S.A.: A Visitor's Guide to the Companies that Make Your Favorite Products, 328 pp., $16.95
The World Awaits, 280 pp., $16.95

Automotive Titles

The Greaseless Guide to Car Care, 272 pp., $19.95
How to Keep Your Subaru Alive, 480 pp., $21.95
How to Keep Your Toyota Pickup Alive, 392 pp., $21.95
How to Keep Your VW Alive, 464 pp., $25

Ordering Information

Please check your local bookstore or call **1-800-888-7504** to order direct and to receive a complete catalog. A shipping charge will be added to your order total.

Send all inquiries to:
John Muir Publications
P.O. Box 613
Santa Fe, NM 87504